Kenneth D. Brown is Professor Emeritus of History at
Queen's University Belfast. He is a Fellow of the Academy
of Social Sciences and author of *The English Labour Movement
1700–1951* (1982); *A Social History of the Nonconformist
Ministry in England and Wales 1800–1939* (1988) and *The
British Toy Business* (1996).

'Herbert Gladstone, youngest son of William Ewart Gladstone, the political colossus who bestrode the late nineteenth century, has languished in the shadow of his father, although he attained one of the great offices of state, the Home Secretaryship, in 1906. Herbert had exercised considerable political influence over the emergence of Irish Home Rule, and his crucial work as Chief Whip in consolidating and revitalising the Liberal Party culminated in the Liberal electoral triumph of 1906. He served as the first Governor-General of the Union of South Africa, and here the author of this book defends Herbert against the criticism that he supported a government that paved the way for apartheid. This study, based as it is on an exceptionally wide range of sources, is a particularly fine type of political biography.'

Professor David William Bebbington,
University of Stirling

THE UNKNOWN GLADSTONE

The Life of Herbert Gladstone,
1854–1930

KENNETH D. BROWN

I.B. TAURIS

LONDON • NEW YORK • OXFORD • NEW DELHI • SYDNEY

I.B. TAURIS
Bloomsbury Publishing Plc
50 Bedford Square, London, WC1B 3DP, UK
1385 Broadway, New York, NY 10018, USA

BLOOMSBURY, I.B. TAURIS and the I.B. Tauris logo
are trademarks of Bloomsbury Publishing Plc

First published in Great Britain 2018
Paperback edition published 2020

A catalogue record for this book is available from the British Library.

A catalog record of this book is available from the Library of Congress.

ISBN: HB: 978-1-7883-1024-6
PB: 978-0-7556-0092-2
ePDF: 978-1-7867-3298-9
eBook: 978-1-7867-2298-0

Library of Victorian Studies 11

Typeset in Garamond Three by OKS Prepress Services, Chennai, India

To find out more about our authors and books visit
www.bloomsbury.com and sign up for our newsletters.

CONTENTS

ACKNOWLEDGEMENTS

This book has been several years in the making and I have been much aided by the many archivists who guided me with unfailing courtesy through the various documents listed in the bibliography. Quotations from the Glynne-Gladstone papers appear by kind permission of Mr Charles Gladstone; from the diary of the first Lord Ponsonby by permission of Lord Ponsonby of Shulbrede; from the diaries of Margot Asquith by permission of Christopher Osborn; from the Trevelyan and Runciman Papers by permission of the Librarian, Robinson Library, University of Newcastle; from the C.P. Scott Diary by permission of the University of Manchester Library; from the Crewe and Hardinge papers by permission of the Syndics of Cambridge University Library; from the archives of the National Liberal Club by permission of Bristol University Special Collections; from the Milner papers by permission of the Warden and Scholars of New College, Oxford; from the Herbert and Margot Asquith, Bryce, Harcourt, Morley, Murray, Ponsonby and Selborne papers by permission of the Bodleian Libraries, University of Oxford. I apologise if I have failed to acknowledge other copyright holders.

I am also indebted to the following: the warden and staff who make working and staying at the Gladstone Library such a delightful experience; Professor David Bebbington of Stirling University who read the entire manuscript and offered innumerable helpful suggestions from his unrivalled knowledge of the Gladstones; Professor Ritchie Ovendale, formerly of the University of Aberystwyth, who kindly read the chapter on South Africa; Dr Robin Darwall-Smith for directing me to important material in the archives of University College; and to Dr Andrew Brown of Queen's University for help with the technical matters that persistently baffle me.

LIST OF ABBREVIATIONS

BL	British Library
BLO	Bodleian Libraries, University of Oxford
BLPES	British Library of Political and Economic Science
BUL	Birmingham University Library
BUSC	Bristol University Special Collections
CCC	Churchill College Cambridge
CUL	Cambridge University Library
FRO	Flintshire Record Office
GG	Glynne-Gladstone
HJG	Herbert Gladstone
HNG	Henry Gladstone
LUL	Liverpool University Library
NA	National Archives
NCO	Nuffield College Oxford
NLS	National Library of Scotland
NUL	Newcastle University Library
RLM	Rylands Library Manchester
SANA	South African National Archive
SRO	Scottish Record Office
UCO	University College Oxford

LIST OF PLATES

Plate 1 Hawarden Castle. Credit: Alamy.

Plate 2 Parliamentary tennis match. Credit: Getty Images.

Plate 3 Herbert Gladstone MP. Credit: Alamy.

Plate 4 A Gladstone family group. Credit: National Portrait Gallery.

Plate 5 Margot Tennant. Credit: Victoria and Albert Museum.

Plate 6 Herbert Gladstone as home secretary. Credit: Getty Images.

Plate 7 The Campbell-Bannerman Cabinet in 1906. Credit: Alamy.

Plate 8 The London Eucharistic Procession of 1908. Public Domain.

Plate 9 Suffragette leaflet. Public Domain.

Plate 10 Herbert Gladstone in court. Credit: Alamy.

Plate 11 Dorothy Gladstone. Credit: Alamy.

Plate 12 The Rand Strike. Public Domain.

Plate 13 Belgian refugees in London. Public Domain.

Plate 14 Little Munden church and graveyard. Public Domain.

CHAPTER 1

Hawarden to Westminster

In the flickering light the father's shadow, distorted by the presence on his back of an excited 11-year-old, lay dark and heavy over the cradle in which lay his newest-born son, peacefully sleeping, the light occasionally glimmering on his barely discernible ruddy gold hair. It was a shadow which the baby, soon to be christened Herbert John, was never fully to escape even though his future was to include stints as under-secretary for Ireland, commissioner of works, chief Liberal whip, home secretary, and first governor-general of South Africa. This was by most standards an impressive record until set against that of the father, William Ewart Gladstone, who at the time of Herbert's birth in January 1854 was chancellor of the exchequer and was eventually to serve as prime minister on four occasions, the dominant figure in British public life for the better part of half a century. A more difficult act to follow would be hard to imagine, even allowing for the fact that in British politics very few sons, Winston Churchill certainly and William Pitt the Younger and Neville Chamberlain possibly being the exceptions, have outshone their fathers. Nor in fact did Herbert Gladstone ever show any inclination to eclipse his parent. The intense emotional and psychological empathy between the two men fuelled the son's lifetime commitment to honouring and defending the name, principles and achievements of the father, a word which he invariably capitalised in his own correspondence. Even his autobiography was mostly a spirited defence of the Grand Old Man's actions, wrapped up in some personal reminiscences of his own.[1]

Destiny may have decreed that Herbert Gladstone should be forever overshadowed by his illustrious father but temperament also ensured that he was happiest working behind the scenes. Most have been content to leave him there, agreeing, if only tacitly, with the dictum that politicians like actors appear taller before the footlights than offstage. Herbert's relatively peripheral role in his own published recollections was a matter of personal choice but it was mirrored in the memoirs of his many political contemporaries in which he was rarely deemed worthy of more than a passing reference. As Liberal chief whip he was by definition working backstage. As a minister between 1905 and 1910 he was, in common it must be said with most of his cabinet colleagues, overshadowed by the personalities and policies of more extrovert characters like Churchill and Lloyd George, while his departure to South Africa in 1910 removed him for the most part from the British public gaze. Subsequently, neither his wartime work with Belgian refugees nor his intriguing against Lloyd George for the soul of the Liberal Party in the 1920s attracted much contemporary interest. With the passage of time Herbert Gladstone slipped even further into the shadows and he was almost alone among those holding office in the pre-war Liberal Governments in failing to attract a later biographer, unlike several comparatively junior colleagues.[2] His sole monument in the graveyard of historiography remains that penned in 1932 by Sir Charles Mallet, a sometime Liberal MP and a writer of modest ability who was not Lady Gladstone's first choice author and whose book is coloured throughout by its author's intense dislike of Lloyd George.[3]

For Agnes Gladstone, the excited 11-year-old perched on her father's back in January 1854, that first shadowy glimpse of her newborn brother always remained a special memory and she referred to it frequently in later years because, as she put it, 'I never before had entered into the intense joy that such a sunbeam brought to an old sister's heart.'[4] If that sentiment now seems mawkish and overblown the new infant's arrival was certainly a matter for great family rejoicing, which somehow never dissipated and bathed him in warm and loving surroundings throughout his childhood and beyond. Victorian politics were still a relatively leisurely affair, allowing Gladstone senior time for scholarly work but as chancellor he was still much engaged in affairs of state, not least the outbreak of the Crimean War shortly after Herbert's birth. Furthermore, like most Victorian fathers, he was content to leave the daily responsibility for his seven surviving children to his wife Catherine (nee Glynne). Nevertheless, his diaries reveal that he kept a keen and affectionate eye on their progress. 'God bless him', he wrote on Herbert's third birthday in 1857, 'he is at this moment a remarkable child whatever he may hereafter be.'[5] A similar pride was evident when the boy reached his eighth birthday, Gladstone predicting that 'he will hardly be an ordinary man but seems to have both breadth and depth', a comment perhaps prompted by his recent discovery of Herbert engrossed in reading the latest news from America.[6]

Gladstone had a lofty view of paternal duty, especially when it came to religion. A high Anglican, his sense of the Divine presence and purpose shaped every aspect of his own personal life and frequently informed his public utterances. His piety was more than matched by his wife's and while their beliefs could not be forced upon the children, family prayers, regular biblical instruction from Gladstone himself and church attendance twice on Sundays left no doubts as to the Gladstones' convictions or their aspirations for their children. In this as in all other matters the parents together set the tone for the family. Gladstone also instructed all his sons in arithmetic, languages and geography, although by the time Herbert came along politics were depriving him of the necessary time. Even so, he did what he could and after one lesson he again noted that Herbert 'has very considerable gifts'.[7] For his part, Herbert was certainly not conscious of any neglect by his father. Even in old age he could still write vividly of the delight he and his siblings experienced when Gladstone joined them for tree-felling, games, a seaside trip or an impromptu concert, the latter instilling in Herbert a lifelong love of music and singing. When their father abandoned, however briefly, the outside world of public affairs and entered theirs, the children, Herbert remembered, were 'like little dogs who never resent exclusion but are overjoyed when they are allowed in. Our affection was secured.'[8]

In 1868 Gladstone became prime minister for the first time. Personally involved with several of his government's major measures, he maintained a comprehensive eye on all its business and regularly attended the House of Commons. For her part Catherine tried to be present when he spoke in parliament and to accompany him at the numerous official and social functions required of a prime minister. But if the parents were thus often and increasingly occupied or absent there was still plenty of fun and affection to go round, for the ties between the children were also strong and reinforced the secure surroundings in which Herbert's formative years were spent. He himself was just about entering puberty when his father became prime minister but older brothers Willy and Stephen, born respectively in 1840 and 1844, both took an almost paternal interest in him, particularly after he started school. With Harry (formally Henry), his senior by only 18 months or so, Herbert formed almost from birth a fraternal bond of astonishing strength and durability which, as their voluminous correspondence indicates, survived all the vicissitudes of adult life and was severed only by death. As boys they were inseparable, delighting in exploiting the possibilities of the family home and estate at Hawarden Castle, just outside Chester. Together they roamed the nearby countryside, climbing trees and learning to shoot and fish, activities which seeded in Herbert a love of field sports and the outdoors which he was never to lose. Predictably, he never cared much for the chancellor's Downing Street residence, his birth place, complaining because it was 'so dirty' and 'we can't climb any trees'.[9] Of his sisters, he was probably closest to Mary who watched over his early career with particular interest and in whom he tended to confide his most intimate thoughts on those rare occasions when he chose to express them at all. But affection for Agnes and Helen also bubbles through the surviving family letters. They wrote frequently to each other, effusive and mutual expressions of birthday wishes; concerns for Herbert's health, magnified no doubt by memories of the meningitis which had carried off another sister, Jessy, in 1850; regrets that a particular family treat had been missed; and exchanges of gifts and cards, including on one occasion rather thinly disguised Valentines received by both Mary and Stephen, behind which they immediately detected Herbert's boyishly mischievous hand. Outside the immediate family, similarly close ties developed between the Gladstones' offspring and the 12 children of Catherine's sister, Mary Glynne, wife of the fourth Lord Lyttelton. The cousins were frequently in each others' company for holidays, games, outings and parties. The families were so close that they even developed their own private language, Glynnese, and the Gladstone children saw far more of their Glynne and Lyttelton relatives than they ever did of their father's Gladstone kin.[10]

The constant at the heart of this vibrant family dynamic was Catherine Gladstone, not merely the wife of a rising politician but a remarkable woman in her own right. She was no stranger to the world of high politics since the Glynne family itself was related to a number of important political dynasties. She well understood, therefore, the demands of government on her husband. A devout woman, Catherine was outgoing and gregarious, sympathetic to those in less fortuitous circumstances than her own. Domestically she was untidy and not much interested in externals, but little escaped her with regard to the children. After Mary Lyttelton's unexpectedly early death in 1857 Catherine became virtually a surrogate mother to the Lyttelton nieces and nephews, one of whom recalled that, with her, 'children felt always, especially in times of anxiety or distress, that somebody had arrived who was going to help to solve difficulties, to light up the road and incidentally to make fun for all concerned. She radiated tenderness.'[11] A grandson noted similarly that she had the gift of being able to reinforce a child's self-respect and self-belief.[12] While none of her extended family was excluded from her capacious affections, her own two youngest boys, her 'sugar plums' as she called them, undoubtedly claimed a special place in her heart and about Herbert especially, she once said, there was something so special that it 'seems to go my soul'.[13] As his correspondence with her confirms, that intensity was reciprocated and together with her husband Catherine remained Herbert's emotional focus well into his adult years.

Not surprisingly, therefore, she found it difficult when William arranged for Herbert and Harry to go to Hunstanton in Norfolk to be tutored by the Rev Church, who had taught the older Gladstone boys and five Lytteltons during his previous incumbency near Kettering. Catherine wanted to keep them at home with a tutor but, the decision made, she affirmed to her sister that she meant to be very brave 'but it is trying, the going away of the younger pair [...] I own to crying at the very thought.'[14] What the nine-year-old Herbert thought about the decision is not recorded. He could not have been particularly keen on leaving the freedom of Hawarden, the warmth of his family or the company of their dogs to whom he was particularly attached. On the other hand he appreciated that most Victorian boys from his social background followed a similar educational path. There was also the not inconsiderable consolation that Harry was going with him.

Church's school was a small affair with never more than a handful of pupils. The regime required them to rise at 6.30 a.m. and work for seven to eight hours. Herbert was not particularly studious and preferred games but he was an outgoing child who made friends quickly enough. Not all of them, however, were to his father's taste, Gladstone finding it necessary in April 1863 to chastise both his sons for their bad language, a habit acquired, he suggested in his diary, from a boy at Church's school. 'They seem sorry and their culpability is not great', he added.[15] In all probability their remorse was genuine, springing from the great respect which they had for their father but for all his artless charm and openness, Herbert at least was not above being disingenuous, or perhaps politic. Notwithstanding his teacher's inclination to bad temper and frequent recourse to corporal punishment, he told his father in October 1863 that Church was very kind and that he liked him very much.[16] Harry, however, told Willy that while they were getting on as well as could be expected they were 'not very happy yet'.[17] Herbert confided to Catherine that school was not very nice compared with the comforts of home, adding rather plaintively that he and Harry had no flannel on which to grow their mustard and cress, except for the very small piece which they shared for the purposes of washing.[18] From September 1864, however, Herbert had the piece of flannel to himself, for Harry followed the family tradition by moving on to Eton, leaving his brother to make the long journey to Hunstanton on his own for the first time. He seemed to cope better than his family. Gladstone noted in his diary that the boy went off 'in a brave and manful spirit'.[19] Mary wrote the next day saying that they had all stayed on the platform waving their handkerchiefs until the train disappeared into the tunnel.[20] Stephen summed up the general family feeling. 'We were all sorry to lose you though we were very glad to see how bravely you went off.'[21] Herbert appears to have reconciled himself easily enough to his brother's absence and by Christmas 1864 positive reports on his academic progress prompted a serious conversation with his father about following in Harry's footsteps.

By the time Herbert actually got to Eton in the summer of 1865 reform of Britain's great public schools was very much in the air following publication of the Clarendon Commission's report a year before. The incumbent headmaster of Eton, Edward Balston, was hostile to its recommendations but in 1868 he was succeeded by John James Hornby, who was more favourably disposed to change. By this time and with constant letters of encouragement from home, especially from Stephen, who wished that he 'knew enough grammar to be able to give you more help in it & in Latin prose', Herbert had successfully negotiated his way into the 'remove', notwithstanding a period of serious illness in 1866.[22] Thereafter, and despite several offers of help and visits, mainly from Stephen since Willy had been elected to parliament in 1865 and held minor office from 1869, Herbert does not appear to have done much more than necessary to keep up in school, even though Hornby was widening the curriculum to include science and extra-curricular subjects for the senior boys. There is no evidence, for example, that Herbert ever attended any of the voluntary science lectures introduced in the 1860s and while even as a schoolboy he was an eloquent and copious letter writer, those surviving from his Eton days suggest that his primary enthusiasms lay outside the classroom. The only current of educational reform that did seem to catch him up was the growing emphasis on sport, for he greatly enjoyed cricket although he was no more than a modest player, averaging ten runs an innings for the school's lower club in 1870. He also rowed a little and joined both the music society and the rifle club, shooting so frequently during the school holidays that on more than one occasion Harry expressed concern that there would soon be no rabbits left in the Hawarden countryside for anyone else to bag. Herbert even contemplated joining the Eton Volunteers in 1870 but decided against it because the uniform cost £4-10-0d, an interesting comment on the relatively parsimonious allow-ance he was receiving from home, even though his father had, from 1868, been prime minister. He also developed a great liking for mountaineering, whose hazards, graphically described in his letters, caused considerable anxieties to his sisters. 'I was hourly in dread on the arrival of your stick dipped in your blood', wrote Mary in September 1869, and Helen conceded that while his expeditions sounded delightful, she was all too glad that he had not 'tumbled over precipices & cracked your precious skull'.[23]

She did have reason for concern the following year, however, when Herbert, away climbing in Wales, became so unwell that Catherine's maternal instincts drove her urgently to his bedside at Dolgelly, where she slept on the floor, casting aside all the considerations of decorum or dignity which might have been expected of a prime minister's wife. A few months later Herbert was again taken ill, this time at school. The problem, about which he was subsequently conventionally discreet apart from one passing reference to his 'bread basket' appears to have been some sort of bowel obstruction. Towards the end of September a second doctor was called in to 'have a look & a poke' and extended rest was recommended. Personally Herbert seems to have been more concerned for his mother who, he told Harry, was 'missing Papa and all of you' and that he had caused her 'dreadful worry'. In the same letter he did concede that it was 'horrid missing all the fun at Hawarden', adding almost incidentally that while the latest medical reports were good he was still confined to bed since the doctors feared the development of an abscess which could cripple him for two or three years.[24] He remained bed-ridden over Christmas, prompting an unexpected bunch of grapes from Queen Victoria, then perhaps more favourably disposed toward Gladstone than she was later to be, and an anguished complaint from Helen about his inability to return home for the holiday. A week or two later he reported to Harry that the main lump in his bowel had gone although there was a possibility that a smaller one remained.[25] Even after he was allowed out of his bed, he remained under medical observation for several months and had to seek the doctor's permission to resume cricket in the summer.

As he began his final year at Eton in the autumn of 1871 he faced the tricky question of his future. Harry had left in 1870 to join his grandfather's business, Gladstone, Wylie and Co., in London. Herbert, however, was evidently expecting to emulate Willy and Stephen by going to Oxford. After that, he had notions of business or the foreign office. Aware that by the time Herbert finished at university, entry to the civil

service would have become competitive on the recommendation of the Northcote-Trevelyan Report, which he himself
had commissioned, Gladstone senior, who always sought to
shape his sons' lives as closely as his own father had directed
his, told his youngest son that it was not worth going to
Oxford unless he intended to take his degree.[26] His concern
was less with Herbert's ability than with his application.
A poor school report strengthened these doubts and
prompted him to suggest to Catherine that Herbert should
be removed from Eton because for all his charm and merits he
did not yet know what effort and hard work were. Stephen
apparently had similar reservations, telling his brother that it
would be pointless to go to Oxford 'if one is idle' because it
'is rather a tempting place for idleness'.[27] As ever, however,
Catherine championed Herbert's cause, artfully explaining
that she would not even have ventured to contradict her
husband save that he had been so busy that he had perhaps
had insufficient time to study Herbert as he would have
wished. She acknowledged that neither Herbert's ability nor
his application matched Willy's but on the other hand, she
urged, he had tried his best and he had been ill for a
considerable time. Her diplomacy paid off. Towards the end
of April 1872 there was another long conversation about
Oxford, after which Gladstone concluded that Herbert's
attitude was now 'very satisfactory'.[28] Harry offered practical
advice, suggesting that his brother abandon cricket to prepare
for the entrance examination. While Herbert was certainly
willing to do this he was well aware of his limitations.
Notwithstanding his father's instruction in theology, he
felt that he was not well up in the Old Testament and
mathematics were even more of a worry. Up to the 1850s the
subject had been purely voluntary at Eton and while this had
changed by Herbert's time, it was still regarded as markedly
inferior to Classics and only three hours of instruction were
provided each week. One contemporary described the maths
class as 'a rag, boys shying books at each other [...] no one
ever learnt anything'.[29] Gloomily, Herbert told Harry that he
would have to take up algebra. As ever when it came to

matters of the mind, it was Stephen who weighed in with the most useful advice, urging his brother to stick to just two maths subjects and concentrate on the general paper, tackling only topics about which he felt confident. 'It is always best at Oxford in any examination, especially where you only want to pass, not to venture any guesses, nor to attempt questions with which you are not familiar.' Almost as an afterthought, perhaps an unnecessary one in Herbert's case, he urged him not to overwork.[30] When it came to the test itself only Herbert's rote learning of Euclidean geometry compensated for some astounding mistakes, indicative not only of his own ignorance but also of the standards then provided by Eton and required for Oxford entrance. Ruefully he told Harry that amongst other errors he had suggested that three-quarters of a yard was two feet. 'The mathematical man was very sarcastic about it.'[31] However, in the general paper his musings on topics ranging from the conquest of Mexico to telegraphs, steam engines, balloons and gunpowder were good enough to secure a place to study Classics. Harry was delighted. 'Well done thou good lad,' he wrote on hearing the news. 'I am glad – how jolly – you lucky fellow. I envy you awfully now [...] Stephy was quite right, he said a fortnight ago that at any rate the General Paper would pull you through.'[32]

In October 1872 Herbert followed the path previously taken by his father and two of his brothers and went up to Oxford. Once in the town, however, he turned into the High Street and University College, rather than into St Aldates and Christ Church as the others had done. His father thoughtfully sent him a set of guidelines for student life which included devoting the Sabbath to religious literature, studying for seven hours a day, daily prayer and financial prudence. Now Herbert was always dutiful and respectful, but as the prime minister's son he was never going to be short of social opportunities and there were of course plenty of old Etonian acquaintances already at Oxford. He entered into college life with such vigour that within a month Harry was chiding him for the absence of letters, asking plaintively 'are you so

busy?'[33] The answer was self-evident, Herbert replying that
he had multiple invitations for breakfast or wine and was
throwing himself wholeheartedly into college sport, having
played football against Harrow, hoping to play for Oxford
Etonians against Cambridge, and planning to row in a boat
race.[34] Later in his first year and by now having resumed
a more frequent correspondence with Harry he described a
lavish Bullingdon Club dinner, following which he was driven
home in an unlit carriage by a drunken cabman. 'How we
arrived alive I don't know', he confessed.[35] In the summer he
played cricket so often that he had to reassure his father that
it was not interfering with his work. Nor did he allow his
musical interests to lapse, for he continued with the cello he
had taken up some years before and eventually hired a piano
for his rooms. An equally enthusiastic music lover, Harry's
regular visits to see Herbert often incorporated attendance
at a concert.

As for his studies, Herbert did not initially find the
curriculum to his taste, displeased to discover that he had to
read Virgil rather than Homer. Longer-term, there was the
question of whether he should try for honours or a mere pass
when the time came in 1874. He did not fancy his chances of
honours since he had never studied Greek composition,
believed himself to be deficient in Greek grammar and found
philology disturbing. But the decision was not for him alone.
The family also had views. 'There was a discussion last night
about your going in for Honours', Harry wrote in February
1873. 'Nothing was decided – but Willy as you know is strong
for your going for a pass while Papa rather inclines the other
way [. . .] it would be well I think to have Stephy's opinion.'[36]
Agnes's husband, Edward Wickham, headmaster of
Wellington College, also advised him to aim for the pass.
However, the recently appointed master of University College,
George Bradley, had loftier aspirations. As a matter of course,
he expected all his undergraduates to attempt the higher level
and he was unwilling to make an exception, even for a prime
minister's son. A short discussion between the two ended in a
decision that Herbert should go for honours.

In writing to express his pleasure at this outcome, Stephen raised a further question and one which had also been exercising their father for some time.[37]

> I often wonder if you are any further towards making up your mind *what to do*. In spite of its trials & disappointments I don't believe that any life is so full of interests & hopes, ever rising afresh, as the clergyman's, provided he has a vocation to clerical life. And if you felt any drawing that way I'm sure you would find it so.[38]

This was entirely understandable advice from a man who at a very early age had felt called to the Anglican priesthood. But although he had been confirmed into the Church of England in February 1870 and the family social circle included prominent churchmen like Lord Acton and Scott Holland, Herbert felt no such sense of vocation. He certainly accepted fundamental Christian doctrines such as human sinfulness and salvation through the atoning work of Christ's death and resurrection but he seemed relieved to learn from his father that the evangelical term 'being saved' could be interpreted simply as belonging within the Christian fold.[39] Spiritual matters rarely engaged his passions in the way they did with his parents: at least if they did stir any deep feelings within his soul, he did not talk or write about it. On the other hand, it has to be said that Herbert's deepest emotions were seldom shared with anyone, even within the family. Nor is there anything to suggest that he suffered from the temptations and guilt that plunged his father into the agonies of private spiritual turmoil recorded in his diaries. All the same, the reality of God was a given in Herbert's mental firmament, providing a sense of the eternal and immortal even if, except in times of extreme personal anxiety, He seems to have been essentially a rather remote presence, albeit one whose authority and nature required and received regular acknowledgment in the form of private prayer, scripture reading and attendance at divine worship. Apart from these observances, always dutifully and sincerely carried out, Herbert's faith manifested itself primarily in his adherence to principles and an ethical code, although superficially this sometimes appeared to be no more than the conventional respectability so influential in determining the timbre of both private and public Victorian life.

Most pressing in his own mind in the spring of 1874, however, was the pending ordeal of examinations. He declined Agnes's offer of a study base at Wellington College, preferring to remain in Oxford over the Easter vacation. Despite frequent letters of encouragement from the family and especially his mother, he remained gloomy about his prospects. His pessimism deepened once the examinations actually began at the end of May. 'My hopes of a second', he told Harry after two or three days, 'have been knocked on the head.'[40] By the time he finished he had abandoned hope of getting any classification at all, even fearing that he had failed altogether. His concerns proved ill-founded, though only just, as he was placed in the third class, a result about which his family remained curiously silent, perhaps because it fell short of the seconds achieved by his brothers and well short of the first secured by his father. It is perhaps unsurprising that after such difficulty with the Classics and a viva in which he was 'on the rack before five men for forty minutes' he switched, probably on his father's advice, to study history for his final two years.[41]

The ever-supportive Willy promptly sent his own history notes to Oxford along with a recommended scheme of study, but although Herbert replied that he would utilise it, he clearly found the prospect unappealing. 'The amount of work I have to get through', he told Harry, 'is appalling to one of my reading capabilities', and as he entered his third year there was little in his letters to suggest that study would be allowed to interrupt his extracurricular activities.[42] He entered two field events in the college athletics competition, though no races because he had a tendency to asthma after sustained exercise. He reported regularly on his billiard matches in the winter and on his cricket in the summer when he turned out for two college teams. There were accounts of fines imposed on him by the proctors, the officials responsible for student discipline, and the smuggling of his dog into college, a breach of rules which, had it been discovered, would also have been penalised. An escapade involving fireworks in the quadrangle, the destruction of a don's door and several smashed windows led to the sending-down of two men and lesser punishments for others. Herbert may have been only a minor participant but he was greatly relieved to escape detection. Nor did the hectic social pace slacken when he returned to Hawarden in the long vacation of 1875 and gave himself enthusiastically to village cricket, lots of shooting, daily organ practice, singing with the local glee club and parties and balls so numerous that he took dancing lessons.

Yet beneath the frivolity there were signs of change, a growing seriousness sparked by the realisation that his undergraduate days were soon to end. In one of his more thoughtful letters he observed that the passage of time was changing the family. Stephen and Harry were developing their careers, Agnes was married, uncles Stephen and Henry were dead and, therefore, 'one ought to get reconciled to the idea that life is not all a delightful boyhood.'[43] If that reality had been slow to dawn on him, in its new light and with finals now only a year away he started going to the British Museum to study. When he returned to college at the start of his final year his peers commented on his withdrawal from college life and increased attention to his books. It would, he wrote to Harry, be a hard grind and he would be glad to get the exams out of the way, although he would then have to face the real commencement of life. 'With few intervals school and university pass easily and lightly [...] the fearful final examination and the hard work one has in order to pass through this eases off the feeling that boyhood has entirely passed away.'[44] So intensively did he now apply himself that at the end of the term his tutor told him he was overdoing it and advised him to take a break. But books were not the only source of his learning. Herbert's adolescent antics seem to have somewhat puzzled his father but as he began to mature and draw on his parent's knowledge and experience, their relationship developed a more comfortable level of mutuality and companionship, underpinned by a powerful familial affection. As finals loomed ever closer Herbert was writing to ask his father's opinion of Pitt as a financier while much of the Easter vacation was spent together in long and frequent walks with historical subjects as the main topic of conversation. His application, which even entailed a self-imposed absence from the cricket pitch, did not go unnoticed by the college master who confided to Agnes his own hopes that Herbert would do as well as his efforts deserved.[45]

Herbert had never been one to blow his own trumpet, possibly because the family usually blew it on his behalf, and he was as usual downbeat about the examinations.

> I have done beastly badly. I have had very bad luck. We have had 6 papers, not one of which has suited me, and hardly any questions out of the books I have been grinding at. As regards the examination I am quite disgusted, but do not much excuse myself of neglecting in reading.[46]

By the time he got round to posting this, however, the results were known and scrawled across the top, almost as an afterthought but with no other comment, were the words 'first class'. To Catherine he opined that the award of a first-class degree was utterly unexpected but privately he was actually very pleased. He had worked hard for it, resisting what he described years later as the temptations of sport, music and socialising.[47] His father was equally delighted, describing it as 'a success which his modesty forbade him to anticipate. It was a joyous surprise.'[48] Mary thought it 'frantically exciting'.[49]

Herbert celebrated with a summer excursion to Austria and Switzerland although the question of his career still remained unresolved. It was a matter which had been exercising his father for some years for even in 1874 he had noted that he would be 'glad when this is more advanced'.[50] Swayed perhaps by his enjoyment of the outdoors, Herbert's had flirted briefly with the idea of becoming a land agent but by June 1876 he had reverted to his earlier notion of going into business alongside Harry, combining this with a fellowship at All Souls for which it had been suggested he compete.[51] In the event the fellowship went to a Balliol man, but Herbert decided to try again, supporting himself by accepting a lecturing post at the recently established Keble College, whose first Warden, Edward Talbot, was a relative by virtue of his marriage to Lavinia Lyttelton, Herbert's cousin. Preparation for the second competition was interrupted, however, when in a typically generous gesture Herbert offered to accompany Stephen, whose health had completely broken down, on a voyage to the Cape Colony. Ironically, during the course of this trip he himself fell ill again, much to the alarm of his mother who feared a recurrence of his old trouble, quite unnecessarily. Although Herbert always kept a precautionary aperient close at hand it was some time since he had been troubled by what he had once described with unconscious irony as his 'old seat of disorder'.[52] The trip represented too lengthy an interruption of his studies, however. He again failed to secure the All Souls fellowship and had perforce to concentrate on his lecturing. The annual salary of £100, plus £30 from his tutees, probably did not seem a great deal when he was looking after Harry's finances and investing considerable sums on behalf of his brother, now away in India for new employers. Nor does he seem to have regarded academic life as a long-term proposition and early in 1879 he confided in Harry that he was now veering towards a political career. Harry does not appear to have been in the least surprised, urging him simply to make sure he stood for election in a strong borough. Some months later Herbert described how his father had taken the opportunity during a family holiday in the Dolomites to talk

> most kindly about the future – marriage & occupation. About the first nothing at present can be said – about the second a good deal. I am perhaps in danger of leaving too much to chance & trusting that some opening may turn up. I admit that I don't see my way clearly though I know my own mind

pretty well. I did not say much at the time but I shall write
from Oxford. He took the line of assuming a hankering after
political life on my part – of pointing out its disadvantages &
of showing that it is rather the writer & the clergyman who
have influence & the greater opportunities of usefulness at the
present time.[53]

Gladstone's own note of this conversation concluded simply
that in Herbert's remarks he detected 'some leaning towards
the line of politics'.[54] In one sense of course this was not
particularly surprising. In all walks of life it was common for
Victorian sons to follow the same careers as their fathers and
politics were no exception. On the other hand, as a student
Herbert had shown little interest in public affairs and while he
had joined the Oxford Union, unlike many aspiring
politicians he had taken little part in its proceedings and in
his letters overt political comment, save a natural concern for
his father's fortunes, was rare. What swung the balance was
the Ottoman Empire's increasing resort to the repression of
minorities, especially Christians, as it sought to stave off the
symptoms of its own decay. Herbert fully shared his father's
outrage when Turkish troops slaughtered thousand of
Bulgarian civilians in 1876, just as Herbert was completing
his final examinations. One Keble colleague testified that the
Eastern Question then became something of an obsession
with him and years later he himself confirmed that his
political life had been birthed in events in Bulgaria in 1876.[55]
It was not insignificant, therefore, that during that same 1879
holiday in which he had confided his aspirations in his father,
he also spent several long evenings with Mary and Lord Acton
discussing issues of tolerance and the rights of minorities.

Early in 1880 Herbert suggested that he might work as his
father's political secretary. While he perhaps saw this as a
useful starting point for his own career it was also something
of a family tradition, for at one time or another several of
the Gladstone children filled this role, just as Gladstone
himself had done for his father, even after his own entry
into parliament. Should the preliminary experiment prove

satisfactory, Herbert told his mother, he would wish to continue with it, subject to the approval of the Keble warden.[56] But events had already begun to assume a momentum of their own. By late 1879 it was becoming clear that Disraeli's Conservative Government could not survive and that a general election could not be long delayed. Even as he contemplated the prospect of becoming prime minister for a second time, Gladstone found time in December 1879 to discuss with party colleagues potential parliamentary openings for Herbert.[57] Some of the family were consulting even higher authority on the matter, Stephen telling his mother that he was praying that Herbert would be guided aright, adding that his brother would be well aware of the bed of thorns on which every honest politician had to lie.[58] Following the dissolution of parliament and the calling of an election, Herbert dined in London with party notables and then in March 1880 he met a deputation at Liberal headquarters in Parliament Street. The upshot was an invitation to stand for the Harrow division of Middlesex. After telegraphing his father, who seemed somewhat taken aback to learn of this development, he accepted. Harry was as surprised as his father that Herbert should agree to fight a double-member constituency against two prominent Tories, Lord George Hamilton and Octavius Coope. But when Mary heard the news she went 'nearly went mad [...] in a boiling state of excitement', though she noted that Herbert 'sat all day staring with big eyes into vacancy'.[59] Certainly her brother seemed somewhat overwhelmed, less perhaps by the turn of events than by the challenge which he now faced. 'I could not refuse', he noted in the irregular diary which he began about this time, 'though I felt annihilated. The cause was so great & the opportunity such as I should never again have. What a chance for anyone!'[60] But the immediacy and scale of the challenge left him struggling to formulate his ideas on the great public issues of the day.

Nevertheless, he had shown in preparing for his Oxford finals that he could exert himself when necessary and he now threw himself vigorously into electioneering. In the midst of an agricultural depression the Liberals' proposed extension of the parliamentary franchise to rural labourers was significant but their main focus was on criticising Disraeli's foreign policy. Herbert launched his own campaign on 18 March at the City Liberal Club, making in Mary's view a 'capital' impression. He had undertaken little in the way of public speaking before but over the following five days he made 27 speeches in different parts of the constituency, revealing a hitherto unsuspected ability as a stump orator in the face of crowds almost uniformly hostile. Mary was impressed by what she saw and heard. In Kilburn, which was noisy and boisterous, he was 'excellent'. A meeting in Harlesden was 'rapturous' and Herbert's speech 'astonished me'. Finchley was 'horrid' with fights during which pepper and other missiles were thrown. Tottenham and Enfield were 'fearful' because patriotic crowds broke into 'Rule Britannia' every time Herbert opened his mouth. Holborn Town Hall and Mill Hill were less rowdy and he was allowed to display his 'remarkable gift'.[61] When it came to the vote, however, he was well beaten, much to the surprise of the national press, Mary and indeed Herbert himself, his disappointment compounded by the knowledge that in the country at large the Liberals won a substantial victory. Some consolation perhaps was provided by the resignation of Disraeli and the Queen's eventual grudging invitation to Gladstone to form a new administration in the spring of 1880.

It would be easy to dismiss Mary's comments on her brother's performance as sisterly bias but she was by no means alone in her view. Lord Acton told her of the senior Liberal Robert Lowe's assessment that there had been nothing to choose between Herbert's speeches and those of his illustrious father, while another mutual acquaintance opined that Herbert had nothing to learn as a speaker, notwithstanding his inexperience and limited political knowledge. Acton himself thought Herbert's defeat as good as a victory because of the way in which he had conducted the campaign.[62] Such judgements perhaps influenced James Kitson, the industrialist who dominated Liberal politics in

Leeds, where Herbert's father had won a seat but then
vacated it in favour of Midlothian. Herbert replied positively
when Kitson asked if he would care to stand for the vacancy
and he was unanimously adopted at the meeting of the
Liberal caucus. After delivering half a dozen speeches in
two days he was returned unopposed on 8 May. Edward
Hamilton, one of the prime minister's private secretaries,
noted in his diary that Herbert had had a magnificent
reception in Leeds and promised to make his mark on the
political world.[63] Catherine told the Liberal intellectual
James Bryce that she was 'much moved' by the outcome,
while the new prime minister himself was delighted by the
enthusiasm his son's speeches generated, especially among
working men.[64] At the same time, however, he made it clear
to Kitson that Herbert's decision to enter political life was
'not of my instigation. He has done it by a deliberate choice
which he has made for himself with my full approbation.'[65]
That may have been so but Gladstone had certainly pulled a
few strings on his son's behalf.

CHAPTER 2

Ireland and Back

The path to Westminster was well trodden by the political families with whom Herbert had mixed from earliest childhood and in this sense election to parliament involved a virtually seamless transition. The benches of both Houses were predominantly occupied by men whose presence, like his, had previously graced the classrooms of the great public schools and the lecture halls of the ancient universities. If many of the faces were familiar so, too, were the rhythm and timbre of parliamentary life, for the session normally filled only a few months of the year, though affairs of politics, often accompanied by those of the heart and loins, formed a continuous thread in the lives of the Victorian social elite. It was inevitable that as an eligible bachelor and son of the prime minister the new member for Leeds should be much sought out by those seeking political influence or a husband for an unwed daughter and Herbert's gregarious nature and natural charm added to his appeal. The intermittent diary that he started in 1880 bears witness to a hectic and sustained round of dinners, weekend house parties and theatre visits together with musical evenings to which Herbert contributed both his voice and his cello. Interspersed with these were shooting parties, tennis and frequent visits to Lords cricket ground from which his own game apparently drew some inspiration since his batting for the parliamentary team was generally more successful than his efforts at Oxford, though this probably reflected the inferior quality of the opposition as well.

He was much in demand, too, in his new constituency where he was naturally regarded as the next best thing to his father. Fortunately, Kitson was a seasoned political organiser, well able to steer him through the maze of correspondence, invitations and solicitations which an MP invariably received and the two men became good friends, notwithstanding the considerable disparity in their ages. Constituency affairs had to be juggled with the demands of the family estate and parliament which in his first session he attended assiduously. One fairly typical diary entry from his early months as an MP recounts how he sat through a lengthy overnight debate, voting in three divisions before going home in order to change, wash and eat. He then returned to the House, lunched with Lord Rosebery and then spoke at the Stepney Working Lads Institute before dining at the Criterion.[1] Rather against his father's advice, he decided not to address the House during his first session. He knew full well what constituted a good parliamentary speech and also that any effort of his would inevitably invite comparison with his father, one of the finest orators of his day.[2] Yet, as his father understood, the longer Herbert delayed, 'cogitating with much pain & grief', the greater the magnitude of the task appeared.[3] Finally on 24 March 1881 he rose on rather shaky legs to speak against an opposition censure of the government's declared intent to withdraw British troops from Afghanistan. Sir Charles Dilke led so ably for the government that Herbert felt it necessary to begin his own speech by apologising for following him, hardly a promising opening. His own half-hour contribution could at best be described as solid, relying too much on closely written notes which he found difficult to follow in his edgy state of self-consciousness.[4] The thrust of the Conservative case was that the proposed withdrawal would weaken Britain's ability to protect India against Russian expansionism. Herbert dismissed this on the grounds that Russia respected public opinion too much to invade India and was in any case incapable of such action without command of the sea. The following day the opposition resolution was defeated but Herbert seems to have been more relieved by the fact that he had broken the ice though he felt that his 'much labour' had produced only 'a tiny mouse'.[5] The prime minister's pleasure in Herbert's performance might also have reflected relief, not least because in 16 years an MP, his older son Willy had made no impact at all, rarely contributing to debates. 'Father's face when he turned round to me at the end, I shall never forget', Herbert noted with some feeling.[6] Edward Hamilton noted the nervousness but generally thought Herbert had inherited much of his father's charm of voice, put his thoughts together clearly and delivered them excellently.[7] John Morley, then editor of the *Pall Mall Gazette*, agreed, while Lord Spencer declared that Herbert had the makings of a real orator.[8] Although such responses were consistent with accounts of Herbert's speeches during his election campaign, platform and parliamentary oratory presented different challenges in terms of the expectations of their audiences and the formality of proceedings. If on the face of it his maiden speech was well received the emotional effort and nervous tension which accompanied it clearly affected him deeply and always thereafter played on his mind, disinclining him to speaking at all, thereby contributing to his reputation as an ineffectual performer on the floor of the House. Over the next few years he rarely joined in a debate and when he did his touch was sometimes unsure. In August 1883, for example, he was much criticised for failing to explain the principles behind a minor Irish measure whose second reading he was introducing for the government.[9]

Even so, as Mary Gladstone noted, some Tory ladies in the gallery were much taken with Herbert's maiden performance, though their views may have been based less on the speech than on the eligibility of the speaker. At least one leading society hostess thought him very good looking and the working-class girls in his own constituency had similarly taken a shine to him.[10] Whether he was himself conscious of this (and he always believed his relatively short stature something of a drawback) Herbert certainly enjoyed feminine company, often commenting in his diary on the charms, both physical and intellectual, of the various women he met. Thus Mrs M., encountered on the tennis court during a house party, he judged to be 'very attractive', while the Misses Lord and Miss Whittingham, fellow guests at a dinner party, he described respectively as interesting to talk to and pleasant to look at.[11] It was another, however, who seems particularly to have caught his eye at about this time. Gladstone senior was very close both politically and personally to the Scottish MP and industrialist Charles Tennant, and their families socialised frequently. Herbert dined often at the Tennants' London home and Sir Charles's son, Eddy, was probably his closest friend. So often was Herbert in the company of Eddy's sisters, Laura and Margot, that in March 1881 a rumour circulated in London's clubland that his marriage had been settled with 'Miss T'. Given that Margot was only 17 at the time it seems likely that the story, which was utterly baseless, referred to the slightly older Laura.[12] Yet Herbert was strongly attracted to the vivacious and somewhat unconventional younger girl. His diary lapsed in the summer of 1881 but when he resumed writing he included a summary of the missing weeks. After shooting at Hawarden he went to Scotland, first to fish the Spey and then to stay with the Tennants at their ancestral home, The Glen. It was, he recorded, two weeks of 'pretty shooting, splendid lawn tennis in the covered court & wild larks when we should have been in bed. The Miss Tennants very delightful; Miss Margot perhaps in particular. Most sorry to leave.'[13] Nor, apparently, was the interest all one way. Herbert certainly did not possess the predatory animal magnetism of a lothario, but sociable, musical, sporting and with a warm, outgoing personality, he had much that did appeal to the opposite sex. Margot was clearly flattered to have sparked the interest of the prime minister's son. For all her youthfulness, however, she seems even then to have been weighing up the prospects with a maturely calculating eye, for she was not short of suitors. Mary Gladstone also visited The Glen at this time and, finding

Margot confined to a couch with a smashed knee, talked with her for a long time about politics and, she specifically noted in her diary, about 'Herbert in particular and whether he is ambitious'.[14]

Margot's query was well founded, for Herbert had been slow to decide upon a political career and he had not been motivated by thoughts either of personal advantage or ambition. Even so, by the time the convalescent Margot raised the matter he had already been given something of a forward push when his father, ignoring his colleagues' warnings about nepotism, appointed him a Civil Lord of the Admiralty, or junior whip. The appointment required him to be re-elected but so soon after a general election and in a solidly Liberal constituency this was little more than a formality and he was returned unopposed, resuming his seat in the Commons on 24 August before heading off to his pleasurable diversions at The Glen. Shortly afterwards his father asked the Irish secretary, W. E. Forster, to take Herbert as his assistant. 'Of what use he may be to you remains to be proved; but I do believe he will be a pleasant & cheering presence.'[15]

Ireland had barely featured in the 1880 election campaign despite that island's enduring miseries, exacerbated from the 1870s by a sustained agricultural depression. Yet the country's condition and future were to dominate the parliament of 1880–5 and thus the first years of Herbert's political career, not least because the election saw some of the moderate Irish MPs replaced by men of a more militant disposition whose filibustering tactics turned Westminster into something of a bear garden, exhausting its members and generally, as Herbert later wrote, causing the government express to lumber along like 'a blocked, half empty goods train'.[16] Brought up with a profound respect for parliamentary convention Herbert found this constant obstructionism repellent, though he went too far in a public speech at Hornsey when he suggested that the Irish members' tactics were part of a malicious conspiracy coordinated by the Tories. As before, it seems that he found a freedom and passion outside that he seemed unable to display inside the House of Commons where he subsequently and very meekly withdrew the offending words.

Meekness was not overly evident in Ireland itself, however. Encouraged by the Land League, set up in 1879 by Michael Davitt and Charles Parnell, violence was escalating against evictions for the non-payment of rents. Gladstone's government responded positively when in April 1880 the Irish members demanded compensation for tenants evicted because failing harvests made it impossible to pay their rents. The principle accepted, Forster piloted an appropriate measure through the Commons only to see it rejected by the Lords. Suggestions that the violence be met with force were divisive in the cabinet but early in 1881 coercive measures were forced through, tempered by the introduction of a second Land Bill. Although this granted much of what the Land League demanded with respect to rents and land rights, it ignored wider issues of economic development and the relief of distress. More significantly, it excluded from its provision tenants *currently* in arrears, much to the displeasure of the Land Leaguers, although some of them did not particularly wish to see agrarian hardship diminish because it was a potent recruiter for the wider objective of national independence. Following an inflammatory speech from Parnell in October 1881 the Land League's leaders were arrested and imprisoned in Kilmainham Gaol, provoking the launch of a no-rent movement. It was at this juncture that Herbert was delegated to assist Forster and made his first visit to Ireland.

His assignment was not completely out of the blue, for throughout the spring of 1881 he had kept his father well posted as to the general eagerness of Liberals for the Land Bill and the two men frequently discussed Irish affairs. A great deal of scholarly ink has been spilled analysing the prime minister's ultimate espousal of home rule in 1885 and whether it represented a sudden conversion or the outcome of more considered mental processes. Either way, he was already discussing Ireland with a son whose own ideas, while still being moulded by events, circumstances and personal experience, were already further down the road towards the principle of home rule than Gladstone's own. Herbert was initially somewhat reluctant to speak out too freely without prior consultation, but through Harry the prime minister intimated that with respect to Ireland Herbert should be free to talk about what ought to be done and also what was likely to be done. 'Father points out that it would not do for him to make important announcements through you.' He particularly stressed the prime minister's wish that 'you shd. form and state your own opinions.'[17] Noting that it would 'awkward if I got the reputation for being his mouthpiece', Herbert took this at face value.[18] In April 1881 he used a speech at Leeds to advocate giving the Irish people complete responsibility for the management of their own affairs, 'the root trouble', as he wrote later, being 'English autocracy'.[19] Yet there remained the matter of the form Irish self-government might take, as well as more immediate issues of law and order. Herbert struggled with what was to become a classic Liberal dilemma, how to uphold the rule of law in the face of violence spawned by what were, in his view, justifiable grievances. In going to Ireland, he told Harry, he hoped to gain a better understanding of the agitators and to see how far people were justified in attributing wrong-doing to Dublin Castle, the seat of British administration.[20]

First impressions, however, were alarming. He arrived in Dublin just as the news of Parnell's arrest broke and while bad weather prevented any significant public demonstration, the Castle guard had been doubled and he felt it necessary to arm himself with a revolver. Within a fortnight he was wondering whether he had committed himself too far at Leeds in recommending that the Irish be given complete management of their local affairs.[21] Immersing himself in police reports he also concluded privately that coercion was necessary.[22] But while he deplored violence and wished to suppress it, his underlying sympathy for the Irish people remained undiluted. At the end of October he attended the trial of a man charged with murdering a policeman during a riot. Personally he thought the evidence of guilt was conclusive, especially as the defence's chief witness was a Fenian sympathiser who had conducted the post-mortem without proper authorisation and before anyone else had a chance to examine the dead officer's injuries. The jury, however, decided that the evidence was insufficient and found the accused guilty only of being one of a crowd. For Herbert this outcome underlined the difficulty of relying on the jury system when the bulk of the population clearly had little time for the property arrangements it was designed to protect. Yet at a human level his sympathies lay firmly with the prisoner in the dock. 'Poor fellow has he ever had any hopes beyond a rise of his miserable wages or an extra pint of beer?'[23] Government, he noted, may not have been responsible for the man's actions but it was responsible for the public house where he got his drink and for the policies which had led to the riot in the first place.

Returning to Hawarden briefly in November and informed by what he had witnessed in Ireland and gleaned from the various official papers he had examined, he feared this father was 'too sanguine' about the situation.[24] Back in Ireland he travelled through some of the most turbulent areas of the south and west, though his hopes of remaining anonymous were soon dashed. Conversations with scores of land agents, policemen, magistrates, landlords and tenants confirmed his belief that government policy was working, though he thought more could be done to reduce further the incidence of agrarian outrages.[25] Equally, however, these encounters reinforced his conviction that the root cause of Ireland's woes was the culpability of the landlords. 'Everything that I have seen & heard of them as a class', he wrote to his mother, 'makes me think that they have not been half enough abused for their want of backbone, nerve & common sense.'[26]

During the Christmas holidays he again spoke privately with his father about Ireland and lectured, badly as he thought, on the subject at the Manchester Free Trade Hall. Margot was in the audience but there was little time for social niceties as he returned to Dublin on Boxing Day, accompanied by his sister Helen. By the time he quit Ireland for good at the end of January 1882 he had composed several reports for his father as well as helping Forster and his officials to prepare prospective Irish bills. Yet he did not contribute to the Irish debate that opened the 1882 session of parliament. He was prepared to do so, he noted in his diary, but the discussion ended somewhat abruptly and there were enough ministerial speakers.[27] While this may have been factually accurate it contained a hint of post-facto rationalisation. Apart from Forster no one on the Liberal benches could match either the breadth or the currency of the direct knowledge which Herbert had acquired during the previous three months and it seems likely that his silence reflected his discomfort in the House of Commons: it was after all only a few months since his nerve-wracked maiden effort. It is possible, too, that he felt inhibited by his awareness that he was not totally at one with his father with respect to coercion. The prime minister had not been in favour of the Coercion Act because in his view it could be effective only against secret societies, not open ones like the Land League. Herbert was well aware of the sensitivities of the actual term 'coercion' but still favoured strong measures because he was increasingly convinced that the violence had more to do with revolutionary aspiration than mere economic distress. Nor did he believe that the Coercion Act itself had been entirely ineffective and when at the end of March 1882 Forster made a controversial speech suggesting otherwise, he judged him to have been both indiscreet and inaccurate. Coercion, he noted in his diary, 'has succeeded in these most important particulars, namely the enforcement of rent payment & the re-establishment of the Common Law as the only recognised law.' Like his father Herbert also regretted that Forster had expressed himself so publicly. 'It does not do to make any confession of weakness & I think Mr F was wrong to acknowledge the power of the League & the impotence, supposing it to exist wh. I do not, of the Gt.'[28] Whether this incident influenced his father's attitude is not clear but a few days afterwards Herbert noted with some satisfaction that he seemed to be coming round to his own view that the no-rent campaign had failed and that ongoing crime was primarily revolutionary in intent.[29]

On 22 April Herbert met with the Nationalist MP, F. H. O'Donnell, who agreed that the Land Act was working and suggested that an amendment to deal with the matter of tenants in arrears would be a major step forward. He further intimated that the Land League wished to withdraw the no-rent manifesto because Parnell himself feared that the crime associated with it would get out of hand. Herbert asked whether the Irish members would desist from their agitation if the government accepted a formal Irish declaration against crime and in favour of law and order. O'Donnell indicated that they would, adding that as Nationalists they would be 'content with a fair grant of Home Rule'. Herbert then assured him that he was willing to do everything to find a way forward for Ireland but stressed that 'of course I came to see him solely on my own responsibility.'[30] Despite this assurance it seems highly unlikely that he was acting without at least tacit encouragement from his father, and certainly he immediately sent an account of his conversation to Forster. But the Irish Secretary distrusted O'Donnell and was not persuaded. Joseph Chamberlain, who had been formally charged by the cabinet with handling negotiations with the Irish, asked Herbert for a report of his conversation, prior to a meeting with his own intermediary, Captain O'Shea. O'Shea confirmed much of what O'Donnell had conveyed to Herbert, whose own views, particularly with respect to coercion, were now beginning to soften. In principle he considered it base to come to terms with men regarded as criminals purely for party political advantage but pragmatically he thought that if what O'Donnell said was true then it would be foolish to reject the possibilities out of hand. 'This being so', he wrote in his diary, What is the use of continuing broadside coercion & of keeping Parnell & Co in prison – a new departure is necessary [...] Father has been much interested in what O'D(onnell) has said & doesn't cast it aside by any means. He is more sanguine than Mr F(orster) though of course not so confident as Mr C (hamberlain).[31]

Writing at length to Harry at this time he reiterated his belief that the Land Act was working well and that the no-rent campaign had effectively broken down. Yet there were residual problems with rent collection and crime, which he attributed to the current system of government in Ireland, the operation of coercion, the increasing number of evictions and the incarceration of people's leaders. New measures, he said, were under consideration.[32]

The new departure was formally announced in *The Times* on 3 May 1882 when the imprisoned Irishmen were released. Parnell agreed to uphold law and order, and the Land Act was amended to include the tenants in arrears, arrangements which signalled the effective start of tacit government collaboration with the constitutional nationalists, and in Herbert's opinion, the first necessary step towards home rule. To the surprise of both the Gladstones Forster promptly resigned in protest, though it is possible that having survived two assassination attempts he feared a third. Events seem to bear him out, for his successor as Irish Secretary, Lord Frederick Cavendish, was barely off the Dublin boat before he was stabbed to death in Phoenix Park on 6 May, along with Thomas Burke, the permanent Irish Under-Secretary. The murders had an added personal significance for the Gladstone family because Cavendish's wife was Lucy Lyttelton, one of the cousins who had figured so prominently in Herbert's childhood and his diary contains several musings on her fortitude and bravery, along with repeated and fervent denunciations of those who had made her a widow.

The assassins were members of a hitherto unknown group, the Irish National Invincibles. Never short of physical courage, Herbert immediately offered to return to Ireland. Twice the prime minister recommended him to the Viceroy, Lord Spencer, who spurned the offer as unnecessary, adding that any Gladstone would be a likely target for extremists.[33] As was intended, the assassinations threatened to widen the gulf between England and its unhappy neighbour, Parnell's prompt denunciation of the murderers doing little to offset the widespread view which Herbert detected among his constituents that the Irish were 'inhuman & shd. be killed off'.[34] The editor of *The Times* certainly did his best to stoke up such sentiments, demanding draconian action and the reversal of all existing remedial measures, recommendations which drove Herbert to his diary in a rare display of anger with the editor for whom 'no words are too strong for condemnation, no lash too severe [...] inspired by the devil.'[35] Yet in truth his own convictions were shaken, especially by the personal dimensions of the murders, and he confessed to Harry that never before had he 'felt the urge to devote my life to hunting down remorselessly & to death one's fellow men'.[36] But somewhat paradoxically the murders ultimately ushered in a relatively quiescent period in Irish affairs although initially a new Coercion Act giving Dublin Castle greater powers to deal with disorder provoked even greater savagery. Parnell refused to condemn the violence and while the Land League was disbanded, it was replaced by the National League working explicitly for home rule. Gradually, however, as the Arrears Act began to have an impact Spencer and George Trevelyan, the latest Irish Secretary, managed to bring the disorder under some degree of control.

With Irish affairs less pressing, Herbert was freer to pick up the threads of his personal life. He had remained a regular visitor at the Tennants and on a couple of occasions in February and March 1882 noted long talks with Margot. There is no indication in his diary or correspondence as to the nature of these conversations but there can be little doubt that for the first time in his life he was seriously smitten. He partnered Margot to the Tennant family ball in July and to several other summer parties. In October he went to The Glen for 12 days although the midnight romps were less frequent and rowdy than previously because Margot (the only other member of the company mentioned by name in his diary) was incommoded by an injured arm. He was back in Scotland for New Year's Eve, which, he recorded, he never enjoyed more, L and M being 'very kind'.[37] The party dispersed a few days later and a pencilled diary entry notes

that after Lady Tennant's departure for Glasgow, 'Margot & I
followed alone. We had a romantic journey to G. & never did
I find the time pass in a very slow train so quickly. M & I had a
long talk.' The next two lines have been heavily inked over,
leaving a single line noting simply 'shorter interview with M in
evening'.[38] Two days later Margot left The Glen, taking with
her, it might be inferred, Herbert's dashed romantic hopes.
Whether the inking over of the diary entry was done at the
time or later is not clear but the very action suggests that
what had transpired between himself and Margot at the
morning meeting was so intensely private that he determined
no-one should ever know of it. It seems more than likely,
therefore, that he had broached the issue of marriage and that
after agreeing to think it over she turned him down in the
evening. Herbert was an avid correspondent, particularly
with family members, but not a hint of this is to be found in
his communications even with Harry. However, one letter
from Mary is suggestive. Referring to a private note from
Herbert, she replied that he could be 'certain that what you
tell me shall be locked in the innermost recesses of my heart &
never revealed to my life's end and thereto I plight thee my
troth.'[39] Her letter is undated and assigned in the Glynne-
Gladstone papers to the 1870s. But there is no obvious reason
for such a dating while both the sentiment and the language of
Mary's letter suggest strongly that Herbert had confided
something deeply personal in her. Given that he preserved
virtually all his correspondence it is interesting that the letter
which prompted Mary's response cannot now be found,
suggesting perhaps that he removed it from the family papers,
a step entirely consistent with his attempts to obscure his
diary entry of 10 January.

   Even had he been so inclined, there was little time for
moping as he had a busy round of constituency engagements
to occupy him: several speeches and institutional visits, a
dinner and a lecture, an address to the Leeds Chamber of
Commerce, receptions for deputations and opening the
annual Yorkshire and Lancashire tournament in his capacity
as chairman of the Leeds Chess Club. One of the speeches,

delivered at the Leeds Albert Hall on 19 January 1883, contained a strong message on Ireland, though in his usual self-deprecatory fashion he thought it lacked both form and polish. Another followed in which he argued that Irish self-government could be claimed on the grounds of justice and reason but could not be gained by force. While not even the most fervent nationalist could expect a separate parliament immediately, he said, there was no reason why the principle should not be discussed. For himself he did not believe that the establishment of a Dublin parliament would threaten the Queen's authority in Ireland. Furthermore, he warned, the demand for home rule would only intensify unless Westminster addressed the issue on its merits.[40] He had already hinted the previous autumn that he was ready to support Irish self-government so long as the supremacy of the Imperial Parliament was maintained.[41] However, these latest remarks, delivered with that abandon which he rarely displayed in the House itself, were too much for some of his colleagues. Forster thought he had overstepped the mark while George Trevelyan thought it implied divisions in the government which would encourage the Nationalist drive for home rule, adding rather threateningly that it would diminish the friendly regard in which Herbert was held by the party leaders.[42] Repeatedly imploring Herbert to be more measured, Hamilton told him that most Liberals believed he had been indiscreet and that he had not only damaged his own prospects but hampered the Dublin administration.[43] None of this cut much ice with Herbert, however. He had no personal political ambitions and was unrepentant, asserting that he had spoken out of conviction and on his own responsibility.[44] Even before his Leeds speeches Nationalists had been urging the Liberals to embrace his ideas, T. D. Sullivan noting that wisdom was often to be found in the mouth of babes and that he hoped 'the old man would take heed to the words of his son and act on them'.[45] In fact the prime minister, who could hardly have been unaware of Herbert's views given their frequent conversations about the subject, was virtually alone among Liberals in supporting

Herbert, arguing that he had every right to express his own
views and encouraging their publication for wider circulation.
Herbert's popularity with the Irish may not have endeared
him to some fellow Liberals but it did reflect how rapidly he
had emerged within a short space of time as an influential
voice in the most important political dialogue of the day,
a conduit between the Irish and government, a constant
prompt in the prime minister's ear and a man whose speeches,
certainly outside of Westminster, could cause waves. All this
had come about without any conscious effort or intent on
his part, and without his ever saying much in the House of
Commons or occupying a significant official position: indeed
in 1883 he rejected a suggestion from his father that he succeed
Lord Richard Grosvenor as chief Liberal whip. Such an
appointment would certainly not have gone down well with
those Liberals who found his continued public utterances on
Ireland distasteful. Another speech at Acton in July particularly
vexed Spencer and Trevelyan. Hamilton believed its effects
had been exaggerated but he still thought Herbert very
pig-headed in wilfully refusing to see the danger of being
indiscreet. 'He won't submit to the penalties attaching to
being a son of Mr G and a member, however, subordinate,
of the Government.'[46]

Early in 1884 Chamberlain came up with a plan for Ireland
combining minimal coercion with devolved administration
via county councils reporting to a Central Board, proposals
which found some support, although Dublin Castle had
reservations. Parnell saw it as a positive step towards home
rule and the prime minister, who according to Herbert had
in 1882 virtually conceded the principle of giving a large
measure of local government to Ireland, was supportive.
However, he was somewhat distracted by affairs in the Sudan
and Afghanistan, as well as a complex Redistribution Bill and
with the exception of Lord Granville, the Whigs in the cabinet
opposed Chamberlain's plan. With little prospect of anything
coming from the scheme, therefore, Parnell turned instead
to the Tories, who were making encouraging noises about
Ireland and who, from his point of view, had the massive

advantage of controlling the House of Lords. In June 1885 the Irish helped carry a Conservative amendment to the budget, a defeat which prompted Gladstone's resignation. The Irish imbroglio had tried the government sorely and policy disagreements had so divided Liberals that several ministers had already offered to step down. But an immediate election was not possible because electoral rolls incorporating new voters enfranchised by the 1884 Reform Bill were not yet ready. Lord Salisbury therefore took office as prime minister in a minority Conservative Government although his administration was effectively one long election campaign.

Discussing the situation with his father shortly after the Liberals' resignation Herbert opined that they should offer Parnell a parliament, to which Gladstone responded simply 'I think we must.'[47] But with Chamberlains's plans in the air and Parnell apparently flirting with the Tories neither man knew exactly what the Irish now wanted. In a letter dated 21 July 1885 Mrs O'Shea claimed that Parnell now favoured a scheme along the lines advanced by Herbert in his most recent speech at Leeds but Herbert himself was sceptical, as he noted after another discussion with his father in early August.

> The question is what do these men want & what will they evolve? Do they wish things to remain unsettled? To wait upon events? Or will they agree upon a thorough going measure of self-Gov't which the Liberals under their old leader can give them?[48]

Herbert had growing doubts about Parnell's good faith and was not inclined to follow his father's suggestion that the Irish leader be contacted via intermediaries to establish whether he was still in favour of some form of local government reform. 'I do not take this line & told Father that [...] Parnell is now playing a wholly personal & selfish game – that he is vindictive & will never forgive his imprisonment.'[49] In fact, Parnell had already met with the new Irish Secretary, Lord Carnarvon, a meeting which led him to think he might get something from the Tories. Nevertheless early in November he finally forwarded a document to Gladstone indicating that the Irish now had higher expectations than the Central Board for which they had been prepared to settle in January. Gladstone, however, had already begun to think about turning home rule into a legislative proposal, although he was acutely aware of the danger of splitting his party. In mid-October 1885 he set out his latest thinking in a letter marked 'private' and 'supplied to Herbert', the intention being that Herbert should communicate its contents to Henry Labouchere, a leading radical close to Chamberlain.

> I can go so far as to give you my own impression as to my Father's views, derived from observation & from consultations with him at times.
>
> I feel sure that he has reflected much before coining the words of his address relating to Ireland & that he means to stand by them in both the main particulars ie first to uphold the unity of the Empire and surrender or compromise nothing that is essential for it, secondly that there is no limit to the powers he would gladly see, compatibly with this condition, given to Ireland for the management of all affairs previously her own.
>
> Father is, as I think, in no way disapproving of the efforts of the nationalists to get the Tory Party to take up their question. I have however heard him say that unless they wish permanently to sink or swim with the Tories, they had better bring the matter to a very speedy upshot. I doubt whether he would commit to the gratuitous launching of a plan by him at this present stage to be the best way to forward it. From his Address he seems to expect that Ireland may through her representatives speak plainly and publicly for herself.[50]

There was nothing in this with which Herbert disagreed but while he concurred with his father on the objective the means and timing of its achievement still separated them. Herbert was particularly keen that something be said more publicly and promptly but he realised that this could happen only if the Liberals had a parliamentary majority and if they could be assured of Irish cooperation.[51] Also, as he pointed out to Harry in November, he was afraid that

> the Br. Public & the ordinary MP may complain that a mine has been sprung on them when the proposal for a separate legislature is made (given a favourable election) seeing that according to our leaders we are by way of dealing first with procedure. Cd it not be said that it wd be admirable to deal, if possible ie assuming Parnell reasonable, with the I.Q first?[52]

Harry responded immediately that 'your remarks re I.Q. seemed to impress him & I think he will take an opportunity of making it clear that I. Q. may come before anything else.' He added that he had found their father that very morning drafting a rough bill.[53] However, the Liberal leader was not prepared to act on Herbert's wish that something substantial be said about the detail of the proposed legislation. His preferred course at this stage was to leave the ground clear for Nationalists to negotiate with the Conservatives. In a further letter dated 14 November and marked 'secret', Gladstone acknowledged the force of Herbert's suggestion but went on to assert that

> It is dangerous for me to give out anything however obvious it may be, which could be carried to the Government that they might outbid it.
>
> It is beyond all doubt that if 1. The sense of Ireland be adequately declared in a certain direction and if 2. The Liberal Party is placed by the Election in a position to take up the question, then there ought to be early communication with those who would be the organs of Irish desire.
>
> You might state your opinion to this effect, and your opinion also that this is my opinion. But remember to do nothing that can indicate a desire on our part to draw them off from communicating with the Government if they are so inclined.
>
> I conceive that the obvious bases for any admissible measures would be

(1) Irish Chamber of Irish affairs

(2) Irish representation to remain as now in both Houses but only for Imperial affairs

(3) Equitable division of Imperial charges by fixed proportions

(4) Protection of minority

(5) Suspension of Imperial authority for all civil purposes whatsoever.[54]

Another letter to Herbert, dated 10 December and preserved in the papers of Lord Rosebery, reiterated Gladstone's opinion that, because the Tories were currently in government, they should be allowed an opportunity to settle the Irish question in conjunction with the Nationalists since a plan for Ireland *ought* to be introduced by the government of the day and no constitutional principle would be threatened by letting the current cabinet remain in office. 'You will be sure to be right as to my opinions while you keep on these lines.'[55]

It seems likely that these letters were intended to help Herbert prepare for the election campaign, which finally got under way on 24 November. His manifesto to the voters of Leeds West, the new constituency which had replaced his old one as a result of the Redistribution Act, concentrated almost exclusively on the Irish issue and his views got a further airing in *The Times* on 12 December. His letter stressed that while he could not countenance separation, if the majority of Irish people wanted to have their own parliament, then justice and wisdom demanded that their wish be granted. Three days later he travelled to London, calling briefly with Bryce before meeting with Labouchere and Wemyss Reid, editor of the *Leeds Mercury*, to acquaint them with his father's thinking. Then he met Dawson Rogers of the National Press Association together with one of his editors and 'gave them the situation' before returning to Chester.[56] Rogers had requested this meeting in the hope of receiving some guidance as to what he might publish to clarify the current Liberal position on Ireland which to him seemed confused, not an ideal condition in the context of an election campaign. Herbert seems to have chosen his words quite carefully but Rogers and his editor placed their own interpretation upon them and on 17 December the national press carried the sensational news that Mr Gladstone had come out in favour of home rule. In fact there was little new in what the press reported. What was novel was the idea that home rule might actually be an imminent and realistic proposition. Herbert noted in his diary, apparently with a certain amount of self satisfaction, that

> fat all in the fire. Standard publishes 'Authentic plan' of Mr G., & the evening papers & telegraph agencies go wild in the afternoon. Hn flooded with telegrams & all the world is agog [...] How very odd it is that people refuse to see their house is ablaze till the fire engines come to put it out. Every man of sense saw what was coming in I. this election, & what wd. have to follow. The inevitable is on us, that is all. So far as I can see the leakage has been considerable. L must have let out a good deal, R a certain amount with discretion, & the NPA has sent the whole lot out. This is what it says & it is an accurate report of my 'private' interview. Father quite *comps*.[57]

Herbert's father was indeed so undisturbed that in the midst of the furore he found time to finish writing a theological article and the following day Herbert again noted his father's apparent equanimity.[58]

These diary comments might seem to support the notion that Gladstone had deliberately given Herbert both the freedom and the material to communicate with the press, to fly what became known as the Hawarden Kite in the belief that their reports would allow him to gauge Liberal feeling before publicly committing himself to home rule. In fact, all Herbert did was to give his own opinion as to his father's views which, as he told Hamilton, he had been authorised to do subject to his own discretion.[59] This authorisation is clear from the letters of 14 November and 10 December. The record also shows that more than once Gladstone had expressly discouraged Herbert from appearing to be his spokesman, encouraging him to develop and express his own views on Irish affairs. But while unswervingly loyal to his father and operating as his go-between with the Irish and with radical critics in the party, Herbert was no cipher. There is no reason, therefore, to dispute his own claim that in talking to the journalists on 15 December he acted entirely of his own volition. As he wrote later to his cousin

> The Irish question is the one question on which I feel very deeply and with reference to which I can sacrifice my opinions to nobody [...] I have acted and spoken freely on my own responsibility for five years; when convenient the Tories have endeavoured to associate my Father with my views, but I have spoken my mind so persistently that if our own political friends choose to consider whenever I say or do anything in connection with Irish matters that I am made use of by my Father for his own purposes and ends they overlook my right to full political liberty governed only by my own sense of responsibility and they do him a cruel injustice. My rights matter nothing except to myself and I can look after them. But injustice to him is a crime in my eyes.[60]

His motives were undoubtedly mixed but driven primarily by his own long-held conviction that Irish self-government was warranted on both moral and practical grounds. Believing also that his father was the only Liberal with sufficient political weight to drive through so controversial a reform, Herbert was acutely conscious that his parent was 75 when he resigned in June 1885 and that his health would inevitably decline. To this was allied the realisation, shared by his father, that such a measure would likely split both Liberal opinion and the Liberal Party, a message reinforced by Dilke who had publicly declared that he and Chamberlain both thought any settlement between Gladstone and the Nationalists unacceptable and that it would be better to keep the Tories in power. If home rule failed Herbert knew that his father would retire, leaving the party prey to the Chamberlainites who, disenchanted with

Gladstone's leadership and yearning for more radical policies, were also seeking to gain control of the National Liberal Federation (NLF), thereby raising the possibility that any policy split would be mirrored by an organisational division. Herbert later told Kitson that his real purpose in speaking to the journalists had been to forestall this possibility by forcing the NLF to come out unequivocally in favour of home rule.[61]

These then were the thoughts swirling around in Herbert's head as events gathered momentum during the protracted general election campaign of late 1885. What brought them to bursting point was a communication from Wemyss Reid suggesting that the radicals' wished to keep the Tories in office because they wanted the Irish question shelved and Gladstone prevented from forming a government, a view independently confirmed to Herbert by former Liberal minister, Lyon Playfair. For Herbert, this slight on his father was too much. It outraged him. So also it did Harry, who told Hamilton that the 'simply atrocious' Chamberlain and Dilke had put personal ambition before patriotism.[62] Reid's appeal to Herbert to do something publicly to frustrate the radicals and help the party by sustaining Gladstone might most obviously have been made to the party's chief whip, but as an opponent of home rule Grosvenor was unlikely to be helpful. Accordingly, therefore, Herbert took matters into his own hands and gave his controversial interview. Labouchere may have pondered whether Herbert's action had been mere stupidity or intentional 'by order of Papa' but the kite was neither a plot hatched at Hawarden between Herbert and his father nor a case of stupidity on Herbert's part.[63]

In explaining his actions to Lady Cavendish, however, Herbert did concede that he had perhaps erred in not realising how the journalists to whom he spoke would report the discussion. They had, he complained, jumbled

> up into one Authoritative Statement much of what I had said – distinct beliefs, possible opinions, contingent policy without stating the contingencies, qualified ideas without the qualifications, and they headed most sentences with *Mr G*

thinks, holds, and so forth [...] I had no idea that an unauthorized account of a confidential talk with me was to be immediately sent as a bald statement to the papers.

But his motivation was quite clearly spelled out.

You may say I was to blame for not being more careful – justly perhaps. One lives and learns and I shall be in future more on my guard [...] I have betrayed no confidences. I have not intrigued against anybody for myself or for any one else – *though I have done something to stop the intrigues of others.* Where I have made mistakes, it has been in over-rating the discretion of men whose direct interest it may have been to be indiscreet.[64]

Sir William Harcourt may have sneered at Herbert's motives but he clearly understood them, telling Chamberlain afterwards that 'the chivalrous Herbert', fearful of a plot to keep his father out of office, 'thought it his duty to defeat this plan and took his measures accordingly.'[65]

Predictably, the Hawarden kite was interpreted in some quarters as a deliberate attempt to win over the Irish and the public airing of Gladstone's imputed views did swing Nationalist support back towards the Liberals. Herbert's actions, however, came too late to have any significant effect on the election, which gave the Conservatives 249 seats and the Liberals 335. This left the 86 Irish members in a position to keep either of the other two parties out of government but to keep only one, the Liberals, in office. With his government still in a minority at Westminster and his cabinet rejecting Carnarvon's recommendation to bring in home rule, Salisbury's position was clearly untenable. In January 1886 he resigned and William Gladstone became prime minister for the third time. Herbert's appointment to a junior post at the War Office, where he found Henry Campbell-Bannerman to be both a kind and an efficient chief, was perhaps an indication that his actions had not displeased his father and also of the value the new premier placed on his son's role as the link between himself, the Irish and Liberals in the country and parliament.[66]

In March the prime minister put two Irish measures to
the cabinet, one extending the land purchase scheme, the
other calling for the establishment of an Irish parliament.
Herbert was untroubled by rumours that the second proposal
might provoke unrest in protestant Ulster, but he was alert to
the dangers of a Whig break-away and of disagreements with
the Irish over the suggested financial arrangements. Even so,
he was highly optimistic when the first Home Rule Bill was
introduced in the House of Commons on 8 April although the
widely acknowledged brilliance of his father's speech did not
convince all of the government's own members or supporters.
As Frederick Cavendish's older brother, Lord Hartington
had strong personal reasons for rejecting any settlement with
the Irish Nationalists while John Bright opposed as immoral
what he saw as a concession to violence. The debate ebbed
and flowed over two weeks, dragging Herbert's hopes back
and forth with it, although even for this cause which he had
long championed on many a public platform, he could not
overcome his mental block and contribute to the swelling
parliamentary clamour. In early May he told Harry that
Chamberlain was being difficult and that unless some
concessions were made the bill would fail. Later in the
month he thought things had turned in the government's
favour but when the final vote was counted 93 Liberals,
including Chamberlain, followed the Conservatives into the
'no' lobby, thereby ensuring that the bill was lost.[67] Even
Herbert's brother Willy had doubts and in the ensuing
general election, the government's only recourse in the light
of its defeat, he stood down and brought to an end his
undistinguished parliamentary career. In Leeds Herbert
naturally concentrated almost exclusively on the Irish issue
and the electors did not let him down. But their sentiments
were not shared nationally. There was little time to organise
effectively and many seats went uncontested by the confused
and divided Liberals, while the Tories generally opted not to
oppose anti-home rule Liberals. Consequently, the Liberals
were reduced to 191 seats while the Parnellites won 85.
Against them were ranged 316 Tories and 78 Liberal

Unionists. Neither Gladstone's resignation nor the defeat dented Herbert's own convictions about the rightness of the cause. 'The present system of Gov't in Ireland is bad from its inception & there is enough to be said about it now to condemn it ten times over', he told his mother shortly after the campaign ended.[68]

The election over, Herbert cleared out his room at the War Office – he had not been in it very much during the government's brief life – and headed to Hawarden for a fishing break. Chamberlain, he noted was as 'vicious as ever & is bent on squashing out Father. I hear he has marked me down for vengeance. I don't care a rush for him.'[69] A more immediate consequence of his loss of office was felt in his pocket, however. He had long been financially dependent on his father but otherwise his only regular income had been the small official salary he had received from May 1882 when he was made a paid whip. A generous gift of £5,000 from his father in March 1882 brought in some investment dividend but now he found himself writing to Harry in some embarrassment about his finances. Over the past few months, he said, he had repaid a £600 loan to his father, spent £180 on elections and £50 on a wedding present for Mary, who at the age of 38 had announced in the midst of the kite crisis that she was to going to marry the curate of Hawarden, Harry Drew. In addition Herbert had forked out his subscription to the Reform Club, purchased a new cello and honoured a call on his shares in the National Liberal Club (NLC). He was, he confided, desperately short of ready cash. With the generosity that always characterised his relationship with his siblings and especially Herbert, Harry made the appropriate response, thereby allowing his brother to enjoy that autumn's music festival at Leeds free of financial worries, and once again in the company of the Tennants. Although his attempt in 1883 to further his relationship with Margot had been rebuffed, friendship with her family had continued to provide a welcome respite from politics. In the seasonal rush of social events, Herbert appeared for a time to take particular pleasure in the company of Margot's sister, Laura, though she was never more than 'Miss T' in his diary and even that was curtailed when she married his cousin, Alfred Lyttelton, in May 1885.[70] Her death early the following year was a dreadful shock and in an attempt to raise his friend's spirits, Herbert invited Eddy Tennant to accompany him to India where, he explained, Harry would put them up comfortably and arrange plenty of shooting.[71] It was a mark of the passing years, however, that Herbert afforded himself the luxury of this trip only after he had reassured himself that the Drews, Stephen and Willy would all be on hand to care for the ageing parents at Hawarden.

CHAPTER 3

Into the Wilderness

Herbert returned from India at the end of 1886 to find Irish affairs still very much on the front burner and he predicted that its fate would soon occupy all their attention.[1] He was right. As one of those most closely identified with the home rule cause, he was snowed under with invitations to speak almost as soon as he arrived in England, the torrent building up to such an extent that he complained it was as if he had a hundred throats. In July 1887 he excused the brevity of a note to Eddy Tennant on the grounds that speaking engagements were still pressing so heavily on his time, adding that nothing but animosity towards the government's Irish policy, 'a miserable attempt at Cromwellianism', was keeping him going.[2] The Cromwellianism to which he referred was associated in particular with the Salisbury Government's Coercion Bill and the appointment in March of Arthur Balfour as Chief Secretary. As Scottish Secretary Balfour had put down a crofters' revolt with some force and he appeared equally resolved to crush the Irish Nationalists' Plan of Campaign, which encouraged tenants to pay withheld rents into a central fund to fight evictions. His approach effectively amounted to the selective introduction of martial law and the attendant risks became apparent in September when three civilians were shot by policemen firing on an illegal assembly at Mitchelstown in County Cork. The Tories' inept handling of Ireland was providing so much intellectual and emotional ammunition that for once Herbert felt sufficiently well-armed to overcome his parliamentary fears. In a lengthy and impassioned attack on the Queen's Speech in February 1888, he tore into the government, accusing it of bad faith with respect to law and order and of hypocrisy in condemning tenant outrages but not the crimes of the landlords, and then pouring scorn on its resort to force and its failure to introduce the promised local government measures for Ireland. The Conservatives, he concluded, had misled the electorate but the struggle would continue until they either granted home rule or gave way to those who would. When he finally sat down the following speaker commented that he thought his speech the bitterest he had ever heard in the Commons.[3] In October Herbert's peroration at Bristol attracted some 500 listeners who cheered him for five minutes before he began and then, when he had concluded after 70 minutes, pulled him in a cart to another venue and prevailed on him to make a second speech.[4] Small wonder that the Tory MP, Sir Matthew Ridley, dubbed him the 'enfant terrible' of the Liberal Party although in fact his most cutting comments were often directed against Liberal Unionists, whom he described in October 1888 as 'illiberal disunionists'.[5] The announcement that he was to speak at a home rule rally in Ulster in December raised serious local concerns about public order and indeed his own personal safety, hardly surprising given the general protestant hostility to what was perceived to be Rome rule.

Herbert was not the only one whose passions were roused. *The Times* had long been keeping the anti-home rule pot boiling, sensationally claiming early in 1887 that Parnell and other Nationalists were implicated in criminal activity associated with the land war and then publishing a letter purporting to show that the Nationalist leader had approved of the Phoenix Park murders. Refusing Parnell's demand for a select committee to investigate these claims, the government instead set up a commission of inquiry, tantamount to putting the whole Nationalist movement on trial. Herbert took a strictly pragmatic view of the first charge, thinking it understandable that those accused had denounced crime only in a qualified way and while he agreed that the outrages committed during the land war were shocking he wondered why the actions of landlords, perpetrated under the cover of the law, did not seem to rouse anything like the same degree of moral indignation. As for the letter, his belief that it was a fake was confirmed in February 1889 when a Dublin journalist admitted to forging it. Although the commission did not formally report for a further year, this confession exonerated Parnell and raised his stock among Liberals to the extent that in November 1889 he went to Hawarden to discuss the shape of a future home rule measure with Herbert's father. However, events were subsequently given a fresh twist when Captain O'Shea filed for divorce against his wife on grounds of her adultery with Parnell. The Irish leader did not defend the case: he had been living openly with Mrs O'Shea and had fathered children by her. Herbert professed to be shocked by Parnell's conduct but he must have had his suspicions and certainly admitted later that he had known much more than his father about the matter.[6] Under the widespread public opprobrium which followed, Parnell was virtually abandoned by the Nationalists and the Liberals had little choice but to follow suit by distancing themselves from their most promising ally. Yet that did not entail any relaxation of their onslaught against the government's Irish policy. Another incident involving the use of police firearms against civilians provided grounds for a parliamentary motion in 1890 to reduce the financial estimates for the Royal Irish Constabulary. Leading for the Liberals, Herbert stressed that his target was not the policemen but the policies which made their actions necessary. It was, he said, 'an atrocious thing to arm a civil force with revolvers and cutlasses, and rifles, not against criminals but against the people in case of political disturbances'.[7] Ultimately he drove Balfour into an humiliating climb-down by producing a telegram showing that, contrary to the minister's previous assertion, no action was planned against the relevant commanding officer.[8] It was an impressive performance on Herbert's part, the more so because it took place in an arena where he rarely shone.

He was equally prominent when the government finally produced an Irish Local Government Bill in 1892. He took almost an hour to damn it, in principle because the wishes of the Irish themselves had not been considered and in practice because there were so many differences between it and the comparable measures applied to England and Scotland. It was, he concluded, drawn up in its own interests by Dublin Castle, the 'birthplace of so many ill-fated measures for the government of Ireland. There is no mandate for this Bill.'[9] In an article in *Nineteenth Century* he added a pragmatic argument, pointing out that the measure would do nothing to reduce the disproportionate amount of parliamentary time taken up by Irish business.[10] A similar piece in the *New Review* concluded that the logical resolution was devolved government for Ireland.[11]

The *Nineteenth Century* article rested on his estimate of how much time a devolution of Irish matters would free up for the consideration of other pressing matters. Among these he referred specifically to those of concern to working men, a theme he had floated a year or two before, arguing at Bacup in October 1890 that political leaders needed to develop a closer relationship with labour.[12] Such sentiments were in part a response to a new assertiveness amongst workers, manifest in the London dock strike of 1889, the spread of trade unionism in previously unorganised trades, and growing interest in the idea of independent parliamentary representation. As one journalist put it in 1891, 'until the last year or so no single member of either side of the House thought it worth his while to inquire precisely what the working men through their Unions, wanted and how they hoped to get it.'[13] But Herbert also had a deep instinctive empathy with working people, evident for example in his patronage of the National Physical Recreation Society. In a lecture delivered under its auspices in 1890 he stressed the deleterious effects on health of poor housing, bad air and unhealthy employments. Those in a position to do so, he declaimed, were bound to do all in their power 'to make the lives of the artisan and labouring millions of men, women and children brighter and happier, healthier and more hopeful'. Still active on the games field himself, albeit with no great success since his batting average for the House of Commons cricket team in 1888 was only 11, he concluded by advocating compulsory physical education in schools.[14]

Significantly, the question of working-class parliamentary representation was one of a number of topics which figured increasingly at this time in Herbert's conversations with his father who had already been seeking to broaden the Liberal agenda even before the Parnell divorce scandal. Herbert seems to have shared this desire, telling diners at the National Liberal Club in 1891 that home rule was a 'given' and thus not so much spoken about because the party was turning to other equally important questions.[15] Motivated in part by a desire to outflank Chamberlain and his radical cronies, the older Gladstone condoned, albeit rather vaguely, the Newcastle programme, an attempt to construct a broader platform accommodating Liberalism's various faddists and interest groups, and endorsed by the NLF. Herbert certainly shared his father's distrust of the party's radicals but he had little time for the Newcastle programme, protesting vigorously when NLF officials suggested some years later that it had been his father's brainchild.[16] But if he did not himself care for that particular agenda he was increasingly certain that Liberalism needed to reach out more generously to labour, partly on principle and partly as a matter of strategy. He was frequently reminded by his local party organiser, John Mathers, that his own constituency contained many working-class voters and that he could not afford to ignore their developing appetite for collective action in their own specific interests. But Herbert's advocacy of working-class parliamentary representation as set out in a paper he drafted in 1892 was too enthusiastic for some senior Liberals. Much put out by its content, chief whip Arnold Morley sought Bryce's view. Bryce was equally alarmed, fearing that the article would encourage the advocates of working-class separatism and be fatal to the Liberal Party.[17] He urged Herbert to balance his support for increasing the number of labour MPs by inserting an explicit statement of opposition to the idea of an independent party. Bryce was an old friend but his opinion was far less important to Herbert than that of his father who deemed his son's effort to be 'capital'.[18]

Herbert's widening range of concerns, particularly with respect to labour, was very evident in the manifesto he produced when Salisbury called a general election in the summer of 1892. There were references to registration reform, the payment of MPs, one man-one vote, licensing reform, working-class housing, the enforcement of employers' liability, popular control of elementary education, disestablishment, free trade and a reduction of working hours on the railways. Ireland, however, still occupied the primary place, Herbert neatly pointing out that the Tories had opposed the Liberals in 1886 on a programme of no home rule, no coercion and no buying-out of Irish landlords, since when they had passed a Coercion Bill, paid out £38 million to landlords, and given no measure of self-government to Ireland. Herbert's majority went down but his vote was about the same as it had been in 1885, a reasonable enough outcome given that on that occasion he had been unopposed while this time round his opponent, a significant local employer, spent money freely and used a fleet of carriages to carry voters to the polling stations. Furthermore, the election coincided with a dispute between the local Liberal corporation and its gas stokers, which probably did not help the Liberal cause. Considerable credit was due to Herbert's local party officers who had had all their arrangements in place well in advance and had kept their workers in a high state of readiness. Mathers thought that the reduced majority came about because the Tories, knowing they could not hope to unseat Herbert's father, went all out to defeat the son instead. Herbert, whose slender financial means were stretched by the campaign and saved only by Harry's generosity, attributed the outcome less to anti-Irish sentiment than to his own alienation of the extreme temperance lobby upset by his abandonment of the principle of the local veto.[19] He was probably right, for home rule failed to rouse the electorate as it had done in 1886 and nationally the Liberals secured only a small majority over the Conservatives, 274 against 268. Nevertheless, the return of 47 Liberal Unionists meant that to form a sustainable government the Liberals would require the backing of the 70 or so Irish Nationalists, putting home rule, it seemed, firmly back on the legislative agenda.

In constructing his fourth administration Gladstone naturally appointed party heavyweights to the senior positions. The Home Office went to Herbert Asquith, who was offered Herbert as Under-Secretary, a position which, the new prime minister said, his son much desired. Now there is no doubt that since the Liberal defeat in 1886 Herbert's standing both within the party and in the public consciousness had risen significantly. He had been very prominent on the platform and more vocal in parliament. Encouraged perhaps by his impassioned contributions to Irish debates he had spoken more often and asked far more questions than hitherto, though admittedly on matters of varying degrees of triviality – would cricket be allowed in Hyde Park; could the minister provide a record of ships lost over the last century; what did the minister know of a constituent who had died from syphilis following vaccination? But it was a recognition of his growing stature that in May 1891 Arnold Morley asked him to chair the NLC's political committee, a post requiring a strong individual in touch not only with the Liberal leadership but also with party headquarters. Later in the same year the party's chief political organiser, Francis Schnadhorst, invited Herbert to join a number of Liberal front-benchers in a select team to revive Liberal fortunes in London. An under-secretaryship in one of the three great offices of state, while open to the charge of nepotism, was equally a logical and merited recognition of Herbert's standing. He himself, however, was initially unsure, telling his mother he thought he could achieve more out of office than in.[20] Rumours of his hesitancy clearly got out because local party activist, Joseph

Henry, wrote to say he hoped they were untrue.[21] The prime minister seems to have been either downright disingenuous or merely somewhat optimistic in telling Asquith that Herbert actually wished to work at the Home Office, but it certainly was the department that had most to do with the labour affairs in which he had become particularly interested and which would therefore provide him with the most scope for action. Conscious perhaps that as recently as 7 May he had published an article on the eight hours question in the *Workman's Times*, Herbert havered, fearing that his views on this and other industrial questions might be too advanced for the new Home Secretary, but a conversation served to reassure him and he finally accepted the post. A couple of years later he conceded to his father that his decision had involved no sacrifice 'because my interests & sympathies were there, & I thought the work wd. give me some opportunities for usefulness.'[22]

His first opportunity soon arrived. The collapse of the Liberator Building Society in 1892 ruined many small investors and subsequent revelations about its crooked financial underpinnings prompted the suggestion that building societies be subjected to the same controls as friendly societies. Asquith agreed and set up a departmental committee to examine the possibilities of appropriately amending the existing Building Societies Act. As chairman Herbert handled the representations from individuals and institutions, and in consultation with his chief, developed various drafts of the necessary legislation.[23] When the bill came before the House in 1894 he handled the committee stage with surprising skill, displaying flexibility with regard to amendments and firmness in keeping the House focussed on the fundamental objective of safeguarding borrowers and investors against fraud. He also had to deal with a rather put out Registrar of Friendly Societies who, as the bill was couched, would be required to present an annual report on building societies to the home secretary, a slight on his status because formally he was responsible to the Treasury and had therefore always reported to parliament itself. Herbert was

not worried about bureaucratic sensitivities but in the end he
effected a neat compromise by recommending that the
Registrar continue to submit an annual report to parliament
and at the same time send a copy to the Home Office.
The *Leeds Mercury* was justifiably proud of its local MP,
observing that in handling the bill Herbert had shown ability,
tact and perseverance.[24]

For the most part, however, Asquith himself took on
the bulk of his department's parliamentary work and while
Herbert did have to take his turn at dealing with questions
when his chief was absent, perusal of the departmental files
suggests that many matters never passed from the desk of this
most hands-on home secretary to Herbert's. This was true,
for instance, of one of the government's most significant
labour measures, the Employers' Liability Bill, for Herbert's
initials appeared on very few of the relevant files and he did
not accompany his chief in meeting important deputations.[25]
His public profile was equally low with respect to the
administration's other main labour bill, the amendment of
the Factory Acts, but here he did make several significant
contributions behind the scenes. Asquith set about this
particular task by establishing three departmental committees
to examine working conditions in the chemical, pottery and
quarrying industries, and a fourth to consider the use of white
lead in manufacturing. Herbert had direct responsibility for
the last two of these, overseeing the relevant administrative
arrangements, selecting witnesses, consulting personally with
departmental and external experts, and considering the views
of the workers themselves. Thus after receiving representations from the National Amalgamated Union of Labour
and talking to his own officials he extended the remit of the
white lead committee to include both red and yellow lead and
the subsequent recommendations on all three products were
incorporated into the revised Factory Acts.[26]

His backstage work on quarry safety was less straightforward, hampered by the department's statistical deficiencies.
Even before he could begin considering the subject he had to
get his factory inspectors to compile something as basic as a

complete list of quarries in their respective areas. Having secured this and then mulled over the accumulated evidence, it was on his personal recommendation that the safety regulations, hitherto applicable only to those quarries deploying machinery, were made universally applicable.[27] Less productive was another inquiry into the use of phosphorous in match-making, a matter to which public attention had been drawn by a strike of women at the Bryant and May's factory some years earlier in 1888. Having overseen the necessary administrative arrangements for the committee's work Herbert was soon well on top of things and amongst other recommendations urged that manufacturers be compelled to keep a record of workers' employment dates and to provide them with frequent regular medical inspections. This was a humane and rational suggestion in view of the substantial evidence that extended exposure to phosphorous could have detrimental and long-term effects on health. In the face of strenuous objections from the employers Asquith caved in, but Herbert was vindicated later when it emerged in 1898 that Bryant and May had for several years been systematically covering up deaths from phosphorous poisoning among its employees.[28]

Another matter to which public attention had been directed by adverse publicity was the contemporary prison system in which Chief Commissioner Edward Du Cane presided over a regime widely regarded as sterile and reactionary. Charged by Asquith to chair a departmental inquiry, Herbert was once more frustrated to find that the available judicial statistics were as unhelpful and inadequate as those relating to industry. Before the committee could even begin its work he found it necessary to have his officials gather additional preliminary information, which he then used to shape the scope of the inquiry. The original mandate was to investigate the general condition of prisoners but having taken into account his new data Herbert quickly decided that such a limited remit was pointless and impossible without taking into account the wider context of prison legislation and its application. Steering carefully through this much broader inquiry, Herbert led his colleagues to produce over two dozen recommendations, including a reduction in the use of the harshest dietary punishment, increased government support for prisoners' aid societies, more books and conversation time for prisoners, the re-establishment of Sunday exercise, special treatment for drunkards, the raising of the admission age for reformatories, extended powers for visitors' committees, better staff training and regular inspection. Small though each may have been in its own right, cumulatively these recommendations amounted to a humanising of a hitherto severe, uniform and soulless administration. Du Cane's resignation followed very quickly, unlamented by anyone, although Herbert, always loyal to those with whom he worked, did speak kindly of him. This report on prisons was probably Herbert's most significant work at the Home Office. It appealed to his underlying compassion and caught his interest to such an extent that well into the tenure of the next Conservative administration he could be found in the House defending the Home Office against charges that its implementation of the recommended changes had been tardy.[29]

Asquith seems to have been well pleased with his lieutenant, particularly the amount of time and effort that he had put into the background work for the amendment of the Factory Acts. He also thought there was value in the scheme which Herbert, chastened by his unfortunate experiences with his departmental committees, devised to establish a new industrial department and reorganise the way the Home Office collected its statistics. His proposal was modest, intended only to improve the efficiency with which figures were gathered. It did not address at all the fact that they were gathered solely to measure year on year achievement. As it happened, lack of time meant that the plan was shelved and while in essence it was implemented later in the 1890s, in the longer term it was to be the Board of Trade which developed the use of statistics as an analytical tool for policy formation.

Herbert's time at the Home Office came to an end in 1894 when his father resigned as prime minister. Given the closeness of the 1892 election result the older Gladstone was initially reluctant to put a detailed home rule proposal to the cabinet, but colleagues insisted that a committee be established to draft the necessary legislation.[30] Privately, Herbert had come to the view that what might have been feasible in the mid-1880s was now impossible because opinion in Ireland itself had hardened but he was torn between respect for his father's inclinations and his belief that the party rank and file would be disappointed if home rule were shelved.[31] There was never any doubt, however, that he would support the second Home Rule bill when it was introduced on 13 February 1893, although he did not participate in the debate. Unionist filibustering kept it going in the Commons for 82 days before the bill was passed, whereupon the Lords promptly threw it out by an over-whelming majority. Gladstone wanted to dissolve and fight an election on the issue of the peers versus the people but not a single minister supported him. Thus, already divided from his cabinet colleagues, the prime minister then found himself almost alone in opposing his chancellor's wish to increase the naval estimates and in February 1894 he resigned.

He was not invited by the Queen to discuss his successor. While the Liberal MPs probably would have preferred Sir William Harcourt, the Queen sent for her own favourite, Foreign Secretary Lord Rosebery, who had the backing of most cabinet members and the Scottish wing of party as well as being favoured by the influential London press. In the reconstructed government Herbert was offered promotion to cabinet rank as first commissioner of the Board of Works. Perhaps this was a genuine acknowledgement of his quiet achievements at the Home Office, or perhaps merely a token nod in the direction of the recently departed prime minister since Rosebery, who himself had once occupied the same post at the Board of Works, regarded it as having 'neither dignity nor importance' and described it as 'the least of all the offices'.[32] However it is interpreted, it disappointed the Nationalists who had told Herbert privately that they hoped he might replace John Morley at the Irish Office.[33]

Cabinet rank brought with it new honours and burdens, the former including a privy councillorship, the latter a by-election (unopposed) occasioned by his promotion, and the inevitable flow of requests to use his influence to secure office or titles. The brevity of Rosebery's administration was to leave new ministers very little time to make their mark, but Herbert once more demonstrated some administrative flair, averting a threat to the amenities in London's Richmond Park and securing a pay rise for his department's employees. He also took up with some gusto a redevelopment scheme for Parliament Street, originally drawn up several years before by a Conservative administration. Developers had already introduced two private member's bills seeking parliamentary sanction to develop the site around the House of Commons but they had been unable to raise sufficient finance. A third private member's bill was currently before the House and under pressure to respond to it Herbert convinced Chancellor of the Exchequer Harcourt that the government should take over the powers of compulsory purchase which the bill proposed to confer on the private company. That was as far as he was able to get before the government fell.

Although his post was amongst the least important in the cabinet and lasted for only a year or so, Herbert, by common consent an amiable and unthreatening individual, frequently found himself at odds with his leader. While he received Reginald Brett, Rosebery's nominee to office in the department, in a cordial enough spirit, news of his doubts about Brett's suitability got back to the prime minister.[34] On another occasion his ruling about cycling in Hyde Park provoked Rosebery to send him a note expressing surprise 'after our last conversation on the subject'.[35] Rosebery was even more annoyed when he was left in the dark about the site selected by Herbert for a statue of Oliver Cromwell, an ignorance which he said could have severely embarrassed him with the Queen. His curt final request to Herbert that 'I hope in future that you will keep me informed' drew an immediate apology.[36]

These were minor matters and the fact that Rosebery even allowed them to annoy him reveals more about his temperament than about Herbert's competence. By turns diffident and hyper-active and plagued by insomnia he proved unable to provide strong leadership, especially as he himself sat in the House of Lords. He dithered and then abandoned completely the question of how to prevent the upper House overriding the wishes of the Commons. His chancellor's efforts to curb the nation's alcohol consumption failed to satisfy the more extreme prohibitionists whilst simultaneously antagonising the Irish over whom publicans and brewers had considerable influence. When he tried to make special provision for Ireland he was accused of neglecting English interests. John Morley attracted similar complaints of neglecting English interests when he tried to help Irish tenant farmers. On top of these difficulties, Rosebery's imperialist sympathies were too much for many Liberals, including Herbert himself, and he was further undermined from within by the hostility of Harcourt, who led the Liberals in the lower House. The antipathy between them was well illustrated when after a long bout of indisposition Rosebery sent round a note thanking people for inquiring after his condition. On the envelope in Harcourt's own hand is a terse note: 'I didn't inquire.'[37] Rosebery's lack of iron finally led him to resign his premiership in June 1895 over a minor parliamentary reverse. The Queen promptly invited Salisbury to form a Conservative administration. Having agreed to do so, he called a general election in July.

The contest was a disaster for the Liberals. Unemployment, even amongst skilled workers, had been running at high levels since the start of the year, agricultural prices remained low and considerable resentment had been generated in Lancashire by the Indian Government's imposition of a tariff on imported cotton goods. Liberal coal-owners had opposed a proposal to introduce an eight-hour day for miners while brewers had been equally alarmed by proposed licensing reforms. Any credit the Home Office might have hoped to bank with organised labour through its various administrative reforms had been largely forfeited in 1893 when Asquith first deployed 400 London policemen and then sanctioned the dispatch of troops to control rioting during a strike at Featherstone Colliery in Yorkshire. On 7 September army fire killed two men, adding a further grievance to the list that fuelled the demand for independent working-class representation at Westminster, manifest in the establishment of the Independent Labour Party (ILP) and the publication of the Fabian Society's influential pamphlet, *To Your Tents O Israel*, both in 1893. The political climate was thus very unfavourable for the Liberals and with no unifying issue to hold them together Herbert thought that defeat would perhaps be good for them. He may have felt vindicated when his party secured only 177 seats against 70 Liberal Unionists and 341 Conservatives. Of 114 seats in Greater London and the six cities of Birmingham, Glasgow, Manchester, Leeds, Liverpool and Sheffield the Liberals won a paltry 17. Herbert's was one of them, though his campaign was by no means straightforward. Guided as ever by the faithful Kitson and well served by his local party organisation, he had nursed his constituency carefully but its voters were not immune to national events or the heightened divergence of interest between workers and employers. The local Tories also poured considerable amounts of money into the fight and even Harry's generous cash injection did not lift Herbert's spirits very much. Letters he wrote during the campaign were littered with pessimistic terms like 'desperate', 'hard fight', 'awful evening', 'result is not certain'.[38] The contest was also marked by an unusual degree of personal unpleasantness, including the delivery of a couple of black-edged 'in memoriam' cards mourning his forthcoming parliamentary demise. They were premature in the sense that he retained his seat but in another they were almost prophetic of the dark times that lay ahead as the familiar political and personal landmarks in his life began to shift.

Politically, the Liberal Party, moulded by the father whom he revered, appeared to be in a state of virtual melt-down. *The Times* was hardly a disinterested observer but its 1894 diagnosis remained broadly accurate for several years afterwards. The party, it commented, was 'chaotic [...] fettered in all sorts of informal ways by all sorts of incompatible engagements and destitute of any coherent body of conviction or any intelligible principle of action.'[39] On the left, the radicals, despite lacking effective leadership and split between traditionalists and modernists, remained a constant irritant with their efforts to gain control of the party and commit it to a more advanced programme. Others believed that it was the precisely the adoption of 'a programme' that had brought about the electoral defeat and argued for a reversion to a more focussed political strategy, concentrating on a specific issue. In a speech at Guildford in December 1897 Herbert was critical of this latter view, arguing that they should be Liberals first, and home rulers, prohibitionists or anything else second.[40] Asked about the party's current stance on home rule he replied that nothing had changed but significantly he declined to state whether it would be at the forefront of the party's next election manifesto.[41] Such strategic ambivalence amongst the advocates of home rule served only to add a further dimension to the party's broader divisions over the very principle itself.

Such internal dissensions might have been less serious had the party not at the same time been suffering from a lack of stable leadership. For all his undoubted abilities, Rosebery was a weak prime minister and a year or so after he resigned the premiership he renounced the Liberal leadership as well without troubling to consult with his colleagues. Harcourt was his somewhat reluctant successor and he also struggled in vain to draw the Liberal factions together before he, too, resigned. There was some force behind the question put to his son in November 1898: 'Does anyone out of Bedlam think a Liberal victory possible at a General Election if the present state of affairs continues?'[42]

On the personal front Herbert had to cope with his father's departure from political life. William Gladstone's decision to retire in 1894 was perfectly understandable for a man then in his ninth decade and indeed it had long been anticipated, even encouraged, by some in the family. But its actual occurrence was for Herbert, as his father noted, 'sad [...] & hard'.[43] It meant the loss of his mentor, the man he admired above all others, for whom he had acted as private secretary, through whom he had gained insight into the workings of the political establishment and with whom he had constantly discussed policies and issues. 'I never feel', Herbert explained to Harry, 'that I have grasped or can grasp all that he has been to us, it is all so great.'[44] Normally self-controlled and cheerful, he admitted that escaping the 'darkness' into which his father's retirement had plunged him was a slow process. 'Whatever the future may bring forth, nothing in this world can bring to me the joy & pride [with] which for 14 years I have worked for you'.[45] Both psychologically and emotionally he felt utterly deflated, telling Hamilton in July 1894 that he had lost interest in politics and did not much care if he gave them up or they gave him up.[46]

Although his promotion to the cabinet afforded some diversionary activity its benefits were diluted by his differences with Rosebery, short-lived because the new administration lasted only for a year or so, and overshadowed as Herbert was increasingly absorbed by the care needs of his father whose remarkable constitution was at last beginning to fail. Invitations to The Glen, to shoot in India and to holiday in Europe all had to be spurned as more and more of his time was divided between London and the family home. True, there was always a sibling on hand at Hawarden to help out, for Gladstone had done all he could to ensure that his children remained close at hand.[47] As village rector, Stephen lived just across the road from the castle while for several years after her marriage Mary and her husband lived with the senior Gladstones. When Stephen moved to nearby Buckley as vicar in 1897 Harry replaced him as rector, whereupon the unmarried Helen gave up her college post in Cambridge to devote herself full time to her father's care, a task she did not find easy, telling Mary that the only way 'was to set one's teeth and go on from day to day.'[48] But if the practicalities of daily care fell most heavily on Helen, Herbert felt most responsible for the decision-making, partly because he was the only unmarried son and partly because of the specially close relationship he had with his parents. Eventually, therefore, he insisted that a residential housekeeper be employed to help out. If doctors advised a change of scenery as potentially beneficial for the parents, then someone, often Herbert, had to accompany them. A visit to Cowes, where rather against his own better judgement he took them in January 1898, left him particularly heavy hearted. Father, he wrote, 'has gone down in spirit and it left me lower than I would like to admit [...] The really trying part just now is the unknown future & anxiety from day to day, how he & to a less extent she will get through it.'[49] The pressure which he felt was well illustrated in a letter from Mary in April 1898, recounting that her father had asked for Herbert and Harry. Told that they were both away he 'sighed heavily. Both Henry and Herbert gone. Dreadful.'[50] By this time Gladstone's decline had manifested itself in facial cancer and as the inevitable end approached, there was the added strain of fielding constant press inquiries about the condition of such a prominent public figure, with Herbert particularly anxious that every member of the family stick to the same agreed line in order to deter misleading speculation and rumour.

The end finally came at Hawarden on 19 May. A *Sunday Times* reporter who called on Herbert at the London house of an old family friend, Lord Armitstead, where he was making funeral preparations, found him 'quite grief stricken' and wishing to say little.[51] There was not much time for private reflection, however, as the arrangements were both complex and fraught. The villagers of Hawarden were somewhat resentful that their most famous resident was to be laid to rest not in the local church graveyard but, as befitted a former prime minister, in London. This entailed detailed consultation with government and church officers. Even the Queen was involved, though the Gladstone family's loss did little to soften her heart towards a man she had long disliked and she was intensely annoyed that the Prince of Wales was mooted as a pall bearer. Eventually all was settled as Herbert and Harry together met with the officials to finalise details of the lying in state at Westminster Hall. On 28 May they each took an arm in escorting their mother to her place in Westminster Abbey for the ceremony.

Even then, however, Herbert was not free, for the family immediately set about identifying a biographer who could do justice to the patriarch. Long-standing colleague and friend John Morley was an obvious choice but Herbert and Harry both feared that as a dogmatic atheist Morley would not deal satisfactorily with the religious faith which had been so central to their father's life and their own. Herbert was quite clear what he wanted: 'a tribute paid to goodness as much as to service [...] It was due to the long lesson of his life, its control, discipline, self-sacrifice, devotion and boundless energy based on an all pervading and unflagging Christianity in both public and private life.'[52] Eventually the terms and the scope of the project were agreed with Morley: there was to be no discussion of religious belief. But if Morley had to set about his task with one eye on the Gladstones' wishes he was also well aware that others were equally interested in what he might write. Concerned that his long friendship with Gladstone would influence his interpretation of her own uneasy relationship with her four-time prime minister, the Queen let Morley know of her wish that he would 'appreciate the importance of treating the subject impartially'.[53] It is not clear whether the Gladstones themselves were aware of this royal interference but their stress levels were certainly not helped when Mary suddenly announced that she was proposing to publish her correspondence with Lord Acton. Herbert was angered by this 'bombshell', viewing it as premature as well as a potential betrayal of intimate family confidentialities and likely to detract from the official biography.[54] It was the final straw for a man who had struggled anyway with his father's retirement from politics and then had to deal with the grief, no less powerful because long expected, of the final separation. He seems to have been left emotionally drained and rudderless. 'I feel', he told fellow Liberal, G.O. Trevelyan, ' like a plant torn up by the roots yet unable at present to measure the infinitely great change which must & will overshadow our lives here.'[55] He never entirely got over the emotion of it all. As an old man he could still write wistfully that 'when the sun was shining we thought ourselves part of it & had a curiously exaggerated view of our own importance. But it all went at sunset.'[56]

Of course he was not alone in his devastation, Helen telling Bryce that the gap left by her father's death would be even keener when they settled back into ordinary life.[57] Yet such a settling was not yet likely, for Catherine Gladstone, too, was increasingly frail and there was little relief for the already stretched Herbert. His relationship with his father had been extremely close but typically Victorian and masculine in that it rarely exhibited the emotional intensity which characterised Herbert's bond with his mother. Catherine had always doted upon both her two younger sons, but as the baby Herbert had been the favourite and her attachment to him intensified as old age reduced the circle of her other relationships. 'When you or Harry write to Mama', Helen told him, 'it counts 10 at least!'[58] On another occasion she wrote that the only instruction she had for Herbert from Catherine was to tell him 'how much she lives on yr. letters'.[59] Herbert was a prolific and generous letter writer but even he quailed when Helen also told him that the more often he and Harry wrote the better. It did not matter what he said, she added, it was the mere fact of having a letter that was important to Catherine.[60] In September 1898 Herbert confessed himself 'dispirited' by the reports on Catherine's health.[61] On one of his increasingly frequent trips to Hawarden the following spring he arrived to find that his mother had had a 'very bad day indeed – the worst I have experienced. She wouldn't leave me alone at all & got much excited [...] She wd. not eat much & could not work either fork or spoon.'[62]

Under this constant duress Gladstone family relationships, usually quite harmonious, showed signs of fraying. The old man's manoeuvrings to keep the children nearby had already caused tension between Mary and Stephen, who had also been put out by Herbert's agreement to a state funeral rather than a local interment. Even Herbert and Harry's closeness was tested. During Harry's long absence in India the Gladstone women in particular had come to turn routinely to Herbert for advice about financial and other family matters. This may appear strange but as a clergyman Stephen was probably thought to lack the appropriate worldly wisdom while Willy had been ill and had died from a brain tumour in 1891. Perhaps Harry found it disconcerting that his sisters tended to defer to the younger Herbert rather than him, although this does not seem to have caused much difficulty between them until Herbert began to feel so stressed in the second half of the 1890s. One source of friction was the handling and development of the Hawarden estate in which Herbert had taken an active interest as a young man. The property had actually belonged to Catherine Gladstone's brother, the childless Sir Stephen Glynne. It then passed to Willy and after his death to his son William, a minor, with the boy's uncles Stephen, Henry and Herbert holding it in trust until he came of age. Initially, Herbert seems to have been content to let Harry take the lead as the older man and with a business background. But with his party in the doldrums and his parents an increasing worry Herbert's interest in the estate was rekindled and there were increasingly frequent clashes between the two men over their ideas and plans for its development, even sometimes over their instructions to staff.

Herbert also found himself bickering with Harry's wife, the former Maud Rendel. This, too, was unusual because she had always acknowledged the unique bond between the brothers and even before her marriage in 1890 had sought to reassure Herbert that she had no wish to weaken it but rather to be to him 'a true sister'.[63] On her wedding day she wrote at greater length in similar vein. 'I want you to feel I shall be a real sister to you. My great deep love for Harry makes you come near me & I want to try & make up a little if you feel you lose anything in him thro' me.'[64] Initially at least she need not have worried. Herbert welcomed her in his usual open way and they found common ground in their mutual passion for music, Maud often providing the piano accompaniment for his cello. However, Herbert's usual affable demeanour was clearly affected by the parental situation in the second half of the decade and he had a number of spats with Maud, all over trifling matters.

Harry was naturally defensive of his wife on these occasions and found a further cause of aggravation in Herbert's growing obsession with golf. Although he was never particularly good at ball games, Herbert had always enjoyed them and by 1895 he had reduced his golf handicap to nine. He played regularly for the House of Commons team and in 1897 was elected captain of the Tooting Bec club. Harry was equally keen but it still appeared to him that Herbert was devoting excessive time to the game. More than once he suggested that it was distracting his brother from more urgent and important matters. But distraction was precisely the point. In something of a political wilderness and stressed by the family situation Herbert found respite on the links, as well as companionship and an outlet for energies that had no other recourse. It was strange that Harry did not grasp this, because when Herbert had once expressed concern at the increasing frequency of their 'intensely hateful' disagreements, even on the golf course, he generously put them down to his own failure to appreciate that Harry had been under pressure at work.[65] Yet Harry seemed oblivious of the extent to which Herbert was now similarly burdened. But then he had the consolation of a wife although his repeated references to that fact also irked his bachelor brother. Herbert confided to Eddy Tennant that Harry kept writing in varying states of marital ecstasy and urging him to marry, adding somewhat sourly that 'we are not all Nabobs else we might'.[66] Things were probably not helped in this respect by the fact that Catherine, too, constantly pressed matrimony upon her favourite son, thereby emphasising the single status of which he needed little reminder. In accepting Tennant's invitation to act as his best man in 1895, Herbert replied rather wistfully that he was beginning to feel 'like an isolated rock in the wilderness – you are almost the last of my friends more or less contemporary to take the great & best step in life.'[67]

By themselves the issues between Herbert and his brother
were essentially inconsequential and ordinarily would have
passed unremarked but Herbert's usually even temperament
was being stretched to the limit by his domestic concerns.
He finally snapped, pouring out his inner frustrations and
feelings in a 'most private' letter to Harry, written at a time
when the pain of his father's recent death was still raw. 'This
year for me has been one of incessant movement, change,
anxiety & distraction [...] since Bournemouth I have felt
incapacitated for politics & have no home life to fall back on.'
Reproaching himself rather unjustly for a lack of application
to work he pointed out that 'I have been hit far harder than
my political colleagues [...] I have had & still have no
inclination or opportunity for political work & shall not
resume it till Oct.' He felt it necessary to justify his time on the
golf course by pointing out with some truth that he had given
up other favourite social activities such as concerts and the
theatre. He was willing to accept correction from his brother
he said but 'don't rub it in just when we may fall out on
ordinary matters. Another thing. You rightly say you do most
of the Hn. business. I have more than you know of perhaps for
everyone seems to come to me about things wh. are small but
wh. yet take time.' He was, he added, willing to take on
anything Harry turned over to him but

> I can't crawl in your wake when you mean to act [...] Your ref.
> to M[aud] is the first indication of that grievance. If my
> demeanour was bad I am unfeignedly sorry [...] But look how
> these things work because of our saying either too little or too
> much to one another. M. naturally was conscious of your
> grievances against me. And she kept pinching me in tiny
> almost indefinite ways wh. I frankly own created in me a
> very unsatisfactory state of mind wh. I daresay made me very
> irritable.

Even in the midst of this confessional Herbert's essential
good nature was still discernible. 'It seems we have all been
bottling ourselves up to bursting point & just fizzing out at the

wrong time [...] I know I owe you an apology [...] Above all know that I look upon our relations for forty years as a precious possession; & that even when hardest pressed I have only wanted to do that wh. wd. retain it unimpaired.'[68]

In the same letter he described his single state with some feeling as the curse of his life. Fit and trim even now in his forties, Herbert had lost none of the charm or good looks which so appealed to women in his younger days. After meeting him at the Kitsons in Leeds Gertrude Bell told her mother that 'he *is* nice. I like him particularly.'[69] In France for a short break with Armitstead in 1897, he made a similar impression on two other young ladies who were so distraught when he left that they were unable to talk of anyone else. The prospect of his return to France a year or so later put them, again according to Armitstead, 'in fearful ecstasies'.[70] However, there is nothing to suggest that Herbert had ever become emotionally involved with any woman after his rejection by Margot Tennant. It is of course possible that he still harboured some feeling for her, but over ten years had passed and apart from a throw away remark to Eddy Tennant that The Glen had a special place in his heart and memory, there is no evidence for such a conjecture. In any case Margot's marriage to Asquith in 1894 put her out of reach. It seems far more likely that he had consciously determined not even to look for a wife and he specifically told Harry in 1898 that he had no 'entanglements', despite frequent pleas from family and friends to marry.[71] 'With every word said to me on that subject I agree', he wrote at about the same time. 'The difficulties lie deep. That they are not & cannot be known is an added trouble & so long as this goes on I must put up with the reproach of being a selfish bachelor & a bachelor for selfish purposes.'[72] The reference was clearly to his mother's condition and it is apparent that he was selflessly prioritising her, as he did also his father in his declining years, over any desires or concerns of his own.

Catherine was certainly his first consideration when out of the blue he received an unexpected offer from Henry Campbell-Bannerman who had effectively taken over the

Liberal leadership when Harcourt, sick of Rosebery's constant interventions from the sidelines, finally abandoned it in October 1898. On 5 April 1899 Tom Ellis, the party's chief whip, died unexpectedly. Campbell-Bannerman wasted no time in consulting senior colleagues and then offering the post to Herbert at a private meeting just a week after Ellis's death. Herbert was happy enough, he assured Campbell-Bannerman, that he would be permitted to retain his freedom of thought on key political issues but he pointed out that other commitments such as his various company directorships (in 1898 he and Harry had acquired an interest in a Russian oilfield in the Caucasus) and the maintenance of the family estate at Hawarden would also make demands on his time. Above all, he said, 'the frail condition of my mother is my first duty', adding that if his private affairs got too much he would resign.[73] But loyalty to the party, which in essence his father had created, prevailed. No one, he told his sister-in-law, had been harder hit than himself by Ellis's unexpected death because the pressure to take on the chief whip's work was too great to resist 'even were I disposed to refuse [...] Nothing can be more repulsive to me than much, perhaps most, of the work & it means to me an absence of freedom practically till the end of the next Liberal Gov't.'[74]

It never seems to have occurred to him that he was far from an obvious choice. An internal promotion might have been expected but Campbell-Bannerman seems to have had a low opinion of the remaining Liberal whips. Furthermore, he himself had only very recently become party leader, unelected and emerging largely because the only other viable contender, Asquith, preferred to prioritise his legal work. Given this background, Campbell-Bannerman doubtless wanted a man whom he knew and trusted and whose politics were, like his own, faithful to William Gladstone's. Herbert fitted the bill admirably. Furthermore the two men had developed an easy rapport during Herbert's brief spell at the War Office in 1886 while his earlier service as a junior whip and his chairmanship of the NLC's political committee until 1897 had provided relevant experience. Yet it was highly unusual for the whip's position to be offered to an individual who had held a cabinet post and who stood as high in his party counsels as Herbert did by 1899, not least because the job was widely regarded as something of a poisoned chalice. An old friend and member for Accrington, J.F. Leese, referred to it as 'an unselfish and self sacrificing' step, and Kitson took a similar view, telling him that he was the right man for the job although it would be a sacrifice.[75] Joseph Henry thanked him for putting the party's interest above his own.[76] Harcourt's son, Loulou, offered condolences to Herbert for his self sacrifice in putting on the 'hardest and most thankless of all harness'.[77]

Herbert had no illusions about the difficulty of the task but he had never harboured any personal political ambition and such pessimism did not unduly bother him. His official biographer later asserted that he accepted the job because it allowed him to escape the burden of speaking in the House of Commons.[78] This was partly true. Catherine referred more than once to his dislike of parliamentary speaking and Joseph Henry had written as recently as 1897 wondering why he did not participate in debates as often as his position warranted. If he did not, Henry warned, Herbert might be pushed aside when the party came to power.[79] But in fact he had in recent years spoken more frequently and sometimes to good effect, especially on Irish matters. A far more important reason for accepting the post was his sense of duty to his father's party and memory. 'In the matter of whips', he wrote, 'we are in such a desperately bad way that it does not appear to me that I have any option.'[80] Furthermore, the job provided an opportunity to rediscover a sense of purpose and focus which had become increasingly diffuse since his father's withdrawal from public life in 1894. As Leese said, it would give him 'the regular occupation' for which 'I think you have been rather longing lately'.[81]

CHAPTER 4

Resurgence

Herbert may have been under no illusions about the scale of the challenge facing him but within weeks his difficulties were intensified by events overseas. Relations between the Boers and the British in South Africa had never been particularly friendly and had deteriorated into open conflict in 1880–1. Following a major British reversal at Majuba Hill Prime Minister Gladstone had suspended further military action and effectively recognised an independent Boer Republic in the Transvaal. Shortly afterwards the discovery of gold on the Rand prompted a mass influx, predominantly British, into the new republic. In an attempt to limit their influence President Kruger restricted these Uitlanders' access to full citizenship, at the same time seeking to bolster his international position through alliances with Germany and Holland. Cecil Rhodes, Prime Minister of Cape Colony, saw this as confirmation that Kruger was a major obstacle to his own aspirations for a British-controlled federation in South Africa and began encouraging disaffection in the Transvaal. The situation deteriorated further in 1895 when the Jameson Raid, an abortive incursion by troopers of the British South Africa Company (BSA) into the Transvaal, ended in ignominious surrender, a Boer success which drew plaudits from the Kaiser and encouraged Kruger to impose even more stringent restrictions on the Uitlanders. Chamberlain, by now on the

Conservative front bench as Colonial Secretary, demanded their relaxation but Kruger countered with proposals of his own. The developing tension threatened to derail Herbert's efforts to prioritise party rebuilding as Liberals were left floundering for want of a strong lead. Twice at the end of September 1899 Herbert wrote to Campbell-Bannerman, away on his annual retreat in Marienbad, urging him to speak out on the situation. Given their past history, Herbert was highly suspicious of Chamberlain, believing that his proposals were deliberately framed so as to make their rejection virtually certain because the Uitlanders' rights were being used simply as a cover for the administration's determination to establish British supremacy in southern Africa.[1]

After further pleas from his increasingly agitated chief whip, Campbell-Bannerman finally returned to summon a meeting of Liberal leaders on 4 October 1899. With rumour and counter-rumour circulating wildly at home and Boer commandos and British regulars already on the move, the discussion focussed on what the party might do to prevent war and what to do if it did come. Herbert thought there was no real justification for conflict and that Liberals should act as peacemakers by urging Kruger to reconsider.[2] The next day he told Campbell-Bannerman that in the event of a Boer incursion into British territory Liberal support for the government should be presented as consent under compulsion and limited to approving measures necessary to end the conflict as quickly as possible.[3] It was already too late, however, and the talking was swiftly overtaken by events when the Boers invaded the Northern Cape and Natal.

Herbert was at once appalled and undecided. He would brook no Unionist criticism of his father's actions following the reversal at Majuba, later devoting a whole section of his memoir to it, and he also had some intuitive empathy for the Boers' national aspirations. And yet Kruger had overthrown Gladstone's settlements by force and occupied British territory. Furthermore, Herbert did not share the widespread view that the Boers would be a military pushover, predicting a protracted and costly struggle. But whatever his personal thoughts, he had taken the job of chief whip in order to rebuild the party and his overriding priority was to maintain its unity through the crisis. This was potentially tricky, however, for while the enigmatic Rosebery had voluntarily withdrawn from practical politics, he lurked still on the periphery, a highly influential figure, a formidable speaker, far more charismatic and publicly popular than Campbell-Bannerman, and much admired by those Liberals whose own imperialist leanings enhanced his appeal as an alternative leader. Shortly after he became whip Herbert had had a long meeting with the former premier, leaving with the impression that while Rosebery wished to remain aloof he would re-engage with politics in the event of a national emergency. The war presented just such an opportunity and Herbert clearly feared that the leadership issue might thus be thrown back into the melting pot, particularly as prominent Liberals such as Asquith, Edward Grey and R.B. Haldane were all closer to Rosebery than to Campbell-Bannerman on imperial questions. Haldane certainly told Beatrice Webb with apparent relish that the advent of war had smashed the Liberal Party.[4] Herbert's difficulties were not eased either by Campbell-Bannerman's rather casual approach to public affairs. He had to argue against the cancellation of a number of meetings in November, fearing that to do so would distress supporters and buttress their opponents' claims that the current leadership lacked the courage of its own convictions. Significantly, he added that he did not care at all about offending Rosebery's henchmen.[5]

A further consideration was that any Liberal leadership struggle could well let the government off the hook by diverting attention away from the war. Devising appropriate tactics in this fraught situation was not easy. Apart from a vocal minority of pro-Boers and pacifists, most Liberals felt unable to oppose war once Kruger invaded British territory. The line Herbert recommended to Campbell-Bannerman as that most likely to keep the party together, therefore, was to accept the fact of war but to attack Chamberlain for not avoiding it and for being so unprepared.[6] But with British

forces suffering a series of reverses culminating in humiliating defeat at Spion Kop in January 1900, any Liberal attack
on the government could easily be represented by opponents
as unpatriotic or distorted into implied criticism of the
soldiers in the field. A cleverly worded amendment to
the royal address in February 1900 just about held the
parliamentary party together although there were a couple of
defections and considerably more abstentions. But as over
the succeeding months the tide of battle turned in Britain's
favour, the politicians were forced to grapple with the thorny
issue of what to do with the Boer lands now falling into
British hands. This, too, threatened Liberal harmony. Both
Campbell-Bannerman and Herbert thought annexation of
the Boer republics inevitable, but to preserve unity the party
leaders agreed that individuals should be left free to act and
speak as each thought fit, although Herbert shared the
majority view that failure to support annexation would
reduce their ability to influence any peace terms.[7] A speech
to this effect in April prompted one annoyed Liberal to
accuse him of abandoning the last remnants of the nation's
moral grit in order to make it easier to win a general
election.[8] Both Herbert's brother-in-law, Edward Wickham, by now Dean of Lincoln, and his brother Stephen also
took his remarks in this way, remonstrating that he was
ignoring the morality of the war simply to prevent the party
splitting.[9] Somewhat upset, he turned to Harry in the belief
that he would better grasp the problems facing the party
whip, admitting, however, that he had 'strained my views
for the sake of the party'.[10] Liberal divisions were very
apparent in July 1900 when pro-Boers forced a parliamentary division over the war. Campbell-Bannerman tried to
lead a walk out, only to see some 40 of his colleagues,
including Asquith, Grey and Haldane, vote with the
government, and a larger number abstain. Chamberlain
seized on this very public manifestation of disharmony to
press the case for dissolution on a somewhat reluctant prime
minister. Voting in the general election was scheduled to
begin on 28 September.

Herbert was in despair. Criticised by pro-Boers, serving a less-than-energetic leader who had ignored his advice not to walk out of parliament and acutely aware that he was close to compromising his own opinions for the sake of unity, he confided to Harry that he would not be surprised if Campbell-Bannerman resigned, adding that he did not see how he himself could avoid following suit. 'It is a horrible mess & the difficulties are almost hopelessly great.'[11] Nor was he alone in anticipating his chief's resignation, for on the very same day Rosebery was asked by Haldane, Grey and Asquith if he would resume the leadership in the event of Campbell-Bannerman's departure. The imperialist wing of the party, affirmed Haldane, 'have the machinery, the whips & the future'.[12] Since Haldane was also intent on steering Liberalism away from Gladstonian principles, Herbert was obviously relieved to discover that a night's sleep had apparently stiffened Campbell-Bannerman's resolve. After a full day closeted with him, Herbert put pen to paper at 1.30 am the following morning to let Harry know that the party chief no longer seemed inclined to step down, although he himself was still not fully convinced of the Scot's political stamina. Contemplating somewhat forlornly how he was to fight an election with a divided party, he concluded that he would stick to it, despite his feeling that 'Providence hasn't given us a leader'.[13] They had made great efforts to keep Campbell-Bannerman in the saddle, he told Margot Asquith, but he personally longed 'for Asquith's clear & decisive utterances'.[14] He was still gloomy on 4 August when he left London for his recently acquired seaside cottage at Littlestone-on-Sea in Kent.

Given the party's problems since 1895 it was hardly surprising that when Herbert became chief whip in the spring of 1899 he inherited a dysfunctional party machine. The one positive feature, perhaps, was that friction between the Liberal Central Association (LCA) and the NLF, which had relocated next door in 1886, had been eased by the appointment of a joint secretary, particularly after Robert Hudson took that position in 1893. With him Herbert began to forge a highly effective partnership in addressing the party's organisational and electoral deficiencies. He was so single-minded about this that his backbenchers complained, asking through Jack Pease, one of the junior whips, if he would make himself more accessible to them. Junior whips, added Pease somewhat ruefully, were not regarded as adequate substitutes.[15] Unmoved, Herbert remained unheard and often unobserved in the Commons, his mind firmly focussed. He established committees to consider organisation in London and to assist with identifying candidates for specific constituencies. Nothing appears to have come, however, of an initiative to establish a group of district agents, probably because the necessary funds were not available.

Typically, he devoted most of each working day to interviewing potential candidates. They were not always comfortable encounters. A few overly precious individuals had to be discouraged. Some needed to be enticed with financial support or cajoled with promises of a better seat next time round. Occasionally it was necessary to dangle the bait of office. Recruitment would have been easier had he been spoiled for choice but neither the state of the party nor the patriotic sentiment generated by the war were helpful. He certainly could not afford to be too fussy, even trying to persuade the Fabian, Sidney Webb, who was no friend of orthodox Liberalism, to stand for a London seat. As this suggests, Liberalism was a fairly elastic creed but every decision had to be made in the context of the party's various factions. In Mansfield, for example, anti-war Liberals sought to find their own candidate in the belief that the chief whip would 'like to put a jingo into it', hardly a fair comment given his personal distaste for the war, but indicative perhaps of how effectively he had suppressed it in the party's interest.[16]

If finding candidates was difficult the same was true of fund-raising and Herbert's preparations were severely constrained by the sparse resources at his disposal. Few cared to donate when the party's electoral prospects appeared so dismal, while those alienated by the home rule disagreement were reluctant to back the current leadership. When Herbert became chief whip the

LCA's income barely covered its running costs and it then fell by 14 per cent between 1899 and 1900 despite his personal efforts to increase membership. He was so concerned about the state of the party coffers that he even pleaded with Campbell-Bannerman to moderate his stance on licensing as he was afraid of losing the financial support of Liberal brewers like Whitbreads, a warning which he did not share with the party's temperance lobby.[17] With contributions failing he asked 30 friends for £2,500 each towards an election fund. Only seven troubled to reply and even a close friend like Armitstead refused, saying there was no point in contributing when the party was divided and had no hope of winning.[18] However, even in these straitened circumstances Herbert did not stoop to offering honours in return for donations even though his predecessors had sometimes resorted to similarly questionable measures.[19]

It was perhaps a measure of his desperation that he entertained approaches from the ILP and the Social Democratic Federation (SDF) about an electoral accommodation. In the past the Liberals had financed approved working-class candidates like John Burns, but Herbert's own well-attested sympathy for labour representation certainly did not extend to avowedly socialist bodies. After a fruitless meeting with their representatives he concluded that neither had much to offer either politically or financially. 'This was an overture & nothing given or received.'[20] Candidates backed by trade unions were a different proposition, however, since the unions had financial resources and in many cases a membership whose geographical concentration was electorally significant. This was particularly true of the miners, who had provided the largest number of Lib-Lab MPs over the last quarter of the nineteenth century. It was a miner, Sam Woods, sometime MP for Ince, who suggested to James Ramsay MacDonald, secretary of the recently established Labour Representation Committee (LRC), that he would find the Liberal chief whip very willing to support its candidates in some seats.[21] He was right. Herbert was more than open and undeterred by MacDonald's insistence that such candidates stand formally under the LRC name, knowing that most of them were broadly Liberal in outlook anyway. Thirteen fought the election and while only two were elected Herbert secured most of them a free run against Tories, saving several thousand pounds which he would have needed had Liberals stood in those seats.

The energy which Herbert brought to the task of revitalising the party and organising it for the election was all the more remarkable given his enduring domestic difficulties. Time had gradually lessened the pain of his father's loss and his new political responsibilities left him little option but to rely increasingly on his siblings for day-to-day affairs at Hawarden. Catherine, however, remained a persistent concern and pre-occupation. By May 1900 she was delusional and a rapid deterioration followed as old age ravaged both her body and her mind. The following month the family's prayers for a swift release, well-meant and sincerely offered by those who did not regard death as the end, were answered after a brief resurgence of vitality. But if not seen as an end, death was certainly a goodbye and harder for Herbert than most of his siblings because, as Agnes offered comfortingly, 'she always showered such an unbounded wealth of love & pride upon you – the dear luck baby!'[22] As so often in times of particular emotional turbulence Herbert found solace in his faith.

> I dare not think too deeply all she was to me, so utterly unworthy of it do I feel – except that however unworthy my love grew with the years so that she seemed more & more even to the end to occupy & pervade one's whole being, absent or present [...] what a grim thing life would be but for hope & trust in the life to come.[23]

Shortly afterwards he told Campbell-Bannerman that the past few weeks had been a great strain and he was going away for a while.

There was not much time for grieving, however, as preparations for the approaching election threatened to swamp party headquarters. Constituency delegations turned up almost daily, propaganda material had to be vetted and distributed, and demands for speakers became so numerous that only a small proportion could be satisfied.[24] It was a measure of Herbert's leadership that when Haldane attended a breakfast for candidates and workers in March he found them all in surprisingly good heart. It was a tribute to his powers of persuasion that a future minister, Augustine Birrell, agreed to stand in North-East Manchester, a seat never previously won by a Liberal. Birrell's initial reluctance dissolved under pressure from Campbell-Bannerman and Gladstone, two individuals whose 'sacrifices for the party have been so great that I could not for very shame turn a deaf ear to what they had to urge.'[25] Altogether Herbert was able to field 397 candidates backed by some £60,000 which he had scraped together at the cost of some strained friendships.

But if he had done a quite remarkable job in securing and funding even this limited number of candidates and in setting a more energetic tone, time and circumstance, especially the persistence of internal factionalism, both weighed heavily against him and he was utterly realistic about the party's electoral prospects.[26] Likening himself on one occasion to a valet, he explained that it was hard to serve the Liberals when they lived in so many different habitations but he was determined to bring about unity. Yet this resolve was not easy to sustain because the pragmatism it required sometimes led critics to misunderstand his own position. There was no doubting his personal loyalty to the current leader whom he regarded as his father's true heir and his own political sentiments were certainly much closer to Campbell-Bannerman's than to Rosebery's. Even so, he could not ignore the possibility that Rosebery might yet prove to be the delivery vehicle for the unity to which he was committed. For all his flaws, Rosebery had a presence and an appeal that could allow him, should he so choose, to resume the leadership. This explains both why Herbert never entirely discounted the prospect of a Rosebery return and also why he found Campbell-Bannerman's dilatory approach to politics so endlessly irritating. Herbert wanted his preferred leader to lead, more than once urging him to be more active or decisive. But his exasperation grew as the election campaign got underway and Campbell-Bannerman's insistence on his annual summer migration to Europe undermined his attempts to co-ordinate the public appearances of Liberal leaders across the country. It was, he told Hudson, 'maddening' that the party's need for inspiration was being 'smothered in a Marienbad mud bath [...] Our efforts to find a leader are about as successful as Tommy Atkins' efforts to shoot a Boer'.[27] Three weeks before voting was due to start he was telling Lord Spencer, party leader in the upper House, of his desire that Campbell-Bannerman would return to England 'to write a pithy letter on salient points to [...] show the party that he is still alive but he hasn't seen his way to do this [...] I just have to get on as best I can.'[28] Another week passed but with candidates clamouring ever more loudly for a steer he still did not know when his leader would be back. 'Was ever a poor Whip in such a desperate position!' he asked Spencer plaintively.[29] To Lord Ripon he grumbled that he was struggling to keep his head above water and that CB's 'absence is unfortunate'.[30] Already in the post from Marienbad, however, was Campbell-Bannerman's tardy response to his whip's repeated communiques, although its complacent tone must have irked in suggesting that there was little real discord in the party and that it was being made the most of for political reasons.[31]

While a more engaged leader might have been better for Herbert's morale it would probably have made little difference to the election outcome. The Liberals were unable to contest many seats, the Conservatives emerged with an overall majority of 134, slightly more than before the dissolution and for the first time since 1867 there was no swing against a sitting government. Herbert could perhaps take some consolation from the fact that his party had done marginally better than in 1895, generally holding its own in smaller towns but losing out in constituencies where there were dockyards or munitions centres and in big cities. One of the few to buck this trend was Leeds. Despite his national responsibilities Herbert was no absentee MP but it was the spade work done by his local officials which secured large and enthusiastic crowds for his meetings and ensured victory. Recent municipal elections in the city had depleted the Liberals' finances but Herbert's relief was almost palpable when in the end Kitson put in £100 and Harry added a timely £500, sufficient to pull him through financially. Haldane was also pleased. For all their distance on the Liberal spectrum he had expressed a strong hope that the chief whip would retain his seat, another acknowledgement perhaps of Herbert's skill at holding the party's factions together.[32] Labouchere's contemporaneous verdict that Herbert was 'a hopeless head whip' was nothing more than an expression of radical frustration.[33]

The war figured prominently in the national campaign but it was by no means as dominant as the usual epithet of the 'Khaki election' implies, perhaps because Herbert and Campbell-Bannerman for obvious reasons tried to play it down. Nevertheless, Herbert accepted that the electorate had mandated the Conservatives to resolve the South African conflict and felt that the Liberals should not make this unduly difficult, much as the whole business stuck in his gullet. This was entirely consistent with his father's argument of 15 years before that the voters had elected a Conservative Government which therefore had the right to try to deal with home rule. However, in taking a similar line in 1900, Herbert understood the risk of further deepening the rifts within the Liberal Party. Harry for one was dubious, urging him not to let the Liberal front bench appear to be backing the government's South African policy.

As long as you hold on as Whip I shall believe that you have acted for the best, although I may not always see eye to eye w. you. But if a split does come, I pray that you may not find yourself on the Imp Lib side. Meantime you can only act as you think right.[34]

, He was so concerned that he followed up the very next day with a second appeal, almost identical save that the praying had now become begging. Remaining uncommitted, he urged, need not interfere with the drive for unity. 'I can well understand that you may find your position intolerable as between the two sections and may be forced to throw up the sponge.' If this happened, he advised Herbert to preserve his own neutrality.[35]

This was easier said than done, however, for in February 1901 Campbell-Bannerman needed his whip's support to convince David Lloyd George, among the most vocal pro-Boer parliamentarians, not to move an amendment to the royal address proposing that the Boers be given autonomy once the war ended. The following month Grey and Haldane associated themselves formally with the Imperial Liberal Council, a body established the previous year by R.W. Perks, a Liberal businessman and backbencher. In May the pair joined other imperialists in warmly welcoming the visit of Alfred Milner, the British High Commissioner in South Africa. This was too much for Herbert, who like many Liberals had been repelled by Milner's efforts to defeat the Boers's guerrilla tactics by burning the farms of their supporters and herding hundreds of dispossessed women and children into 'concentration camps'. Emily Hobhouse's press revelations about the dreadful conditions endured by the inmates of these camps created a sensation. Campbell-Bannerman could barely contain his outrage, denouncing Milner's policy in June as nothing short of barbaric. Venting his revulsion at a National Reform Union (NRU) dinner, his face reddened and his language became so fierce that, albeit briefly, it pushed Asquith much closer to the Liberal Imperialists: it was time, Asquith told Perks, to unite themselves firmly around Rosebery.[36] The lurking lord, however, still showed little inclination to re-engage although he still managed to add fuel to the fire by announcing that division would prevent the party ever becoming a political force, adding for good measure that attempts to paper over the cracks were nothing more than organised hypocrisy. This was a direct and very public rebuttal of everything for which Herbert had been working since 1899 and he damned it as a comment which 'could never be forgiven'.[37]

Fortunately for the party, however, he was not a man to hold a grudge and as whip he had consistently set aside his personal opinions and feelings in the interests of unity. He had more than once voiced doubts about the current leadership, or lack of it, but he knew very well that Campbell-Bannerman had the support of the rank and file, something re-affirmed at a special party meeting in July 1901. But he was equally well aware of Rosebery's appeal for leading figures like Grey and Asquith and, as he had learned during the election campaign, for some of the party's wealthier supporters. Thus when Rosebery announced that he was to speak at Chesterfield in December 1901 Herbert welcomed the news as 'the biggest opportunity of our time'.[38] He was so excited by the possibilities that he appealed personally to Rosebery to make unity his theme, claiming with justification that he himself had never consciously allowed his personal views to interfere with his duty to the party but had 'worked my best for party unity combined with free statement of differences'. Playing on Rosebery's vanity, he went on to say that he himself had sworn freely at both wings and while neither could be coerced only led, some sections would give way to him 'when they will give way to no one else'.[39]

On the day Rosebery's widely anticipated speech ranged over a number of topics. He condemned the government's conduct of the war and urged that peace negotiations be initiated, before going on to argue the case for national efficiency (much to the delight of its main proponents, Sidney and Beatrice Webb) and urging the party to shed the Irish alliance and other 'flyblown phylacteries of obsolete policies' devised in 1885 or 1892. His reference to these specific years made it very clear that he was deliberately renouncing the Liberalism associated with W.E. Gladstone and Rosebery did subsequently have the courtesy to inquire through Kitson about Herbert's reaction, acknowledging that the line he had taken would be be painful for him.[40] In fact his remark did not draw the anticipated response, for Herbert's devotion to his father did not blind him to current political reality and while he remained committed to the principle of home rule he no longer regarded it as an immediately practical proposition. By his own supporters Rosebery's speech was received with predictable enthusiasm. Grey was so overcome that he promptly declared that he now recognised Rosebery as his leader, which Campbell-Bannerman dismissed as egotism. Herbert thought it exposed flaws in Grey's leadership credentials but indicated that he would still try to moderate.[41] But even Liberals normally unsympathetic to Rosebery also saw in his Chesterfield remarks a basis for party unity and while this surprised Herbert he was certainly willing to capitalise on it.[42] At the same time he worried lest Campbell-Bannerman isolate himself by treating Rosebery's speech in a crabbed or hostile spirit, in which case, he told Spender, 'we'll be put down as small minded people who didn't put the good of the country first.'[43] In the hope of averting this he wrote the same day to tell Campbell-Bannerman that Rosebery's Chesterfield speech was the best he had ever delivered and that while it had faults it provided a sound basis for unity.[44]

Campbell-Bannerman was not convinced, however. He conceded that Rosebery had spoken well on the war but observed that he had skated over Milner and the camps, the two topics about which people felt most strongly. The comments about national efficiency he dismissed as claptrap. Privately Campbell-Bannerman was also annoyed that Asquith had attended the Chesterfield meeting and intimated that he would no longer consult with him. Herbert was even more dismayed when his chief further indicated that he did not propose to make any public response to Rosebery until mid-January, a decision he thought would be interpreted as fence-sitting. If Campbell-Bannerman failed to take the opportunity now to bring the party together, Herbert told Sinclair, the Liberal whip in Scotland, his own best option would be to quit, a threat his colleague did not take at all seriously, ascribing it to a seasonal surfeit of plum pudding and mince pies.[45] Nevertheless, Herbert appealed to Bryce and Spencer as party elders to try and change Campbell-Bannerman's mind, stressing that 'no personal feeling, however strong, ought to bar the way to unity now that it is within reach.' This was certainly a point Herbert had earned the right to make, given the forbearance he had shown towards Rosebery's implicit criticism of himself and his father. He then went on to deplore Campbell-Bannerman's refusal to consult with Asquith, saying that if no attempt at reconciliation was made, the party would break up, in which case he did not see how he himself could continue.[46] Bryce was horrified by this prospect, replying immediately that 'your continuance in your post is the best guarantee of unity so I earnestly trust that on public as well as personal grounds you will retain it.'[47] He appeared far less concerned by Campbell-Bannerman's attitude, although he did agree with Herbert that their leader ought to respond to Rosebery's speech as soon as possible. In fact, on that same day, Campbell-Bannerman initiated a long private meeting with Rosebery. It appeared friendly enough but when details of their conversation appeared in the press Rosebery complained to Herbert about the leak, which portrayed him as the sole barrier to unity. An unrepentant Campbell-Bannerman denied, somewhat implausibly, that he was the source of the story but he certainly shared his version of the conversation with most of his senior colleagues. Despite Rosebery's complaints, Herbert accepted Campbell-Bannerman's account of the meeting, judged the former leader to be 'lamentable', admired Campbell-Bannerman's self-control and declared, somewhat uncharacteristically, that had he himself been present he would certainly have lost his temper.[48]

With Campbell-Bannerman holding aloof from Asquith and Grey, the former holding fire pending the Liberal leader's public response to the Chesterfield speech, the latter openly espousing Rosebery as leader, Herbert was understandably gloomy about Rosebery's divisive influence within the party. It was not, he wrote to his LCA colleague, Charles Geake, 'a pleasant outlook for the go-between'.[49] Subsequent events offered little encouragement. Campbell-Bannerman publicly challenged Rosebery at the NLF meeting in February 1902 and then Rosebery's supporters announced the establishment of the Liberal League to carry out the Chesterfield programme. Rosebery as president and Grey as a vice-president were unsurprising but Asquith's acceptance of a vice-presidency was more worrying, although the latter seemed to hedge his bets by affirming his commitment to mainstream Liberalism. Harry Gladstone, however, thought Asquith about as sincere as a lawyer holding a brief and again urged his brother to stand by Campbell-Bannerman. If the leader did give up, he went on, then Herbert's best option was stick to the old party, get the backing of the best labour and Irish men and draw on the support of Liberals like Spencer and Morley who remained faithful to their father's principles so that 'with Father's mantle upon you, your position would be splendid'. He added almost parenthetically that in such an eventuality Herbert should not worry about his financial position because while his investments were not currently doing well he could always find him some directorships.[50] Herbert assured his brother that he had no intention of deserting either Campbell-Bannerman or home rule and reiterated that he would continue to make sacrifices for the sake of party unity.[51] Yet it remained a thankless task, as the tenor of his correspondence at this time indicates; Campbell-Bannerman could not be persuaded to strike while the iron was hot; Rosebery was thinking of withdrawing from political conversation altogether because his confidences were not respected; Campbell-Bannerman expected too much from those with whom he differed. The advent of the Liberal League did not help either since some saw it as the basis of an alternative party organisation, and Herbert was justifiably miffed when his right-hand man at Parliament Street, William Allard, was lured away to become its principal organiser. In high dudgeon he complained with some bitterness to Asquith, Grey and Haldane that Allard had effectively been bribed, though denials of any involvement from all three, combined with Allard's return to Parliament Street, prompted handsome apologies.[52] The League's activities notwithstanding, Herbert still tried publicly to keep the door open and his willingness to appear on the same platform as

Rosebery in his own constituency in May rather annoyed Campbell-Bannerman, although as Herbert brusquely told him not to have done so would have exposed him to a charge of hypocrisy, given his consistent stand for unity. As it happened, Rosebery himself disappointed the hopes of his followers that the League might lure him back into active political life, while the signing of the Peace of Vereeniging in May 1902 finally ended hostilities in South Africa and removed a major source of contention amongst Liberals.

The day after the Boers first sued for peace the government presented an Education Bill to the House of Commons. It proposed to do away with school boards, except in London, and make local authorities responsible for educational provision, including that currently offered by voluntary (i.e. church) schools. In effect this appeared to be providing a ratepayers' subsidy for Anglican schools, then educating about half the nation's children, and even Roman Catholic schools. Liberals of all persuasions reacted strongly but the most angry were the nonconformists, previously divided over the war but now uniformly aghast and still spiritually fired up by a religious campaign conducted the previous year by the National Council of Evangelical Free Churches. In the House of Commons Lloyd George put himself at the forefront of the Liberal outcry. His energy, manifest in 104 speeches and 193 other interventions which helped stretch the bill's committee stage to 49 days between June and December, was in marked contrast to the apparent diffidence of more senior Liberals. Morley spoke but rarely, as the designated education spokesman Bryce was lacklustre, while Campbell-Bannerman, more concerned perhaps by his wife's ill health, was frequently absent and gave the matter only spasmodic attention. In May he was urging Herbert to sound out the party's imperialist wing so that the front bench might take a common view, but by late September he was wondering vaguely whether they should be more pro-active. In April, on the other hand, he was complaining along with Asquith that neither had been consulted about their parliamentary tactics and asking who was making the decisions.[53] There is no evidence of any reply and it seems that Herbert had simply allowed Lloyd George, already displaying his aptitude for opportunism, to assume responsibility for the parliamentary opposition while leading nonconformist divines avidly stoked up hostility outside. This was an uncharacteristic lapse because Herbert was normally assiduous in organising the party's parliamentary work, selecting in consultation with colleagues appropriate speakers for specific debates, sometimes telling them what to say, and overseeing his junior colleagues in sorting out voting arrangements. But in this instance it seems that he did not so much drop the ball as deliberately allow it to pass him by because for once he *did* allow his personal views to override political considerations. He was, after all, a practising Anglican and thus disinclined to join battle against the bishops, several of whom were close family friends, while he was also coming under pressure from his family. As incumbent of the Hawarden parish church and responsible for the local Anglican schools, Harry Drew was so aggrieved by Liberal opposition to the bill that he threatened to vote Tory for the first time in his life.[54] Stephen and Harry were concerned that the Liberals appeared to have no alternative to what they saw as the nonconformist ambition to establish some form of amorphous state religion in all schools. Herbert seems to have resolved his dilemma simply by opting out. He did not vote save on a few minor points and it was no surprise that in one of his rare moments of interest in the bill, Campbell-Bannerman should ask his Scottish whip in some exasperation 'where oh where are our English whips and [...] who would think of consulting them.'[55]

Herbert's abdication of his responsibilities with respect to the Education Bill may have annoyed Campbell-Bannerman but it was a small blemish when set against his efforts to hold the party together in face of the obstacles, a leader whose inaction disappointed him, the diva-like Rosebery still hovering in the wings, disaffected senior colleagues and a group of MPs until recently often at odds within itself. In a rare moment of candour, Campbell-Bannerman, not normally an effusive man, seemed to recognise as much, writing in February 1902 to acknowledge the debt he owed to his whip. Recognising that it had been a 'a great personal sacrifice for you to go through all the drudgery without fee or fame or any reward except that worthy old sense of duty', he hoped that they could go on together but he would understand if Herbert had had enough.[56] But Herbert had no intention of abandoning his post just when it looked as though it might become less taxing. He was much more settled personally than hitherto and despite the pressures under which he had laboured since 1899 he exhibited none of the fragility and stress apparent in the years after his father's death. Of course he felt his mother's death deeply but in truth it had been a release not only for Catherine but also for him. It ended his self-imposed obligation to put her needs above all others and seemed to free him emotionally. Within a year of her passing he had fallen deeply in love and the swift transformation in his personal demeanour which followed was widely remarked upon and welcomed within the family.

It all happened quite suddenly. After the election dust settled in 1900 Harry treated him to a short break in Paris, in the course of which he evidently raised once more the subject of matrimony. In November Herbert wrote thanking his brother both for the holiday and his wise words but pointing out that marriage had not come to him, although

> each month it seems more desirable for it grows more formidable from an increasing sense of my own difficulties. Ought I? Dare I? Can I? These questions constantly recurring have hitherto prevented anything more than a general yet longing intention. More than that I cannot say now.[57]

In this 'most private' letter the last couple of sentences might be taken to imply that he already had some object in view and certainly only nine months passed before he was in touch with Harry again but this time in a state of feverish excitement.

The unexpected yet hoped for has come! I am engaged to be married to Dolly Paget. It came off last night in the garden by moonlight quite late. Today we drove to see her parents – they were too kind. She is infinitely too good for me but I could not help it [...] I am very very happy [...] the H of C is out of mind just now.[58]

It was indeed unexpected, not only because of its suddenness, Herbert's long-standing bachelorhood and the fact that he was Dorothy's senior by 24 years, but also because of her family background. Although Liberal herself, Dolly's father, Sir Richard Paget, had spent 30 years as a Conservative MP until 1895 opposing the father of his prospective son-in-law. Sir Richard, however, evidently did not let this affect his delight at the news. Scott Holland was equally pleased. 'Was it not wonderful?' he asked Mary, 'I was so staggered, that, in spite of the most positive assurances from the Pagets, I withheld belief [...] He plunges into the High Tory entourage with religious courage. It will be quite splendid for him [...] I am very glad.'[59] Dolly made a favourable impression when she met her fiancee's family in September. It might have been something of an ordeal given her youthfulness, her political antecedents and the fact that she was meeting the offspring of the great W.E. Gladstone, but she was sufficiently self-possessed to carry it off, though Agnes probably spoke for all of Herbert's siblings when she told him that she loved Dolly simply for making him so happy.[60] And happy he most certainly was. Campbell-Bannerman, whose devotion to his own wife was well known, hoped drily that Herbert was still enjoying his 'new interest [...] so much better in every way than beastly politics'.[61]

The attraction must have been instant and powerful, given the rapidity with which the relationship developed after their first encounter at a musical soiree early in 1901. Despite the lure of the golf course and the demands of his political work Herbert had tried to keep up his singing. His baritone voice was deemed good enough to allow him in 1901 to join the Catch Club, first established in 1761 to encourage the part singing of popular music and good enough to attract many members of London's leading choirs. Dolly and most of her family were equally musical and heavily involved with the Babbington Strollers, a west-country ensemble singing mainly for charitable purposes. But if its members were amateurs its performances had been brought to near-professional standard by a musical director, Dora Knatchbull, who before her marriage had been a prize-winning student at the Royal Academy and had subsequently performed internationally as a concert pianist. The nature of the Gladstones' relationship, however, is not easily discoverable. Virtually nothing written by Dolly is extant. A file in the Glynne-Gladstone Papers is wrongly attributed to her, although it relates mainly to Harry's wife, and nothing sent to her by Herbert survives. Given his prolific pen and the sheer number of letters he preserved, it seems likely that Herbert deliberately culled his most personal correspondence in order to protect their married life from future scrutiny. But sufficient clues remain in other letters down the years to indicate the durability and depth of his love for the woman who now brought a feminine touch to his home, provided a much-needed source of emotional support and whose welfare was to become pivotal and instrumental in shaping many of his decisions and choices. They were married in November 1901. Among the numerous wedding presents was a set of Scott's Waverley novels from Campbell-Bannerman, sent naively or mischievously in the belief that his newly-wed chief whip would have either the time or the inclination to wade through all 48 volumes. There was silver from Lord Rendel, an inscribed silver cigarette box from the Tory whips, and a Bechstein piano from Harry. After a honeymoon which each partner separately described to Mary as perfect, Herbert was able to contemplate politics with a new zest and perspective.

If the ending of the war in 1902 removed a major source of in-fighting, Campbell-Bannerman and Herbert could still not afford to ignore either Rosebery or the Liberal Leaguers who still harboured hopes of him, although the signals he was giving out were as confusing as ever. The situation became even more complicated in the early summer of 1903 when an ideological stone was suddenly lobbed into the waters of British economic orthodoxy. For decades free trade had been the cardinal tenet of the country's commercial policy but in a speech delivered in Birmingham on 15 May, Chamberlain challenged it by proposing the adoption of protective tariffs and the promotion of closer economic ties within the empire. The consequential ripples soon whipped up into a storm, simultaneously threatening to sink the Conservatives and causing Liberals of all persuasions to hoist the free-trade flag. Rosebery's robust defence of this traditional party rallying cry certainly raised the hopes of his supporters, although in fact he again held back and offended Asquith and Grey by refusing to join the Free Trade Union (FTU), the body which Herbert organised on Lord Ripon's suggestion to campaign against tariff reform. At the same time, however, and with a general election widely thought to be imminent as a result of Chamberlain's remarks, Rosebery did advise Liberal Leaguers not to allow themselves to be driven out of local associations as this could weaken the imperialist influence within any Liberal majority in a new House of Commons. Herbert, who had met plenty of resistance when trying to coax donations out of Liberal League supporters, was appropriately wary, warning that overtures of friendship from them were merely a cover for their wish to capture party funds in order to influence the selection of candidates.[62] Yet because the sudden prominence of the free-trade issue clearly did enhance the prospects for party unity he had to avoid giving the Leaguers any excuse for claiming that they had been rebuffed. So when Rosebery appeared to hold out yet another olive branch to Campbell Bannerman, Herbert advised his chief to respond in a conciliatory manner. But Campbell-Bannerman made it clear that while Rosebery's return to active politics would be welcome, it could be only on condition that he did not try to dictate what should be said and done by the party. Herbert thought this too strong, appealing to Spencer to moderate because 'we must obliterate our own old dissensions over the war and see R's speech as a declaration of alliance v JC.'[63]

Expectations of an election gave added impetus both to Herbert's campaign arrangements and his reorganisation of the party. Trying to extract some modicum of comfort from the outcome of the 1900 contest he had told Ripon that he had been encouraged by the solidity of the local workers and also by the fact that in some places men who had abandoned the party in 1886 had returned to help their campaign.[64] Nevertheless, as the huge number of uncontested seats in 1900 indicated, organisation in many English constituencies was virtually moribund. In the midst of all his manoeuvring between the party factions and senior figures he made time to speak frequently to local workers, often irritating them by labouring the need to improve their organisations and step up their activities. To the same end he collaborated with J.L. Gardiner of the *Daily News* in preparing and systematically placing appropriate articles designed to chivvy laggardly constituencies.[65] On the recommendation of one of his new sub-committees, the London Liberal and Radical Union was replaced by a new London Federation over which he personally kept a close eye to ensure that resources were concentrated in the most promising seats. However, shortage of money hampered a registration drive in the capital and fund-raising efforts were not always helped by the activities of colleagues. There was, for example, an ill-tempered exchange with Sir William Harcourt's son, Loulou, who diverted into the coffers of the Home Counties Federation and the NRU a £10,000 donation intended in Herbert's opinion for the party. Progress on other fronts, however, was more promising and by 1905 he was able to report that the LCA's income had increased by 25 per cent over its 1899 level. He encouraged Liberal ancillaries such as the Women's Liberal Federation and the Women's National Liberal Federation, while the National League of Young Liberals, founded in 1903, grew to 300 branches by 1906. He also worked effectively to co-ordinate various free-trade pressure groups that sprang up in the aftermath of Chamberlain's Birmingham speech.

Their benefits were clear when in October 1905 the Liberals won the Barkston Ash by-election, Herbert's own creation, the FTU, providing not only supplementary workers but also finance which did not have to be counted as election expenses.

As the political climate became more favourable so Herbert found it easier to secure candidates. In the immediate aftermath of the 1900 debacle he had encountered all sorts of obstacles; home counties constituencies uniformly unwilling, he was told, to accept Roman Catholic candidates, others rejected because they were Jewish, Loulou Harcourt refusing Clitheroe because it was too working-class. A further complication arose as a consequence of free church displeasure with the 1902 Education Bill, for Herbert was bombarded with demands that education be made a test question for candidates. In July 1903 a formal request was made through Arthur Porritt, a writer for the *Christian World*, that the party's candidates include a generous number of nonconformists. It must have been tempting because the previous August a by-election in the safe Tory seat of Sevenoaks had seen a huge swing to the successful Liberal, a Baptist who had made education his main platform. But even though he had strong religious convictions of his own, Herbert had no wish to be recruit candidates with single-issue bees in their political bonnets.[66] While encouraging the Free Church Council to identify candidates, therefore, he tended to direct them to unpromising seats and offered only limited central financial help, a tactic with which he was, he noted, 'much satisfied'.[67]

With Liberal prospects growing ever brighter Herbert told Hudson he hoped to have every constituency fixed before Christmas 1903 and if this proved over-optimistic his notebooks do point to a gathering momentum. By February 1904 he was only four candidates short in the home counties and the difficult Liverpool seats were also fully covered. The improving position allowed him more freedom to influence the selection of candidates and to ensure that other electoral arrangements were honoured at local level. His policy of

linking the LCA's financial contribution to the size of the
local electorate allowed him to control his overall liability in a
defensible way, while offering constituencies a pound-for-
pound matching contribution forced them to try to increase
their own incomes and often to accept a candidate selected in
line with his own broader electoral strategy. He was quick,
for example, to appreciate that tariff reform made potential
allies of the Liberal Unionists and well before the end of
1903 he was pressing Campbell-Bannerman to come to
some accommodation with them. Concerned that again his
leader did not seem to be treating this with appropriate
urgency Herbert dined with Winston Churchill in January
1904 to discuss the matter. Churchill, still at this time on the
Conservative benches, reported to the Duke of Devonshire
that there was no doubting Herbert's wishes to save the seats
of sincere Unionist free traders. 'About fifteen could be
settled quite easily.'[68]

Also well advanced by this time was the understanding
reached with the LRC in 1903. Despite tentative explorations
during the 1900 campaign local resistance often remained an
obstacle to the adoption of working class candidates. In the
North-East Lanark by-election in September 1901 local
Liberals successfully ran their own man against Bob Smillie,
a miner who had the backing of the Scottish Liberal whip
and several Liberal MPs. This prompted criticism in the
progressive press, which Herbert took personally, responding
sharply when C.P. Scott, editor of the *Manchester Guardian*,
took him to task for not doing more to encourage labour
candidates. 'I have risked more for the labour party than any
of my predecessors,' he asserted with some justification.[69]
However, the Lanark by-election convinced labour leaders
that professions of Liberal support for their candidates were
useless if local associations still chose to put up an official
candidate of their own. Herbert was of exactly the same mind,
telling his own constituents that while he could easily reach an
agreement with labour leaders 'the difficulty lies with the
constituencies themselves and in the unfortunate necessity of
providing funds.'[70] Undeterred, he lost few opportunities to

advocate a fairer crack of the whip for labour and as his speech at the NLF's annual meeting in 1902 confirmed, he was not afraid to ruffle local Liberal feathers. He was clear that party headquarters would be supportive if local committees insisted on running a Liberal against a labour man, but he did his best to minimise such eventualities. Thus when in 1902 Clitheroe Liberals resisted his request to give a clear run to the trade unionist, David Shackleton, Herbert outwitted them by getting the election writ moved before they had time to find a suitable alternative. By this time, however, sentiment was hardening in favour of some form of cooperation as Liberals and the LRC found more common ground in opposition to the Education Bill. Early in 1903 the Quaker businessman and philanthropist, George Cadbury, told Jesse Herbert, effectively the chief whip's lieutenant at Parliament Street, that Ramsay MacDonald would like to discuss arrangements for the next election. Reporting back on this meeting Jesse Herbert indicated that MacDonald had turned up with a list of seats the LRC wished to fight. He also told his chief that the LRC had a fighting fund of £100,000 at its disposal and that allowing the LRC to fight 35 seats would save the Liberals about £15,000. Herbert Gladstone believed anyway that labour's strength in the country warranted greater representation in parliament but the prospective financial benefit was an added incentive to meet personally and secretly with the LRC secretary. There was never in his mind any question of a formal alliance, rather just a willingness to give the LRC some clear runs against a common foe. Although the discussions took place primarily with a general election in view, the LRC also secured agreements with respect to a number of by-elections after 1903, with Herbert doing his best behind the scenes to get John Burns, no fan of Keir Hardie or the ILP, to ensure that moderates rather than ILP men were chosen. When the LRC nominated a moderate union official, Arthur Henderson, to fight Barnard Castle in July 1903 Herbert had no qualms about exercising his influence to overrule local autonomy and get him a free run. This provoked the chairman of the

Northern Liberal Federation to deplore in the *Daily News* the way in which Liberal leaders and whips were nursing into life 'a serpent which would sting their party to death'. Given that William Gladstone had so effectively rallied working people to the Liberal flag, he added, it was a 'strange paradox' that his son should be demolishing that work.[71] Morley was equally dubious about Herbert's tactics, writing to Birrell that what with the League's machinations and the labour mess 'I doubt the vast glories that are supposed to be coming with the election.'[72]

In fact no general election materialised in 1903 and the Tory government limped wearily on under the lacklustre leadership of Arthur Balfour, who had replaced Salisbury as prime minister in 1902. He had made a bad start with the Education Bill and Chamberlain's advocacy of tariff reform not only rang the public's alarm bells with its implications of dearer food, but divided his own party. A Licensing Act in 1904 succeeded in reducing the number of licensed premises, but on such generous terms for publicans that Liberals could claim with some plausibility that the government was in the pocket of the drink trade. The following year an Aliens Act appalled many by ending the automatic right of asylum. Herbert's work was certainly made easier by the government's uncanny ability to antagonise with its legislation but his focus on election preparation never faltered. As in the 1900 campaign he ensured that Liberal speakers were systematically organised and their engagements arranged in such a way that every part of the country received at least one visit from a national leader. He was something of a martinet in this respect, too, for when Birrell independently asked Campbell-Bannerman to address one of his meetings in 1905 the Liberal leader replied that he knew 'no master but one & dare not say aye or nay to anything until I have consulted Herbert G'. Having thus consulted Gladstone, whom he described as 'my last ditch' he agreed to go.[73] There was perhaps in this little vignette another example of the faith which Campbell-Bannerman placed in his chief whip's tactical judgement and organisational skill. 'He trusted us almost too much', Herbert later recalled.[74]

But Herbert, not content to confine himself to the nuts and bolts of electioneering, was trying to drive the party forward in another way as well. Talk of an election in 1903 had been sparked by the widespread reaction against tariff reform but he realised that if the Liberals fought on an essentially negative platform they ran the risk of gaining power without having thought about what they might do with it. Herbert himself was no thinker and certainly no visionary. Like his father he was a political opportunist in the best sense, recognising facts and then seeking to harmonise them as far as possible with his principles.[75] But growing unemployment did prompt him late in 1904 to circulate a memorandum advocating a government works scheme to relieve hard-pressed local authorities. Building on the positive response from colleagues he pressed Campbell-Bannerman to establish small groups to consider policy on a number of key issues such as Ireland, agriculture, licensing, education and labour affairs. When Campbell-Bannerman finally came across his letter, buried in a pile of papers on his desk, he thought it a useful suggestion. More politically astute than he was sometimes given credit for, he asked Herbert to set up four such committees but to confine their membership to ex-cabinet members, lest invitations to others be construed as a portent of inclusion in a future Liberal Government.[76]

At the same time Herbert and his chief were cranking up the pressure in the House of Commons. For Herbert this was not a matter of making his own voice heard in the chamber where he had barely spoken for two years, but rather of organising and co-ordinating others from behind the scenes. In conjunction with Asquith and Lloyd George, he orchestrated the harrying of the Licensing Bill throughout 1904 to the point that Balfour eventually had to propose limits on the time allowed for debate. Even discussion on that proposal was stretched over three days by carefully managed Liberal interventions. Liaising with his leader in June about tactics for the following week, Herbert reported gleefully that they had had a great day in the House with the Tories' inability to get their men up leaving Balfour thoroughly dejected.[77] As the 1905 parliamentary session opened, much of Herbert's official correspondence centred on parliamentary tactics and potential opportunities to bring the administration down. 'It would be a pity', he observed, 'to weaken the position through a little want of organisation.'[78] In March Campbell-Bannerman was seeking his advice about what to prioritise in the Commons, feeling that he could not judge anything like as well as his chief whip.[79] In April Herbert was suggesting a meeting of ex-cabinet members to consider which parliamentary issues to raise and who should speak on each subject, especially the controversial Aliens Bill. The incessant barrage of Liberal questions, amendments and resolutions on that bill once again forced Balfour to seek time limits on further debate. When the government dithered over rising unemployment and public manifestations of unrest, Herbert suggested that his leader add to its embarrassment by raising the issue in the House.[80] By the summer Liberal backbenchers themselves were beginning to falter under the relentless pressure from the whips' office but Herbert told one of his junior colleagues that while it was sometimes difficult to drive the party in the House, 'we must stick to it.'[81] Generally, though, he was delighted both with his own organisation and the willingness with which MPs embraced this concerted effort to wear down the Tories. With the summer recess approaching he told Campbell-Bannerman that they were rattling the government about 'like peas in a pod' and that if Balfour chose to resume in the autumn he would have to keep 250 men in the Commons night and day. 'We worried them until 5 this morning', he exulted, 'and will keep them unhappy today and tomorrow.'[82] Campbell-Bannerman was equally pleased with the work of what he termed his 'francs tireurs', replying that he had watched it with intense interest 'and you have chivvied the poor fellows handsomely.' Adding that he was leaving for Marienbad the following day he expressed a hope that Herbert, too, would get some rest 'after your splendid campaign in House and

country since the year opened.'[83] It was an interesting
reflection on the nature of Edwardian politics that Herbert's
own holidays, four weeks in Scotland, were spent partly in the
company of exhausted Conservative ministers and with
Arthur Balfour, whose parliamentary days he had made so
uncomfortable, an excellent host.

Excellent host or not, politically Balfour had clearly had
enough and as rumours of his resignation multiplied, the
King, anticipating a change of government, summoned
Campbell-Bannerman to discuss its likely policies and
composition. The Liberal leader, having confided this
information to his chief whip on 9 September, then resumed
his holidays, leaving Herbert to cope as individuals and
factions began jockeying for place and arguing about tactics.
Liberal Leaguers were against forming a government before
a general election, fearing that the voting might leave the
party dependent for a majority upon Irish support. Privately
Herbert agreed, though for different reasons, telling Bryce
and anyone else who would listen that taking office prior to an
election would let the current government off the hook,
compel the Liberals to select a cabinet from 200 sitting MPs
when he anticipated having 400 afterwards and also run the
risk of losing newly appointed ministers at the polls and then
having to find replacements.[84] However, Campbell-Bannerman, returning to England on 12 November and at last
displaying some of the incisiveness whose absence Herbert
had often deplored, determined that he would form an
administration before any voting began. The next day he
met with Herbert and other senior colleagues to discuss its
membership.

At this meeting Asquith agreed to serve as chancellor. Early
in September, however, he had secretly arranged with Grey
and Haldane in the so-called Relugas Compact that none
would accept office unless Campbell-Bannerman took a
peerage and allowed Asquith to lead in the House of
Commons. Now on 13 November he felt it sufficient merely
to urge this course on Campbell-Bannerman, perhaps
because a year or two previously Herbert had already passed

on to him Campbell-Bannerman's intimation that in the event of a change of government he did not think he would be fit to take on heavy work and would probably opt for a peerage and some honorific office.[85] Given his own persistent irritation at the Scot's frequent absences from the House of Commons and also his belief that he lacked the instincts of a great leader, Herbert had readily accepted both the logic and the force of this argument, although privately he thought any move to the Lords should be delayed for a while.[86] He suggested to Margot Asquith that if Campbell-Bannerman went as soon as he won an election it might be seen as a condition imposed by the Leaguers, whilst the labour men would also resent the instant withdrawal of someone sympathetic to their interests. Trespassing somewhat on their long friendship, Herbert also pointed out to Margot that her husband had not attended the Commons regularly and so did not really know the Irish members with whom Campbell-Bannerman, on the other hand, had considerable influence. Asquith, he thought, had a lot to gain by waiting since it would only be a matter of six months or so before Campbell-Bannerman retired 'upstairs'.[87]

Campbell-Bannerman himself on the other hand still appeared inclined to go immediately to the Lords, replying positively to Asquith's suggestion at their meeting on 13 November although adding that his wife would be the final arbiter. Indeed, he went further, authorising Herbert to direct the Liberal press not to publish anything hostile to the idea of a peer being prime minister. One of Herbert's own draft lists of potential cabinet personnel, probably drawn up in the course of the actual discussions since it is extensively amended, certainly had Campbell-Bannerman pencilled in for the purely honorific post of lord president of the council, indicative of the intention to let Asquith lead in the Commons.[88] Asquith's willingness to serve delighted Herbert, but he knew that Grey's abstention would undermine the man whom he had long seen as Campbell-Bannerman's natural successor, while an administration lacking both Grey and Haldane would lack credibility.

While there were strong reasons for Campbell-Bannerman starting in the Commons, he mused, 'they do not outweigh the effects of Grey's abstention.'[89] The effect he feared most was that the King might be tempted to ask Rosebery to form a government instead.

His concerns grew when Rosebery emerged once more to throw another spanner in the Liberal works in the form of a speech at Bodmin on 25 November renouncing Campbell-Bannerman's advocacy of a gradualist approach to home rule. Herbert felt it necessary to urge his leader 'most earnestly' to remain as friendly and open as possible to 'Berwick and Fife' (i.e. Grey and Asquith), fearing the re-opening of old wounds and the re-energising of old alliances within the party.[90] Balfour, perhaps making the same calculation, formally submitted his resignation with effect from 5 December. The next day Herbert re-affirmed to Margot Asquith that Campbell-Bannerman was going to the Lords, subject only to his wife's final say-so. When this was also floated in the *The Times* Herbert, as authorised previously, telephoned Gardiner at the *Daily News* to say that his paper should not dismiss the idea out of hand.[91] Fearful perhaps that his own standing with some in the party might be compromised he insisted that his own name should not on any account be mentioned over the telephone. Somewhat mystified, Gardiner promptly contacted the Liberal leader directly who told him that *The Times* story *should* be strongly refuted since he was fully determined to remain in the Commons. Lady Campbell-Bannerman, it seems, had spoken. The next day, a thoroughly dejected Herbert, convinced that Grey and Haldane now would remain aloof, told Margot that he was 'in the depths. It is all so wrong & so unnecessary.'[92] He expressed similar sentiments to J.A. Spender, the editor of the *Westminster Gazette*, who suggested asking a former MP and cabinet member, Arthur Acland, to act as a go-between. After a series of fraught discussions and phone calls which went on well into the late hours, Acland's intervention proved decisive. When Margot saw Herbert the next day 'his face (was) shining with happiness [. . .] Grey & Haldane are in', something for which, he said, Spender and Acland deserved gold medals.[93] In his excitement he rather cavalierly overlooked the fact that to get Acland involved he appears to have hinted very strongly at a cabinet post. In the event Acland got nothing and always blamed Herbert for not honouring his promises.[94]

In the midst of all this there was also the matter of what office Herbert himself might occupy. Thorough and competent though it was, his organisational work as whip had been unspectacular and was as yet largely untested at the polls, while only those at the heart of political life grasped the significance of his unstinting backstage efforts to keep the party together. Interestingly, when in 1904 the parliamentary journalist, Henry Lucy, considered the likely composition of the next Liberal ministry Herbert's name did not figure at all.[95] The fact was that, unlike many of his colleagues, Herbert had little personal political ambition. Towards the end of 1904 Jesse Herbert had told him that apart from Campbell-Bannerman no front bencher could reach the popular mind so effectively and that in due course he would certainly be asked to lead.[96] Herbert was utterly dismissive, knowing all too well that even had he entertained any such aspiration, he lacked the necessary mastery of the House of Commons. Jesse Herbert was not at all deterred.

> Though your personal diffidence must weigh heavily against the wishes of others, as yet you have not heard the call of the people and all I ask now is that you will not prevent them from calling. I know the views of many, and they have a strong desire, which with opportunity will become a purpose to give you that call.[97]

Noting in her diary what her husband told her of the 13 November meeting with Campbell-Bannerman, Margot Asquith wrote that Herbert had been

> very humble about himself. CB had offered him the Home Office but Herbert had refused it [...] Herbert said he wanted

nothing special. CB suggested the Admiralty wh. he fancied enormously [...] Herbert is a *dear* – very honest & generous with a fine nature [...] I love his humility.[98]

But when she congratulated him on getting the Admiralty on 6 December he replied that nothing had been fixed.[99] Somehow there was also a rumour of the War Office which Lord Esher, a permanent member of the Committee of Imperial Defence and who had himself turned down War Office posts in 1900 and 1903, thought would be 'a thoroughly bad appointment'.[100] Lunching with colleagues a day or so before, Lloyd George, who had enough ambition for two, was certain that Herbert would get the Home Office.[101] Despite Herbert's previous refusal, Campbell-Bannerman may have calculated that once Grey and Haldane were safely in the fold, respectively as foreign secretary and secretary of state for war and alongside Asquith as chancellor, the remaining great office of state could not also go to someone associated primarily with the imperialist wing of the party. Alternatively, as Herbert explained to Mary, he would have had the Admiralty except that it had to go to a peer once Haldane took the War Office.[102] Either way Campbell-Bannerman turned to his closest political lieutenant and by 11 December it was determined that Herbert should be Home Secretary.

It is inconceivable that Herbert did not discuss his options with Dolly and although there is no surviving indication of her views, she was sufficiently politically aware to know that a major appointment was appropriate for a man of her husband's standing. Harry was also encouraging.

I don't see why you should not have the Home Office. Lyttelton told me that [...] they are looking for you. Of course it is a big post & you may have to bring in important measures. But why not. You have always done very well what you have to do & I have no fears for you in a big office.[103]

Herbert appeared unmoved by the prospect. 'I tried hard to avoid it.' he told Mary. 'I longed for the Admiralty [...] I am in a great dread and the whole work will tumble on me at once.'[104] In reply she was consoling about the Admiralty. 'How you wd. have loved it, the only big office in which there is no nasty competition & rivalry [...] it would have been jolly.'[105] After five years of high-level bickering amongst his colleagues this, if accurate, might possibly explain Herbert's preference for the Admiralty. More plausibly, he already had first-hand experience of the Home Office's enormous and ever-growing remit and the consequential need for its effective representation on the floor of the House. Then of course it had been Asquith who had borne the brunt of the parliamentary work but now it would fall to him. That would not have been very appealing at the best of times, given his dislike of speaking in the Commons, but as chief whip he had legitimately been able to avoiding speaking at all for three years. But once duty and loyalty to Campbell-Bannerman persuaded him that he should accept the Home Office, however reluctantly, he moved quickly to ensure that he got a junior who would compensate for what he himself called his own 'appalling deficiencies' in the House of Commons.[106] He chose Herbert Samuel, MP for Cleveland, whose abilities as a speaker and organiser were already known to him. Campbell-Bannerman was not keen, regarding Samuel as an imperialist, and other rising Liberals like Walter Runciman were also rather put out. Herbert, however, was insistent and got his man.

With the shape of the new government finally settled, Campbell-Bannerman launched the Liberal campaign amid scenes of noisy enthusiasm at the Albert Hall on 21 December. It was agreed that Herbert should remain at the helm until the election was over, meaning that his Christmas and new year were occupied with finalising a programme of national meetings, sorting out last-minute hitches in the constituencies and handling the donations which were now mounting up very healthily, most of them from a few wealthy individuals including Harry. Harry also contributed to Herbert's own fight in Leeds where, somewhat ironically, rebellious members of the LRC were contemplating running a candidate until Ramsay MacDonald stepped in and condemned both the intention and the reckless language local activists had used about the chief whip. In the event Herbert's victory was easy and the Conservative share of the vote lower than in any of his previous fights. Dolly proved something of an electoral asset, having recovered from the various illnesses which had plagued her since their marriage and a tonsillectomy (without anaesthetic) in the autumn of 1905. She was a youthful and attractive presence at her husband's side on the platform, personally addressing a number of women's meetings and charming everyone she met.

Nationally the voting began on 12 January 1906. By the time it ended some three weeks later the electorate had delivered one of the most decisive results in parliamentary history. The Unionists were trounced, their one-third share of the vote being their lowest in six elections fought since 1885. Their 137 MPs were swamped by 400 Liberals. Most commentators had expected a substantial Liberal majority but this was a stunning achievement, the Liberals' best result since 1832. The Unionists had certainly not helped their own cause. Both locally and nationally their party machine was in a poor state, while the outgoing government's policies had alienated several important interest groups. Above all, of course, the espousal of tariff reform had divided their own supporters whilst gifting to the Liberals the unifying cry of free trade. If these considerations made a Liberal victory in 1906 highly likely, few anticipated its sheer magnitude. Herbert's private forecasts were correct in over 350 seats but the Liberals also captured a further 46 seats where he expected either certain or likely defeat. The organisational changes he had instigated proved particularly effective in London and he managed to ensure as well that the Liberal League operated within the main party structure. The comprehensiveness of the Liberal triumph also owed a great deal to Herbert's unstinting labour in finding and placing sufficient candidates of the right calibre in virtually every seat, raising the necessary finance and using it strategically to provide LCA money for about a half of his candidates and concentrating over a half of the total expenditure in just a fifth of the seats. So effective was his recruitment that only 14 per cent of returned Tories were unopposed compared with 87 per cent in 1900 and 91 per cent in 1895. Of course, it had been easier to find candidates as party morale picked up after 1902 but that improvement itself was in large measure a consequence of his success in holding the various factions together during the Boer War and the uncertainties over the leadership, and in his effective management of affairs in parliament in order to wear down the government. Beatrice Webb's dismissal of Herbert as a lazy lightweight and nothing more than a party wirepuller was quite unjustified.[107] The energy and stamina he displayed during six-and-a-half years as chief whip were remarkable. In the ten years after he stood down the party went through five successors.

As Liberal victories mounted up it was typical of Herbert's modesty that he should see them as a vindication of Campbell-Bannerman's policy but in his later, more considered reflections he gave pride of place to the pact he had negotiated with the LRC and which facilitated the return of 40 or so Labour members. Jesse Herbert agreed, describing the results of this arrangement as 'outstandingly good' and asking rhetorically 'was there ever such a justification of a policy by results?'[108] Yet it did not go uncriticised. Some accused Herbert of unnecessarily letting the Labour cuckoo into the Liberal nest from which it might subsequently oust its host. Others argued that the arrangement with the LRC was irrelevant because the Liberals would probably have won every seat in which they stood aside for an LRC candidate. That may have been so but it attributes to Herbert a foresight which neither he nor anyone else possessed, for he could not have known in advance of the voting that the Labour members would merely supplement rather than actually secure a majority for a Liberal Party which by 1906 had, with a brief interval between 1892 and 1895, been out of power for the best part of two decades. There was much to justify Spender's later verdict that as chief whip Herbert had rendered a signal service to the party.[109] As Jack Pease told the NLF in 1905, Herbert's work generally had been quiet and unostentatious: and that was precisely the point.[110]

CHAPTER 5

The Home Office

The election safely in the bag, Herbert returned briefly to headquarters to clear up a few remaining loose ends. He was genuinely surprised to be presented with a parting gift, innocent as ever of the loyalty and even affection that he inspired in his staff. He was characteristically generous in his own remarks while the party's improved finances allowed him to show his appreciation in the form of substantial bonuses.[1] With the last cheque signed, he was finally free to turn his attention fully to the Home Office.

He was of course familiar with its business but that his was now the ultimate responsibility became immediately apparent when the capital sentences handed down at the recent winter assizes landed on his desk for consideration. Over the course of the nineteenth century technological and social change had collectively generated a huge amount of legislation, much of it drafted, administered and monitored by the Home Office. Consequently, the department had grown to resemble a badly designed and over-burdened circuit board connected ever more intricately with the ordinary citizen's daily life through almost annual accretions. By 1906, for instance, its public order duties embraced administration of the judiciary and prisons, supervision of the police, direct control of the Metropolitan force, advice on the exercise of the royal prerogative and the oversight of fairs and open spaces.

Its industrial mandate included factory safety and inspection, workers' compensation, working hours, industrial law, the truck acts and shops. If funding the secret service was still a relatively minor matter, the Home Office was charged with protecting citizens against undesirable foreigners, the misuse of firearms and explosives, together with moral dangers such as prostitution, indecent advertising, public obscenity, excessive gambling, dangerous drugs and intoxicating liquor. Miscellaneous duties spanned the oversight of cemeteries, wild birds, parliamentary elections and proceedings, the licensing of London cabs and taxis and the affairs of the Channel Islands and the Isle of Man.

Precisely because its activities impinged so widely on the lives of the general public, the Home Office was also constantly pestered by the faddists so frequently found among civic-minded Edwardians, temperance advocates, anti-vivisectionists, public decency enthusiasts and anti-juvenile smoking campaigners, or by special interest groups like the Metropolitan Police or London cabbies. This added further to the workload. By the end of 1905 the 22 staff in the departmental registry were handling almost 89,000 incoming and outgoing items a year. During Herbert's first year alone this figure increased by almost 3,000 and he frequently cited the sheer volume of work to explain why a parliamentary question could not be adequately answered or a request for an investigation of a particular issue rejected. In part it was a simple matter of limited capacity. The most recent return (1902) showed that the Home Office had 289 pensionable (i.e. permanent) staff. Even including the 2,784 working for the prison commissioners still left it far smaller than the Admiralty (8,869), the customs service (3,877) or the Inland Revenue (5,388).[2] Technical expertise was also in short supply, a reflection perhaps on the permanent Under-Secretary, Mackenzie Chalmers, whose training was in law, while statistics were still gathered for monitoring rather than planning purposes. There were other gaps as well, prompting Herbert to approach Asquith about the urgent need for additions to his factory inspectorate and the criminal department.[3] He did not get all he asked for but a dozen new posts were approved in March 1906.

By this time the government had settled to its work. Despite Herbert's efforts to encourage some constructive thinking before the election the Liberals had been returned essentially on a negative programme of reversing Conservative measures. With over 150 free churchmen occupying the government benches and another 40 or so members representing the LRC, soon rechristened as the Labour Party, the choice of education and trades disputes as the main legislative subjects for the session was no surprise. For the rest, however, it seems to have been a matter of which minister could shout the loudest, for the cabinet, notwithstanding its reputation as one of the most talented of the twentieth century, had little collective dynamic. Beatrice Webb gathered from civil servants and ministers that it was incoherent and intensely individualistic.[4] At the very start Herbert had warned Arthur Ponsonby, the prime minister's principal private secretary, that he would need to keep Campbell-Bannerman focussed.[5] But Campbell-Bannerman was not a particularly good chairman and he was much preoccupied with his wife's long illness which resulted in her death in August 1906. He did not provide much direction except when he unilaterally ignored the advice of his own law officers and adopted the Labour Party's Trades Disputes Bill. Noting that the cabinet dealt only with what was under its nose, Ponsonby thought 'they simply ignore what is to happen after that [...] The work of the session was heaped up higgledy piggledy like stones on a cart and some of them are now rolling off and some are being surreptitiously pushed off.'[6]

Herbert soon had some contributions of his own to add to the government cart. Most pressing was the framing of regulations for the Aliens Act coming into force on 1 January. East European migration to Britain had emerged as a public concern from the late 1880s when social investigators began to reveal its impact on London's east end where most of the newcomers were settling. Herbert had spoken against an anti-alien motion in 1893 and like most Liberals he had opposed the Tory measure in 1905. Although he accepted that the act was on the statute book and had to be implemented, he was determined to humanise it. Firmly believing that individuals fleeing from religious or political persecution should not be barred from entering the United Kingdom, he personally amended the first draft regulations in order to maximise Home Office discretion in dealing with such cases and discourage the official tendency to apply broad legislative categories to individual immigrants.[7] As an added safeguard he also ruled that the press should be admitted to the proceedings of the immigration boards. The consequence was that the act's more extreme supporters hounded Herbert persistently throughout the 1906 parliamentary session. In February they moved an amendment to the King's speech regretting any reference to the exclusion of foreign workers during trade disputes. Herbert handled this with refreshing confidence, pointing out sharply that if Conservatives wanted this they should have included it in the original bill. The attacks intensified once he published the regulations. On 14 March Sir W. Evans-Gordon, MP for Tower Hamlets and the organising hand behind the British Brothers League, best-known of the various anti-alien organisations, accused him of introducing fundamental changes by regulation and thereby depriving parliament of the opportunity to comment. The Home Secretary, he asserted, had stretched his powers beyond all precedent by absolving individuals from *proving* that they had religious or political reasons for migrating. Sure of the moral high ground, Herbert's reply was both abrupt and dismissive, much to the annoyance of a Tory whip who felt that an opportunity had been missed. 'Herbert Gladstone's new regulations have virtually wrecked the administration of the Aliens Act', he fumed in his diary.

> We had a splendid case and three or four men both anxious and competent to defeat Gladstone in debate: and yet nothing was done [...] Gladstone, who is a pudding, and ill-mannered to boot, was justified in treating the matter as a mere detail

upon which he had not been seriously criticised [...] We ought unquestionably to have attacked the Home Secretary hotly. His offensive and overbearing attitude has made him fair game [...] with luck we will make his position uncomfortable.[8]

Certainly Evans-Gordon, periodically assisted by others, kept up the parliamentary onslaught, often with language redolent with the worst of contemporary British prejudice. On one occasion Herbert was accused of a willingness to allow in to Britain any alien idiot pauper with loathsome diseases to become a charge on the public purse; on another he was criticised for not deporting a Polish Jewess convicted of soliciting (it was her first offence and Herbert was not going to throw that particular stone). Backed by the gutter press, the increasingly frenetic Tory fringe resorted to scaremongering; what steps would the home secretary take to protect the public against recently expelled French anarchists if they sought to cross the Channel; what was he doing about 80,000 Russian Jews purportedly heading to England; had he received complaints that immigrants were frustrating Church Army efforts to find work for locals; what costs were being incurred by the German gypsies currently wandering around the countryside... and so it continued. In 1906 at least, Herbert won the battle. Only 955 immigrants were initially excluded and of the 796 who appealed against that exclusion 442 were successful.[9]

Herbert, however, had other, more constructive, things on his mind, in particular amending the 1897 Workmen's Compensation Act, his principal measure in the government's first session. The amendment supplemented the existing provision against industrial accidents by adding (and defining) occupational disease as a legitimate trigger for compensation. By extending cover to all workmen not expressly excluded (the 1897 act excluded all those not expressly included) an additional six million people were brought into the scheme. Conscious as always of his own deficiencies in debate Herbert concentrated on the industrial aspects leaving Samuel to handle the drafting and discussion of the sections dealing with disease. It was probably a wise decision, for Ponsonby noted after the second reading that while Herbert had successfully steered the bill through the House

> he is not a very capable parliamentarian either in skill or manner. He adopts the view [...] that the Cabinet opinion is everything: the Government and the party in the House & the party in the country must be directed & led by it and must acquiesce & follow.[10]

The implication that Herbert did not trouble to explain things fully in parliament was not unfounded. Although the measure was generally welcomed by MPs, some Liberals were disappointed that outworkers and those employed in dangerous trades were not covered, while others criticised the fact that small employers were not made liable. Nevertheless, the bill successfully completed its parliamentary passage in December and William Robson, the Solicitor General, told Herbert that in all his experience of government work none was better than the Home Office's on the Workmen's Compensation Bill. It was to prove a rare enough accolade.[11]

Together with minor measures dealing with music copyright and street betting, the Workmen's Compensation Act represented a reasonable outcome for the session, but behind the scenes Herbert's main focus was elsewhere. He was no radical when it came to penal reform or the treatment of prisoners but as his 1894 report had demonstrated, he did aspire to alleviate the harsher aspects of prison life, and now as Home Secretary he often intervened personally in quite low level matters. Thus in June 1906 he reduced the number of lashes prescribed by the Dartmoor Visiting Committee for a prisoner who had attacked a warder with a shovel. He had no problem with flogging but believed it should be a deterrent, not a punishment, and that its excessive use would simply encourage those who wished to abolish it altogether.[12] In the same way he demanded a re-think from the Reading

Gaol Visiting Committee which had sentenced a prisoner to flogging with a cat o'nine tails for attacking two prison officers. This, he ruled, was quite unreasonable, given that the prisoner had only just left Broadmoor where he had been regarded as quite insane. He was critical, too, of the practice of solitary confinement, writing later that he objected to punishments 'which cannot be shown to be necessary to deterrence either on the actual or potential criminal. I object to it still more if not being necessary to deterrence it is harmful positively or negatively to physical or moral soundness.' Discipline was necessary but prisoners should be treated humanely with the emphasis on education, training, reason and individual reform.[13] The author John Galsworthy, a leading campaigner against the use of closed cell confinement, told Charles Masterman, Herbert Samuel's successor as Under-Secretary from 1909, that 'with Herbert Gladstone & yourself at the helm this is the moment to make a change. We shall never again get two men in office who can both feel & see.'[14]

When it came to capital crimes many sentences were clear-cut and warranted no recommendation of mercy, but Herbert agonised over others in what sometimes appeared to be a determination to find any justification for a reprieve. A case in point was Leslie James, condemned to death for murdering her newborn infant. Her guilt was incontrovertible since she had admitted the offence but Herbert sought desperately to find some mitigating circumstance, pondering whether her gender, lack of premeditation or even drunkenness might save her. The judge, however, was not for moving and James was duly executed, prompting a howl of protest from one individual at this decision from a Home Secretary who had more reprieves to his credit 'than any Minister who has held your high office.'[15] This may have been an exaggeration but during his four years at the Home Office Herbert reprieved 51 per cent of the 107 individuals sentenced to hang compared with 40 per cent who escaped the noose out of the 162 given the death penalty between 1901 and 1905.[16] In absolute terms it was a small enough improvement but it was sufficient to unsettle the more hard-hearted, not least the King to whom constitutionally Herbert had to submit his recommendations for mercy. Edward VII seems to have accepted some of them almost on sufferance, believing that Herbert was a sentimentalist with a tendency to regard criminals as martyrs.[17] Sir Alfred Wills, the elderly high court judge who had presided over Oscar Wilde's trial, took a similar view, writing in 1907 of his dismay at two reprieves granted by Gladstone, who in his opinion displayed 'a curious tendency to vacillation and weakness'.[18] One of these involved Horace Rayner condemned for shooting William Whiteley, the department store owner claimed by Rayner as his father. Public sympathy for the convicted, who was ill and alleged to be insane, was widespread but Herbert still had to defend his clemency against establishment claims that it was pure sentimentality, arguing stoutly that it was simply inhuman to nurse a man back to health merely to fit him for execution.[19]

Differences of opinion between judges and home secretaries were of course nothing new and Herbert's predecessors had encountered plenty of judicial conservatism in other contexts, although Lord Chancellor Loreburn, expecting Herbert to achieve great things in prison reform, encouraged him to ignore the judges.[20] Herbert promptly enlisted the support of Loreburn and other legal luminaries for the recommendation, originally made by his 1894 departmental committee but which successive home secretaries had failed to implement, that incorrigible criminals be detained at the royal pleasure.[21] In a similarly reformist vein he was also considering a system of detention for adolescent criminals which, by segregating them from recidivists, might reduce the likelihood of their also becoming career criminals. The inspiration behind this was Evelyn Ruggles-Brise, who as prison commissioner since 1892 had been quietly pushing what would become known as the Borstal idea. He had a number of powerful patrons but it was only when Herbert went to the Home Office that he received the consistent political backing which, in his view, made Herbert quite superior to previous incumbents.[22] As early as

May 1906 Ruggles-Brise was commenting at Herbert's request on early drafts of a criminal justice bill, noting with pleasure that it exceeded his most sanguine expectations.[23] The files contain evidence of an extensive correspondence between the two men before Herbert declared himself satisfied, over-ruling Chalmers' reservations and instructing the parliamentary draughtsman to incorporate their exchanges into a bill.[24]

While Herbert concentrated on this aspect of his proposed reforms he asked Samuel to chair a departmental committee to consider another aspect of the judicial system which he believed ripe for change. Although courts had the power to do so, they did not often release prisoners on recognisances of good behaviour, mainly because there was little provision for their subsequent supervision. Herbert set his lieutenant to work on a bill to establish such provision on a systematic and comprehensive basis. The outcome was the Probation of Offenders Act (1907), largely unremarked at the time and not fully implemented until the 1920s but actually a landmark measure in prisoner aftercare and partly responsible for the fact that between 1900 and 1916 Britain's average prison population fell by about half. Samuel certainly deserved the plaudits for his detailed work, but in the background Herbert had mooted the idea, encouraged it through a series of conferences and then simply allowed Samuel to get on with it. It was a powerful example of his lack of ego and his prioritisation of objective over personal kudos.

The other significant legal reform effected in 1907 was the establishment of the Court of Appeal, prior to which prisoners were able to appeal convictions only to the home secretary. Previous attempts to alter this had failed, usually over highly technical legal issues, but when Herbert took office public interest had been stirred up by two particularly high-profile cases. One involved Adolf Beck, tried and convicted in 1904 for fraud but granted a full pardon when another man was found guilty of the offences. Far more controversial was the Edjali case, which cost Herbert many a sleepless night and certainly cemented his determination to change the appeal process. George Edjali, a solicitor and the son of an Anglican clergyman, had been imprisoned in 1904 on a charge of maiming horses in Great Wyrley in Staffordshire, an outcome which also led to his automatic professional disqualification. There were many disturbing features in the case, doubts about the authorship of letters concerning the crimes and alleged to have been written by Edjali but which continued to appear after his imprisonment, inadequate police evidence and uncertainties as to whether Edjali could actually see well enough to have committed the crimes, all tinged with suspicions of racial prejudice because the accused was of Indian stock. In March 1906 a commission of inquiry was appointed on the recommendation of the lord chancellor. It concluded that Edjali's conviction was unsatisfactory but recommended that he should not receive compensation since there *was* evidence to suggest that he had written some of the letters. Although current Home Office principles did not warrant a free pardon, the commission suggested that Edjali might be treated as an exception. True to his humanitarian instincts Herbert seized on this and after sounding out colleagues decided to grant the free pardon, albeit without compensation. By now, however, the case had attracted widespread popular interest, not least because it was taken up by Sir Arthur Conan Doyle to whom the public seems to have attributed the forensic insight of his fictional creation, Sherlock Holmes. In July F.E. Smith, a prominent lawyer on the Tory benches, moved a reduction in Herbert's salary in order to raise Edjali's plight. In arguing that there had been a miscarriage of justice, Smith was careful to attribute it to Herbert's predecessor, but Herbert, evidently under some pressure and perhaps overawed by Smith's fluency, reacted badly. First he complained that had Smith been in the House before dinner, he could have raised the matter earlier, thereby leaving longer than five minutes for his own reply. Informed by Smith that he had in fact been present, Herbert said that obviously he had just not noticed him, compounding his lack of grace by suggesting that delivered in a court Smith's speech would have taken four hours.[25] Even by Herbert's low standards this was ham-fisted but it perhaps demonstrated why he was so keen to secure a change in the whole appeal process.

In leading for the government when the second reading of the Criminal Appeal Bill came on in May, he left the legal technicalities to the attorney general and made a general case on the grounds that the United Kingdom was the only civilised country in the world without an appeal court, although his real motive slipped out when he indicated that the bill would reduce the number of cases going to his department. Nevertheless, he drew a number of persuasive contrasts between the way a court and the minister could deal with an appeal. The former, he said, heard both sides of a case, could take fresh evidence, and hand down a final verdict. A home secretary by contrast could hear only a petition from an appellant, and could neither consider fresh evidence nor quash a conviction. Furthermore, his decision was not final since it could be challenged. As an argument this was clearly self-serving but it was both heart-felt and logical and for once Herbert's speech impressed.[26] In the course of the year the bill became law, although not quite in the form Herbert had hoped. He was unable to resist an amendment which effectively made the Home Office a court of appeal in the first instance by charging it with the task of establishing whether there was a prime facie case for sending anything on to the new Court of Appeal.

Notwithstanding his sometimes clumsy parliamentary performances Herbert put quite a lot on to the statute book in 1907. Two important law bills and a number of lesser measures, including the Deceased Wife's Sister Marriage Act, the Advertisements Regulations Act and a Factory and Workshop Act that brought institutional laundries into the Home Office's inspection regime represented a decent contribution to an administration which for all its majority had achieved relatively little after two years in office and had seen its flagship education measure flounder altogether in 1906. Even so, Herbert had apparently not impressed, Ponsonby noting in the summer of 1906 that while the Home Secretary had worked hard in 'an ungrateful post', he was not regarded as a success.[27] It is true that he made this observation before the Workmen's Compensation Bill had completed its parliamentary passage but his assessment was echoed a few months later by Margot Asquith who included Herbert in a list of ministers she deemed unsuited to their offices, although conceding rather condescendingly that 'they are all good straight fellows and will come on with experience perhaps.'[28] Not so in Herbert's case apparently. Another diary-keeper, his colleague Alfred Emmott, thought that the performance of the cabinet's Liberal Imperialists like Haldane and Grey far outweighed that of men like Burns, Sinclair and Gladstone.[29] Even more striking perhaps was John Burns' private assertion to Beatrice Webb in October 1907 that he expected to be moving to the Home Office the following summer.[30]

In one sense Herbert was perhaps a victim of his own ambitious schedule, being so focussed on working up and securing his bills that he neglected other aspects of his ministerial role. According to Ponsonby he seems to have been a virtual sleeping partner in the cabinet, where he was 'entirely useless for his silence' and 'his inability to keep in touch with questions outside his own department'.[31] Certainly he contributed nothing to the cabinet's discussion of Haldane's proposed army reforms in January 1907 and did not raise his 1904 ideas when John Burns' feeble unemployment remedies were being considered. Burns, admittedly far from being the administration's shrinking violet, thought Herbert was far too deferential in cabinet, although this observation was probably made in the context of education, a topic on which Herbert's habitual reticence was doubtless further reinforced by constant reminders of his family's deep-seated hostility to the government's 1906 bill.[32] Agnes sent him a detailed critique in November 1906, arguing that it had no logic, no foresight, and offered no possibility of compromise.[33] Mary was marginally more amenable but still irritated him intensely by her preference for the 1902 act and support for the Lords' amendments which effectively destroyed the Liberals' measure.[34]

If Herbert had not impressed in the privacy of the cabinet the same was true in the more public arena of the House of Commons. His handling of bills had not always been confident and in some cases barely evident as he deferred to Samuel's superior abilities, although to be fair this was entirely of his own volition and a very honest acknowledgement of his own limitations. There were also signs that some of Herbert's colleagues were frustrated by the slowness with which legislative proposals tended to emerge from the Home Office. A good example was provided by the Licensing Bill, flagged in 1906 as a major initiative. It was of course a highly contentious issue and the Home Office was subjected to a constant bombardment from different vested interests. Herbert, always conscientious, seems to have read most of their missives (or at least initialled them) although their impact is hard to detect. He was not aided either by the reluctance of some of his civil servants to meddle further with licensing. When the London Licensed Victuallers submitted their *Case for the Trade* in July 1906, arguing that things should be left well alone, one official recorded that he thought the pamphlet 'very fair and moderate'.[35] Although Herbert asked for the main points of a bill to be drafted in December 1906 the resulting proposals rather alarmed an apprehensive chief whip who told the prime minister that the government programme was already too crowded. Fearing that it would be rejected by the Lords, he suggested a less complex measure. Herbert concurred that the main point of the bill should be to secure a gradual reduction in the number of public houses by a third with the dispossessed licence holders compensated over a 14-year period. But the necessary revisions delayed things even more and it was November 1907 before the measure was ready. Although the detailed work had been done in the Home Office it was agreed, probably to Herbert's relief, that Asquith should lead the bill through the Commons in the following session.

Delays with reforming working hours in the coal industry also tried colleagues' patience, the more so perhaps because proposals to introduce an eight-hour working day had been coming to parliament for almost two decades. When they resurfaced yet again in a private member's bill in May 1906, the member for mid-Durham, the miner John Wilson, opposed it on the grounds that it would disrupt the industry in the north-east where longer shifts had always been worked and he proposed that it be referred to a select committee. Herbert responded by pointing out that there was insufficient time to get any measure through in the current session but that he would have the economic arguments considered by a departmental committee which, unlike a select committee, could sit all year round. Although this was agreed, the prospects did not appear very promising when another miners' MP, William Brace, later indicated that the Miners Federation of Great Britain (MFGB) would boycott any committee because it believed that its own substantial analysis of the matter was being ignored.[36] In December Campbell-Bannerman told the MFGB that the matter was of great importance and would be taken up by the government, although the miners still took the precaution of bringing their own bill back to the house in April 1907. Their internal divisions were again pointed up when another miners' MP, Stephen Walsh, argued that a measure would have been passed long ago but for the hostility of the north-east miners. Herbert's own contribution to this debate began uncertainly by refuting Walsh's assertion that he had nothing to learn, prompting cries of 'not what he said' across the floor of the House. Then he had to apologise for the fact that his committee had taken longer to report than he wished because was there was so little information available as to the likely effect of the reform on coal prices. While the government supported the principle of the bill, he averred, it was his duty to get it into a very different form before it could be passed.[37] Herbert's committee finally reported in May 1907, following which it was announced that the government's bill would be given only a first reading in the current session. Lord Ripon for one was annoyed by Herbert's apparent procrastination and given the number of times the matter had been examined in the past further delay certainly did not reflect well on the

Home Office. But even without the complication of the different working patterns in the industry, there were substantial differences of opinion as to how exactly the eight-hour day was to be defined. Herbert, a great believer in experts, was clearly influenced by his inspectors who were unanimous that if the time required to descend into a pit and then to come up again (winding time) was included in the eight hours, then each miner would spend less time cutting coal, thereby reducing wages which were determined by the weight of coal cut. Nor were the potential reductions in output appealing to colliery owners, most of whom opposed the eight-hour day. Further discussions took place between the interested parties before Herbert, having already annoyed by his prevarication, announced at the beginning of the 1908 session that he would submit the government bill to the House but not speak to it. The ensuing criticism from some of his cabinet colleagues led to an abrupt change of mind although with hindsight he might have been better advised to stick to his original intention. He addressed only the first clause of the revised bill which outlined how the eight hours was to be calculated, excusing his brevity on the ground that the rest of the measure was as it had been in 1907. This, it was complained, seemed to assume that Home Office bill-drafting was infallible, a point which had been made before and Herbert's misjudgment did nothing to improve his parliamentary reputation.

Such dissatisfaction with the presentation of bills and the long gestation periods sometimes required were symptoms of underlying difficulties in the Home Office. In any bureaucratic organisation mistakes were inevitable as Herbert discovered very early in his first session when the office failed to provide the lord privy seal with papers he had sought in advance of a debate on the Aliens Act. Ripon wrote rather sniffily to complain that the documents had gone instead to Lord Beauchamp and asked that Herbert speak with due severity to whoever was responsible.[38] But it was not simply a matter of the occasional error. During the debate on the Home Office estimates in August 1906 W.P. Byles observed that Asquith had improved the department in 1893, before adding rather darkly that he hoped 'the present occupant would show equal energy and give a momentum to the administration of his department'.[39] Always loyal to colleagues, Herbert defended his officials by referring to the sheer amount of work with which they, and he, had to cope: workmen's compensation, aliens, regulations, vaccination, licensing, all 'hurled at his head almost every Parliamentary day; and then there was also vivisection on which he had been tormented perhaps more in private than in public.'[40] To these he might well have added constant nagging from Labour members to get the qualifications for the factory inspectorate updated and a long-running campaign to secure improved holiday and pension provision for the Metropolitan police. Attempts to deflect the vivisectionists by indicating that he would not legislate until he received the report of the royal commission he had established failed to deter the critics who complained in July 1907 that sufficient evidence had already been accumulated.[41] He was equally reluctant to involve his department when George Cadbury organised a national exhibition in 1906 to expose low wages in trades such as dress- and chain-making. Personally, Herbert was sympathetic to the point of becoming a vice-president of the all-party National Anti-Sweating League set up in the aftermath of the exhibition but although the Home Office was the arm of government most concerned with working conditions, he argued that his officials were already handling so much that they could not undertake another project. When a private members bill on the subject received a second reading in February 1908, Herbert spoke with genuine feeling about the exploitation of wage earners but repeated his injunction against further increasing his department's work load. Consequently, the bill was referred to a select committee and when the government did finally legislate in 1909 it was under the auspices of the Board of Trade. Often overshadowed by other contemporary welfare measures, the Trade Boards Bill was a thoroughly radical innovation, breaking with the orthodoxy that wages should be determined by the market, and by opting out of responsibility for it Herbert missed an opportunity to enhance his own reputation. That, however, was never something that much concerned him.[42]

Perhaps it was a tacit recognition of his department's administrative shortcomings that when Chalmers indicated in 1907 that he intended to retire, Herbert quickly decided that his replacement as permanent secretary should be Edward Troup, the first man recruited through open competition to reach the top job in the department.[43] In making this choice Herbert ignored the claims of the old guard, including Henry Cunynghame, a long serving assistant under-secretary who promptly complained to Asquith, though he did concede that Herbert had done his best to soften the blow 'with that gentleness and good nature which distinguish him'.[44] But gentleness and good-natured charm were not going to galvanise civil servants and Herbert simply lacked the steel to instil an appropriate sense of urgency and dynamism. As chief whip with only one or two main objectives in view he had been able to keep focus and determine the pace and rhythm of his own work as well as that of his subordinates. But as contemporaries acknowledged the Home Office's wide remit generated a huge work load and demanded a lot of its political chief.[45] Herbert found it difficult to keep on top of it all, coming at times perilously close to being swamped by its relentless flow. This was certainly the sense of a letter to Harry written in March 1907.

> My job is not an easy one for a trained lawyer or an all round able man. To me it is fearfully difficult & the only way I stand it is by keeping it off my nerves as far as possible [...] I am hard at the 8 hours bill, & have the Land in Committee & otherwise a Laundry Bill, Probation Bill, Crime, Ct of Appeal. I am also at work on another Bill. How is it possible to find power in my brain for other things in the heat of the Session?[46]

Letters to Harry, or indeed any other family member, were noticeably less frequent in these years, another straw in this particular wind of work overload. Another was a growing unease among local party officers caused by his extended absence from Leeds. More than once in 1907 Joseph Henry urged Herbert to visit the constituency where the Tories had given the Liberals a bad time in recent municipal elections, boosted by Catholic hostility to the Education Bill, the defection of the *Leeds Mercury* to the Labour cause, and then in the summer by Kitson's retirement as president of the local association.

If his local party was feeling somewhat disconnected from him by 1907, Herbert himself was increasingly isolated in the cabinet, not only by the dissatisfaction of some his colleagues but also by the gradual disappearance of its Gladstonian heavyweights, his natural allies. First, Bryce departed to Washington as British ambassador and then in November Campbell-Bannerman suffered the stroke which forced his resignation the following April. The King sent for Asquith, prompting Lord Knollys to speculate that in a cabinet reshuffle Herbert might possibly be among those dismissed.[47] Margot Asquith was quite certain. After an outing with Herbert's wife a day or two after Campbell-Bannerman resigned, she wondered at Dolly's failure to grasp that 'the whole cabinet were anxious to change Herbert. I did my very best for him not because I think him at all suitable nor indeed likely to be anything but a failure but he has done nothing really bad.'[48] Herbert himself was alarmed when Burns told him that the two of them were to lose their posts, prompting a private outpouring of hypocrisy from Margot.

> The universal feeling that Herbert ought to go made me very sad. I fought for him all I knew. He has after all a most loyal & generous nature [...] He never wanted the place & he has done nothing too sorry & he has only been tactless & dilatory & undecided.[49]

Margot's opinions did not necessarily reflect her husband's, however, and by the time she penned this the King had approved the new prime minister's cabinet recommendations, which included Herbert's retention.[50] Asquith was certainly aware of the Home Secretary's less than convincing parliamentary performances, his failure to stir up his civil servants and his passivity in cabinet. Yet weighed against that was a record of solid legislative achievement and Herbert's personal qualities, not least his capacity for loyalty, important to a man just assuming leadership of the government. Had he so wished he could certainly have wielded the axe, for while the King had wanted Asquith to minimise cabinet changes he had no compunction in urging the removal of those he regarded as liabilities. Moreover, Asquith's letter inviting Herbert to stay was far more than conventionally warm in tone, as he enthused to Margot.

> If he said you have done some good work at the HO but it is best to have a change etc. I shd. have been down on my luck but I could not have had any grievance. As it is I am only conscious of the immense encouragement & whatever my failings may be [...] Henry will find in me a loyal & devoted colleague.[51]

The news apparently had a positive effect in Leeds as well because shortly after the new cabinet was announced the local caucus had its best attendance for years, with unanimous support offered to the government's education and licensing bills, together with strong expressions of confidence in the Home Secretary.

Herbert's private secretary in the department was also delighted to learn that press rumours of a new chief were unfounded, although he had never given them much credence anyway since 'the race is rowed on the river'.[52] Samuel felt the same, so appreciative of the way Herbert had given him his head at the Home Office that he turned down Asquith's offer of promotion. The Labour MP, Philip Snowden, rather nastily put this down 'to the fact that it was not considered safe to keep Mr Herbert Gladstone as Home Secretary without an able Under Secretary' but Samuel's own autobiography later made it very clear that he wanted to complete the parliamentary passage of the Children's Bill, his initiative but one which, as always, his chief had actively encouraged.[53] As head of the department, Herbert, he recalled, was always 'most considerate, giving me plenty of scope and constant support'.[54]

In taking the Children's Bill to cabinet Herbert gave both it and Samuel his enthusiastic endorsement, telling colleagues that his under-secretary would lead it through the Commons. In essence the bill condensed over 20 existing statutes into a single whole, dealing with reform and industrial schools, baby farming, child cruelty, juvenile smoking and child offenders, the section with which Herbert himself was most directly involved. Consolidating legislation it may have been, but its scope and nature signified acceptance of state responsibility for child welfare and represented a major contribution to the government's reputation as a reforming administration. It was, *The Times* said, a true Children's Charter, promising more for social welfare 'than much more pretentious measures'.[55] Once it was on the statute book Herbert also let Samuel look after its implementation, intervening only when necessary.

If the Children's Act was Samuel's triumph, the Prevention of Crime Act, which developed the experimental Borstal school into a national system, was very much Herbert's, a project close to his heart and which he had been fostering for two years. Samuel had some input into the drafting but Herbert did most of the donkey work, consulting with the director of public prosecutions, agreeing to let the lord chief justice draft an amendment he had personally suggested, securing the chancellor's sanction, and dealing with the post master general's reservations about the bill's application to post office employees. It was largely non-contentious and on 16 March 1908, after initialling all the papers and raising a few last queries about wording, Herbert told Troup to proceed with it. Royal assent was received in December, after which Herbert was again content to leave its outworking to Samuel and others, although he continued to oil the wheels when necessary, personally challenging for instance the Treasury's rejection of a request from Ruggles-Brise for additional funds for the Borstal Association in 1909.

By the end of the year the Eight Hours bill was also on the statute book. The divided opinions of the miners and the opposition of the employers ensured that its passage through the House was contentious. Herbert prudently left much of the speaking to colleagues, although he did make the occasional significant intervention. When on 9 December Viscount Castlereagh tried to get the entire measure rejected out of hand because it was the first ever attempt by government to curtail the hours of adult labour, Herbert demolished his arguments in what was by his standards a long and quite effective speech.[56] However, his luck did not hold. The following day opponents made sustained attempts to reinstate clauses rejected at earlier stages, forcing Herbert to his feet on 20 separate occasions. The debate grew ever more heated as its climax neared. When Herbert indicated on 14 December that he did not intend to go into detail because they had been 18 days in discussion and he was sick of his own voice, Robert Cecil promptly said that he did not think any bill had ever been commended with less confidence. Herbert Gladstone's latest speech, he went on, was typical of the government's whole approach, perfunctory phrases with 'the rest of the speech, as indeed was the case with all the right Hon Gentleman's speeches, occupied by explaining to the Opposition that, bad as the Bill was, it was not so bad as they thought.'[57] Despite its imperfections, the measure did help improve working conditions for a large section of the labour force and for all his difficulties in both the preliminary discussions and the parliamentary debates, Herbert had at least pushed through legislation where others had failed before. Conscious perhaps of his colleague's torrid time in parliament, Churchill, in the cabinet since April as president of the board of trade, proffered congratulations on what he termed 'a very substantial piece of work'.[58]

The Licensing Bill was equally important, although the powerful nonconformist lobby was not unanimously favourable towards parts of it while nearly everyone was critical of the delay in producing it. In part perhaps this was due to the intensity with which Herbert himself was scrutinising the details; the draft he managed to leave on a train in January 1908 while returning from a funeral in Wendover was copiously annotated in his own hand and he was mightily relieved to recover it before it fell into the wrong hands. When the second reading debate came on at the end of April Herbert, his confidence perhaps briefly bolstered by his recent re-appointment, made one of his longer speeches although it did little to curb Austen Chamberlain's scornful response.[59] When the committee stage was reached in July, Samuel and Asquith figured prominently for the government but it was the Home Secretary who once again bore the brunt of opposition criticism. F.E. Smith, who brought to the House the passion and skill honed in the court room, was excoriating. Many had criticised the bill, he mocked, but it was reserved to the home secretary to destroy it. Its promoters were statistical amateurs, a telling thrust given the home office's lack of such expertise.[60] Thereafter Herbert, never at ease in the chamber, left most of the detailed debating to Samuel and the solicitor general. It was all little more than academic, anyway since the Tories' dominance in the upper house meant that the bill's ultimate fate was never in doubt and true to form the peers threw it out. This latest reverse for the government, set alongside the enforced withdrawal of the latest version of its Education Bill, left the cabinet in despair, and morale was not helped by growing divisions over naval expenditure on which Herbert, despite his wish for the Admiralty in 1905, offered no opinion. In early December there was an extended cabinet discussion about resignation to which again he contributed nothing.[61] In the end the decision was to hold on but otherwise the government had no clear idea of what it wished to do.

The loss of the Licensing Bill could perhaps be set off against the Children's Act, the Prevention of Crime Act and the Miners' Eight Hours Act. But for all their significance, these measures did little to dispel the unease felt by some colleagues at Herbert's ministerial performance and the

doubts were exacerbated during the autumn by an
unfortunate sequence of events which drove him to the
point of resignation, alienated his only surviving allies in the
cabinet, annoyed the King and embarrassed the prime
minister. For good measure, though it probably did not
bother him so much, it angered extreme nonconformists. The
context was a proposed Roman Catholic procession marking
the end of the Eucharistic Congress in London. Although it
was technically illegal for Catholic dignitaries to parade in
public wearing vestments, a blind eye had generally been
turned in the past. Approached by the organisers in July the
Metropolitan Police Commissioner, Edward Henry, had
given them permission to go ahead but believing it to be a
routine event had not informed the Home Office. At the end
of July and again in mid-August Henry was informed by the
Protestant Alliance (PA) that the intention to wear religious
vestments and to carry the Blessed Sacrament through the
streets was against the law. These communications were
acknowledged but again nothing was forwarded to the Home
Office. A few days before the procession was due to take place
on 13 September, the PA published a protest, prompting
articles and letters in the press and on 7 September the King
was petitioned to ban the event on the grounds that it was
liable to stir up religious strife and threaten public order.
Edward, whose interest in the matter had little to do with any
personal religious convictions and everything to do with a
coronation oath committing him to uphold protestantism,
decided that it could not be ignored. Herbert had already
notified Asquith that while the proposed ceremonial
was illegal, similar events in 1898 and 1901 had passed
unremarked and that he did not propose to interfere.[62]
Neither he nor the prime minister, however, could hold to
this course once the King became involved. They soon had
further cause for alarm when the scale of the event was made
clear to them. Troup, returning from leave on 8 September,
received a deputation from the PA and then forwarded all the
relevant information to Herbert, at the time holidaying in
Scotland. What had initially appeared to concern only a few

extreme protestants and some parading clerics, actually involved a papal legate, six cardinals and Catholic leaders from every major European country, and threatened to stir up the deep-seated anti-Catholicism widely prevalent in Britain. At this juncture, therefore, telegraph wires heated up rapidly as increasingly frenetic messages began surging through them, not always without difficulty. Some of the communications were coded and Herbert was hampered by the fact that he did not have to hand the means of deciphering either of two different systems being used. Nevertheless, he decided against returning to London, unwilling to risk being out of contact by sitting in a train for ten hours and perhaps swayed as well by the fact that Asquith was also in Scotland.

On receipt of the dossier from Troup and after consulting together the prime minister and the home secretary each separately contacted Lord Ripon, then in York, in the hope that as Liberal leader in the Lords and a leading Catholic layman he might do something to simplify the procession and so avoid the danger of serious trouble.[63] Begrudgingly, Ripon took the hint and telegraphed Asquith to say that as requested he had contacted Archbishop Bourne but added that the visiting cardinals and other dignitaries would have strong grounds for complaint at the short notice. Angrily, Ripon demanded to know 'what has Herbert Gladstone been about? To have allowed things to go so far & then to stop the procession passes belief. I have been humiliated.'[64] Having slept on it overnight his temper did not much improve and he dashed off a heated letter to Herbert. As the procession was quite clearly illegal, he complained, the Home Office could have banned it, especially since the details had been known for some time. But nothing had been done and now he had received two non-official requests to intervene and place upon the archbishop a responsibility which was rightly the government's.[65] His letter crossed with a telegram from Herbert who now proposed to appeal directly to the archbishop because the police had advised that the publicity surrounding the procession had heightened the likelihood of disorder.[66] Ripon agreed that a personal approach was desirable but emphasised that Herbert should not *appeal* but *direct* and write in his official capacity. At the same time he reiterated to Asquith his annoyance with Herbert whose wholly indefensible stance, he claimed, had been dropped only when the King got involved.[67]

When Herbert got round to replying to Ripon he stressed that he could not have acted any earlier because he did not have any information to hand until 9 September. Nor, he said, did he have any legal authority to ban the procession.[68] As a barrister, Asquith certainly shared that view and indeed had not intervened when as home secretary he had been faced with a similar situation in 1893. He himself approved Herbert's suggestion that he contact the archbishop, asserting later that it was courteous and appropriate to give the church itself the opportunity to excise the offensive elements from the procession. Archbishop Bourne, however, clearly thought it beneath his dignity to deal with a mere home secretary and sent his reply to Asquith, requesting that it be forwarded so that he could meet with departmental officials. On 11 September he agreed to discard the procession's illegal features on condition that Asquith authorised him to say that it had been done at the government's request. With police fears of public unrest now somewhat assuaged, Herbert sent two communications to the prime minister saying that he would let it be known that he had no power to ban the procession and that he would also inform the King of the archbishop's decision.[69]

Edward, however, was looking for scapegoats. He very much resented that Troup, apparently on his own initiative, had told the PA deputation that the matter was being considered at Court when he had never heard an official word about it. He was annoyed with the Catholic authorities for not approaching the Home Office until the last moment. Equally, however, he told Lord Crewe that if Herbert had known the details for some time, then 'he ought to have seen that it was not quite an ordinary case of police arrangements.'[70] Harcourt, also then at Court and apparently inclined to put the boot in, emphasised that the royal displeasure was 'chiefly directed at the devoted head of H G whom he accuses of weakness, laziness etc. etc'.[71] It was all rather unfair. Herbert acted promptly as soon as he was made aware of the details and any tardiness in contacting the King was due in part to the archbishop's decision to reply not to him but to Asquith. Finally, despite the cleric's request to meet Home Office officials he had kept Troup waiting until September 12 before seeing him, at which point Herbert had communicated all he knew to the palace.[72] That information, however, did little to mollify the royal temper, for a couple of days later Crewe reiterated to Asquith that he would find the King 'very bitter about Herbert and longing to get rid of him. I have endeavoured to point out his many official merits and personal good qualities but without much success.'[73]

On 13 September the procession, shorn of its controversial elements, made its way peacefully to Westminster Cathedral, watched by large, enthusiastic crowds and undeterred by a nearby protestant protest meeting. The fallout, however, was considerable. Prompted by Asquith who was due an audience with the King, Herbert demanded an immediate report from Henry. There was some expectation that as a Catholic himself the commissioner might have appreciated the nature of the proposed procession but in fact his religion was purely nominal and his report indicated that the organisers had not clarified the exact nature of the event. Even had they done so, it was unlikely to have made any difference since it emerged that Henry was simply unaware that the Catholic Emancipation Act barred the wearing of vestments or any display of the Host in the public streets. All he had discussed with the church's representatives in the summer had been possible routes, after which he delegated responsibility to the relevant police division. Herbert thought this sufficient to exonerate Henry, although he still thought him culpable for failing to contact the Home Office once he had been given the full details on 31 July. However, Herbert regarded this as a lesser error of judgement and he determined not to sacrifice his subordinate. Instead, as the relevant minister and having been effectively censured by the King, he offered his own resignation, much to the distress of both Troup and Waller, his private secretary. Asquith replied on 23 September that it was no time for hasty decisions and that he was anxious to retain a valued colleague.[74]

The King, however, scented blood. One man in his sights was Ripon, whose own actions were certainly not beyond reproach, for despite his efforts to lay the blame on Herbert it was strange that as someone who must have understood the nature of the procession he had never mentioned it to his colleagues. Asquith was able to sidestep the royal pressure to dispense with Ripon when the octogenarian opted to fall on his own sword. Learning of this likelihood, the King, quite exceeding his constitutional prerogative, further hinted that Herbert, 'weak' and showing 'lamentable want of judgement' might also be sacrificed and dispatched to the House of Lords as president of the council.[75] Asquith appeared quite open to this suggestion which he promptly broached with Herbert. But Herbert saw straight through Asquith's artful suggestion that his elevation would strengthen the Liberal presence in the troublesome upper House. How could it, given his poor debating skills? After talking things over with Dolly, he rejected the idea out of hand, telling the prime minister that while he recognised the difficulty in the Lords and the need for new Liberal recruits, he was not minded to retire. In oddly stilted language he argued that the procession affair was his first serious mistake and that

> to transfer now to a non-effective office & to the Lords, means to the public mind inefficiency in an effective office without the chance of compensating efficiency in another. For these reasons I hope you would not think me wrong in a conclusion adverse to your suggestion.[76]

The promptness and tone of Asquith's response – he quite understood and there was no question of resignation – raises the issue of why he ever suggested such a course to Herbert, especially given the reassurances contained in his letter of 23 September. Perhaps as he had kissed hands only a matter of months before, he did not not yet feel sufficiently secure to ignore the King's suggestion entirely. Or perhaps he was hoping to deflect attention away from his own part in the affair, for throughout he had been in constant touch with his home secretary to agree tactics. Lord Knollys certainly believed that neither Herbert nor the prime minister had come well out of the episode while much of the press comment on the controversy had as much, if not more, to say about Asquith than about the home secretary.[77] Indeed, an article in the Catholic *Tablet* made no mention at all of Herbert but described Asquith's role as disappointing, somewhat unfair on a man who never made anything of the fact that his attention had been sidetracked at a critical stage when his daughter disappeared from her bed, necessitating a night-time search and her discovery, unconscious on a river bank to which she had crawled after a fall.[78]

It is true that once the dust began to settle Asquith did tell his chief whip that he was annoyed by Herbert's apparent lethargy.[79] But that was quite different from wanting to get rid of a colleague whose legislative achievement was not insignificant and whose several qualities were well appreciated by himself and Crewe, the new Liberal leader in the upper House.[80] In particular, Herbert's personal loyalty was not to be lightly discounted by a relatively new prime minister. Despite his superficial grumbling, therefore, Asquith was happy to accept the report which Herbert presented to the cabinet early in October. It pointed out that the Catholic Emancipation Act conferred no power on a home secretary to ban processions and that while the attorney general could act if vestments were worn or rites enacted outside a place of worship, he could do so only *after* the occurrence. After recounting in some detail the sequence of events, the report concluded that while criticism of the delay in dealing with the affair was justified even that was mitigated by the church authorities' initial failure to disclose full details which justified Henry in treating it routinely. The cabinet was satisfied and in a somewhat ironic coda the following year, the King approved the award by the Pope of medals to two policemen for their services during the procession, prompting Herbert to remonstrate mildly with Knollys.[81] By this time, however, the focus of his attention had long since been diverted to public order issues far more challenging than those presented by a religious procession.

The campaign to gain the right to vote for women had a long history but progress had been slow. The formation of the National Union of Women's Suffrage Societies in 1897 (NUWSS) did little to speed things up although the 1906 election was enlivened by some particularly aggressive demonstrations orchestrated by Emmeline Pankhurst's breakaway organisation, the Women's Social and Political Union (WSPU). Moving its headquarters to London in the summer following the election, the WSPU adopted a strategy of direct action, in the process earning its members the soubriquet of suffragettes from the *Daily Mail*. Six months after the Liberals took office Theresa Billington led a posse of women to Asquith's residence in Cavendish Square, slapping a constable across the face when the police moved in and incurring a fine of £10 or two months in prison. When the Labour MP, Keir Hardie, asked that the sentence be stayed as unduly severe Herbert replied that while he thought it justified he did propose, after representations from Asquith and consultation with the magistrate concerned, to reduce the punishment to a £5 fine or one month's imprisonment.[82] He proved similarly flexible when it came to the classification of suffragette prisoners. Unless the magistrates decided otherwise, the 1898 Prison Act decreed that prisoners jailed in default of sureties were to be placed in the second division, intended for those adjudged to be of good character and who therefore should be kept separate from the mass of prisoners who comprised the third division. In October 1906 ten women convicted of causing a disturbance were divided between the second and third divisions. The magistrates, who had actually made no specific allocation order, readily concurred when Herbert recommended, not for the first time, that the women be moved to the first division. Although intended only for those guilty of sedition, seditious libel and contempt, this category specified superior treatment and conditions. In December he issued a general circular reminding magistrates of their discretionary powers and most of the suffragettes arrested early in 1907 for attempting to get into the House of Commons were put in the top category.

Yet as the number of convictions grew, it proved impractical to afford all suffragettes first-division status since the prison system lacked the necessary capacity: there were only two first-division cells in Holloway, for example. From 1908, therefore, but for practical rather than political reasons, the London magistrates generally stuck to the second division although some provincial benches still opted for the third division in cases involving serious violence. But Herbert's original clemency came back to haunt him as precedent was constantly cited as justification for demanding that suffragettes be accorded first-division status as of right. His standard reply was technically and constitutionally correct in pointing out that such matters were at the discretion of the magistrates rather than the home secretary. When challenged on the matter by Robert Cecil in February 1908 he admitted that his initial intervention had assumed that better treatment would have a positive effect but the privileges associated with first-class status had been abused by prisoners and used to encourage further offending. Whatever his own views, he said, he could not interfere with magistrates on a constant basis.[83]

And therein lay only one of several dilemmas. Constitutionally, the home secretary was part of the executive in a system resting on the separation of powers between it and the judiciary whose members could be fiercely protective of their independence, as Herbert pointed out in a 1909 exchange with A.G. Gardiner. Even ministerial interventions confined to instances where it was felt a wrong allocation had been made would require intensive monitoring of the courts and raise the possibility of conflict if a magistrate refused to change a sentence. Intervention was justified only when a court was unaware of the 1898 principle and committed a person of good character to the third division.[84] Practically, the home secretary was responsible for both the prison service and the maintenance of public order. He could not, therefore, permit special treatment for particular groups of prisoners or allow them to disrupt the effective operation of prisons by flagrantly defying the regulations. Politically, Herbert was a member of a cabinet whose members were deeply divided on the issue of women's rights to vote. Asquith was opposed to it, as were Bryce, Harcourt, and Solicitor General Robson, all of whom joined the minority of MPs voting against the second reading of a privately introduced women's suffrage bill on 28 February 1908. Herbert, favouring the enfranchisement of women, supported the bill, convinced, he told the House, that it was impossible 'not to sympathise with the eagerness and passion which activates so many women in this movement. It is impossible not to sympathise [...] with their disappointments, past, present, and yet to come.'[85] Perhaps in an attempt to reconcile his private opinions with his official actions he added that the women's case could not rest on argument alone but must convince the general public, a weasel argument in the view of one Liberal member who suggested that the home secretary wanted to see the fire lit but was taking away the matches. This was somewhat harsh, especially when the following month Herbert ordered that Mrs Pankhurst and five others be released from prison a day early so that they could attend a suffragette rally in the Albert Hall. This was not enough, however, to deter Christabel Pankhurst from ruthlessly exposing the gap between his personal and public positions when she successfully subpoenaed him to appear as a witness in a suffragette case later in the year.

The women's bill of February 1908 passed by 271 votes to 92 but with no government commitment to take the matter forward the activists' frustration grew and arrests multiplied. There were regular parliamentary clashes between Herbert and his critics about the prisoners' classification. With his previous actions repeatedly thrown back in his face, Herbert stuck to his mantra that it was a matter for the magistrates, but increasingly the claim was that the suffragettes were entitled to first-class status because their offences were political. His stock parliamentary answer was that there was no such such thing as special treatment for political prisoners and that while he had been prepared to act when it was a matter of a few isolated individuals, intervention when mass arrests were involved might become the norm and threaten the very independence of the judiciary. He acknowledged that those convicted of seditious offences did receive special treatment but this had never been the case for ordinary law-breakers. To make it so, he argued, would present insuperable difficulties in knowing where to draw the line between trivial crimes and murder. Told that the absence of any concept of political crime differentiated Britain from all other civilised countries, Herbert replied abruptly that 'it is about time that other Governments should imitate us.'[86]

But behind such official avowals, largely unknown to the general public and certainly rarely acknowledged Herbert *was* consistently intervening to bend the regulations governing second-division status in order to meliorate the women's experience in prison. On receipt of a letter about the suffragettes' access to sanitary protection, for example, he commissioned a report into the treatment of menstruating women, following which he ordered a relaxation of the rules to avoid the women incurring additional discomfort. While by no means acceding to all requests he quite frequently over-rode the visiting rules: the widow of a South African politician was allowed a special visit to her daughter even though an additional one had already been permitted to the prisoner's brother; Dorothy Spencer was allowed an extra visit from a potential employer and Mrs Pethwick Lawrence received a similar concession to permit her to discuss private business with her husband; an official who proposed to refuse supplementary visits by a husband to his pregnant wife was brusquely over-ruled; so, too, was another officer who wanted to refuse Adela Pankhurst permission to see her mother and sister. Herbert also allowed Emmeline Pankhurst and her daughter Christabel to receive newspapers in contravention of the existing regulations. In February 1909 restrictions on access to books, which Herbert had never liked because in his view prison was meant to be, in part at least, educational, were relaxed to facilitate the needs of a suffragette studying for a Cambridge degree.

Notwithstanding these and many other small concessions largely buried in the Home Office files, the suffragettes naturally enough exploited any and every example of ill treatment. General allegations of police brutality were commonplace but no opportunity was missed to draw parliament's attention to other alleged incivilities by the authorities. Was it true that Lady Lytton had been forced to endure the constant screams of a nearby condemned female prisoner? Was it healthy to hold women in solitary confinement for all but 90 minutes a day? Why were solicitors refused permission to visit suffragette prisoners in Birmingham? Was it the case that Lady Lytton was released just because she was a peer's sister? Why had the punishment of 14 women charged with breaking prison regulations included incarceration in underground cells? The records show that these and every other similar complaint raised over the course of 1908 and 1909 were investigated on Herbert's personal instruction and explained. The screams heard by Lady Lytton turned out to be the ravings of a female lunatic temporarily held in the same prison. The women in solitary confinement received visits from the medical officer and were allowed two sessions, rather than just one, of exercise per day. The Birmingham prisoners had not requested a visit from solicitors. Lady Lytton had been released solely on medical grounds. The allegation about underground cells was a mere fabrication. Faced with claims of inadequate ventilation in some cells, Herbert ordered that a factory inspector conduct tests, the results of which demonstrated that the amount of carbon dioxide in the atmosphere was lower than that prescribed as the factory standard. Herbert even took Hardie and several others on a tour of Holloway, accompanied by a released suffragette who told the Labour MP at the end of the visit that Herbert was a much-maligned person.[87] When Lady Betty Balfour complained that women were given only

1.5 pints of water each day for drinking and washing, were supplied with verminous combs and made to darn men's dirty socks, Herbert had each point followed up, his officials' report leading him to conclude that all were wilful untruths.[88]

Whatever the truth behind these official responses, and they were of course just as suspect as the complaints which prompted them, they were never likely to be accepted by suffragettes themselves and for the reading public dull factual rebuttals did not make good press. But the opportunities both for official cover-up and suffragette distortion were ratcheted significantly upwards when on 5 July 1909 Marian Wallace-Dunlop refused to take food. Asked by an anxious governor what he should do, Herbert authorised her immediate discharge. Perhaps not unrealistically in view of the parliamentary vote the previous year, he was still hopeful that a political resolution was possible. On the very day that he authorised the release of this first hunger striker, he received a deputation from the Women's Freedom League (WFL) led by Mrs Despard. Nobody, he said, regretted the present impasse more than he did because in his official capacity he had to act in different ways under the law but he hoped what was currently happening would soon 'end satisfactorily to yourselves'.[89]

But any such prospect vanished as hunger striking spread, in the process widening public divisions. Herbert's initial response was to have the strikers' physical condition closely monitored and to release them at the first sign of deterioration. He was reluctant to authorise the alternative of forcibly feeding the women, telling one official who was keen to adopt this that 'it is a choice of evils but the starvation period appears to be the lesser one.' It would also, he noted on the file, provide free publicity for the suffragettes and do nothing to reduce the difficulty of managing them.[90] At the beginning of August he over-ruled the Holloway Visiting Committee's recommendations that forced feeding be started and that one hunger striker be charged with attempted suicide.[91] Yet neither Herbert nor his officials comprehended the logic of escalation inherent in political violence.

He certainly did not understand the women's mindset and like many contemporaries concluded that the most extreme must be mentally unstable. The suffragettes, he told Harry, were giving him much anxiety and while they could be easily dealt with as a body a lot of them were in his view 'almost if not quite mad'.[92] To concede to such 'foolish & excitable people', he told Gardiner, 'would be a disastrous blow at the really large army of sensible, discriminating & patient women'.[93] Steeped in the traditions of liberal democracy neither Herbert nor the Home Office knew how to cope with individuals apparently intent on sacrificing their lives for a political principle. There was also in the official mind a fear that failure to prevent suicide, a criminal offence, might well expose the Home Office to charges. In Herbert's mind elevated ideals of womanhood, innate compassion and Liberal belief in individual freedom fought against his civic and ministerial duty to uphold the law and his moral compunction to protect the sanctity of life. Ultimately he was driven to sanction the use of forcible feeding.

His position was further complicated by the fact that the King, too, had strong views on the women's movement and no reluctance in communicating them to his home secretary, whose finer sensibilities he evidently did not share. In September 1909 he objected strongly when Herbert nominated two women to serve on the royal commission on divorce. His Majesty feared that such an unprecedented step would be seen as 'a suffragette move' and that the presence of ladies would inhibit frank discussion, not a consideration which seemed to bother him when it came to his own relationships with women.[94] A year or so earlier the King sardonically described Herbert's release of two suffragettes as 'very wise' and doubtless based on careful consideration but he still asked why existing methods (i.e. forcible feeding) of dealing with hunger strikers had not been deployed.[95] Across his order for these women's release Herbert scrawled with some apparent resignation that 'sober explanations' would 'be of little avail'.[96]

Whatever the King, and indeed a good number of his subjects judging by the correspondence columns of the contemporary press, thought about forced feeding, it was intrinsically highly controversial. Keir Hardie was particularly prominent in exploiting it to raise the temperature of debate. In October 1909 he inquired whether any of the hunger strikers in Birmingham Gaol were still being forcibly fed, couching his question in deliberately emotive language. Were the women's jaws prised open with a screw gauge, were they strapped down and was an oesophageal tube used?[97] Herbert's written answers were all in the negative but even if true, his assurance that all was done with the utmost gentleness was never going to have the mental staying power of the image Hardie consciously tried to create in the public mind. The following week Hardie asked whether Laura Ashworth had had her mouth forced open with a steel instrument and been handcuffed. Again, the wording was carefully calculated. So, too, was Herbert's reply. A steel instrument had indeed been used but the woman's mouth had actually been kept open with a wooden prop while her handcuffs, necessary to prevent her from breaking more prison windows, had been removed two days before the feeding.[98] Snowden's advocacy was equally artful. Challenging Herbert's assertion that all the hunger strikers in Newcastle Prison were medically examined prior to being forcibly fed, he claimed to know of one who was not. With the facts at his fingertips Herbert asked for her name. Snowden could not provide it. Another carefully phrased question about force-feeding from Snowden on 30 September prompted an equally measured reply from Herbert challenging his use of the word 'force' on the grounds that prisoners did not always resist and refuting the claim that stomach pumps were used.[99]

Outside parliament the campaign was equally impassioned and relentless. The WSPU leaflet *Atrocities in an English Prison* purported to recount how Selina Martin and Leslie Hall had been knocked down, gagged, forcibly fed, kept in irons and frog-marched up a flight of stairs during their imprisonment. The official report which Herbert immediately demanded of the prison's Visiting Committee suggested that Selina Martin had not in fact been responsible for the statement on which the allegations were based, had not complained at the time and did not wish to take the matter further. Leslie Hall confirmed that the statement attributed to her was accurate but she, too, added that she did not wish to make a complaint.[100] This came too late to prevent the Fabian Society from adding further fuel to this particular fire in the form of a resolution so distorted in its claims that Herbert felt compelled to have them refuted in a letter to *The Times*.[101] This in turn prompted a scathing and disproportionate riposte from George Bernard Shaw whose pen quite ran away with his imagination. Gladstone, the playwright thundered, should be given a banquet of the finest food and wine but fed through his nose and the whole proceedings filmed. That, he added, would soon undermine his talent for taking a pleasant view of an extremely unpleasant act.[102] As it happened, Herbert *had* sought medical opinion about the process. When a petition against it was received from 117 doctors, not all of whom it must be said could be traced to their current stated practice address, Herbert sent it for comment to Sir R. Douglas Powell, President of the Royal College of Physicians, and asking if there were alternatives. Powell replied that in his professional opinion the statements it contained were inaccurate and misleading, that there could of course be accidents in cases where feeding was resisted and that the diet was inferior to a natural one, but, he added, the practice had been widely and successfully used elsewhere. A similar point was made by the President of the Medico-Psychological Association who noted that it had been used for years in asylums and even prisons with no ill effects.[103] These purely medical arguments missed the moral or political point that in the case of suffragettes the feeding was being done without consent and thus represented a violation of the individual, but from Herbert's standpoint there was an equally powerful and contrary ethical imperative to prevent suicide. As for Shaw's specific suggestion, he had also submitted himself to a session of feeding via a nasal tube. He described it as being no worse than 'rather unpleasant', with no element of danger so long as one did not resist or struggle.[104] And despite the suffragette publicity it appears that not all did resist, at least according to the daily reports Herbert ordered from the relevant prison doctors. The resistance offered by Theresa Garnett, jailed for taking a whip to Winston Churchill in Bristol, was described variously as technical, trivial and even playful.[105] Mary Allen was reported to have actually assisted the process while Jesse Laws apparently responded quite passively. Tall and muscular with a powerful physique developed through rowing, Laws certainly did not fit the generally propagated suffragette image of frail womanhood. Neither did the 15-stone Violet Bryant, released from Preston Gaol in January 1910. Both women were clearly quite capable, had they so wished, of hurting prison staff who, as Herbert noted somewhat drily on the official report into the so-called suffragette mutiny at Holloway, were themselves sometimes 'slight, refined and one or two are delicate', even if the public probably believed them all to be she-bargees.[106]

However, he was well aware that the prison authorities on whom he depended for his information were quite capable of putting their own slant on events. He did not think much of the allegation that during the Holloway mutiny, for example, a wardress had been bitten, telling Troup that 'of course it was made the most of.'[107] There is no doubt that the official reports played up such matters and disguised a lot of heavy-handed officialdom behind the prison walls, just as the suffragette machine made the most of everything it could. Emily Davison's was a prime example. Imprisoned following a demonstration at a ministerial meeting in Manchester, she was annoyed that she was charged only with assault, for her action had been intended to escalate the campaign by showing the public that it, too, could incur a personal risk by attending political events. Once in prison, therefore, she set about destroying property and breaking windows. When the Visiting Committee went to investigate she barricaded herself in a cell, whereupon a water hose was played on the ceiling and then on the woman herself. In parliament it was claimed she had been soaked for an hour, the Visiting Committee said a couple of minutes. Herbert was not fooled, dismissing as an afterthought the committee's claim that the hose had been used in order to get the woman away from the door lest in forcing it open the staff injure her. Briefly he toyed with sacking the entire committee before settling for a strong personal rebuke to the chairman. Highly publicised in suffragette propaganda it may have been but the harshness displayed by the authorities on this occasion was not necessarily typical. Nevertheless, as Herbert observed to C.P. Scott, if people believed that all those working in the prison service were liars and torturers there was nothing more to be said.[108]

The reality was that the prison authorities like the home secretary himself were facing an unprecedented challenge and longer-serving staff in particular had been reared in the far tougher regime that Herbert and others had been trying to ameliorate. But if Herbert tried his utmost to temper the treatment of suffragettes, moving only reluctantly to sanction their forcible feeding and then watching over it in some detail, his response was inevitably shaped by the knowledge, beliefs and assumptions of the day and those were never going to save him from suffragette wrath. As the public face and political head of the department charged with the care of prisoners, he was bound to attract personal opprobrium. H.N. Brailsford, Secretary of the Conciliation Committee for Women's Suffrage, told Masterman that 'Gladstone is I believe fool enough to imagine that he can crush the movement by heaping indignities on his prisoners. You, if you will stop to think, are not of his mental calibre.'[109] Yet the propaganda and moral fervour of the protagonists obscured an important distortion of perspective. During Herbert's time as home secretary the number of people arrested as suffragettes (including men) rose from 30 in 1906 and peaked in 1907 at 1,125 before falling back to 144 in 1908 and 280 in 1909.[110] Between September 1905 and September 1909 only 20 sane women were forcibly fed in English and Welsh prisons. Over the same period 53 sane and 29 insane men together with 10 insane females were subject to the treatment.[111] Small wonder perhaps that in his frustration Herbert should have described the militants as a 'mere excrescence' in a letter to Emily Hobhouse.[112] It was an indelicate expression but the letter itself throws another interesting light on Herbert's own role, for it was one of a number he wrote in a persistent effort to encourage the more moderate Women's Freedom League, a breakaway from the WSPU. He could not see a solution, he told one member in September 1909, but urged her to bring together all the moderates in an effort to isolate the militants and their self-defeating tactics.[113] WFL leaders were aware of his sympathies and forbearance, blaming the whole situation on Asquith's obstinacy. Herbert was far too loyal to comment on that but reiterated that he was like a policeman required to uphold the law even if it meant that for three years he had been tarred by the militants 'with venom and falsehood simply because I have been discharging a public duty.'[114]

In truth the logic of violence was irresistible and by the time he wrote this his sympathy for the cause was losing the struggle with his obligation to uphold the law, especially after the suffragettes deliberately started to target ministers. Special branch reports that WSPU members were having shooting lessons added another, darker dimension. Official concern grew that the permanent suffragette pickets outside parliament might wittingly or otherwise be used as cover for an assassination attempt on the prime minister. After a high-level discussion in the Home Office Herbert accepted the police view that the pickets had been in place for so long that they could not easily be moved without arousing public anxiety. But clearly alarmed by this further escalation in suffragette tactics he asked Troup to consider establishing a special police organisation to watch the women, identify their supporters, uncover their plans, and provide protection at meetings attended by members of the government.[115] To the same end he also asked ministers to keep the police commissioner posted about their movements.

Whether this did anything to reassure his colleagues is uncertain but his own position was certainly complicated by enduring divisions within the cabinet over the suffrage issue. Well before the women took up hunger striking, Asquith had reprimanded Herbert for telling his constituents that if an amendment to the reform bill in favour of women's suffrage was passed then the government would give it hearty support. That, said the prime minister, went a long way beyond what he had said. Agreeing that if such an amendment were moved the government would not oppose it and, if it were carried, would proceed with it was, he added, very different from 'hearty support' and he stressed that not only he but also several colleagues 'heartily' opposed the whole idea.[116] Asquith's growing dissatisfaction with his home secretary in this respect was evident in his wider solicitation of ideas for handling the hunger strikers.[117] Within the cabinet the opposition to female suffrage had been strengthened by the promotion of Pease, Samuel and Churchill, while others like Haldane were increasingly exasperated by what they viewed as the home secretary's unduly lenient approach to the suffragettes. Herbert himself certainly believed that he was not well supported by his colleagues. Remonstrating in March 1910 with his successor, Churchill, who had claimed the credit for changes in the treatment of suffragettes which Herbert himself had first proposed, he gave vent to his frustration. He did not usually mind, he wrote, who got the plaudits but 'perhaps however if you had been through 3 years of a vexatious and nasty movement which I faced with a minimum of support from my colleagues, you would understand that I felt nettled at the invidious comparisons drawn at my expense.'[118]

But if by the autumn of 1909, Herbert was coming under pressure from his colleagues over the suffrage issue, the whole government was equally pressed on another constitutional front. The furore stirred up by Lloyd George's radical finance proposals earlier in the year had roused strong passions in the country and the peers were threatening to add the budget to the growing list of government measures they had rejected.

Less disruptive certainly but equally fraught in its own way was the question of the government of South Africa. Securing an agreement from the leaders of the various colonies to merge into a single national identity was one of the Liberals' major achievements but with the 1910 inauguration date for the new Union of South Africa fast approaching, the search was on for a governor-general, who would also serve as high commissioner for the neighbouring British protectorates.[119]

Discussing possibilities in September 1909 with Pease, chief whip since the previous year, Asquith intimated that Sidney Buxton was interested and that Churchill had also put himself forward, though Asquith dismissed this as quite unsuitable. Pease thought the prime minister's other suggestion, Lord Pentland, far too minor a figure for such an important position. Quite when Herbert's name entered their thinking is not clear although Asquith had earlier toyed with him as a replacement for Lord Minto as viceroy of India. This apparently had made Morley's blood run cold because in his view Herbert was 'the greatest failure of this government'.[120] But the very fact that Herbert had even been considered for India makes a nonsense of the frequently made assertion that he was later dispatched to South Africa as a consequence of the Eucharistic Procession affair.[121] Nor, despite Morley's reaction, was he sent abroad because he was considered a ministerial failure, an argument which underestimates not only Asquith's appreciation of his colleague's achievement and character, but also the significance of the role itself. South Africa produced between a quarter and a third of the world's total gold output, vital to Britain's role at the heart of an international economy based on the gold standard. Furthermore, it lay astride the long strategic sea route to India and, like the adjacent British protectorates, shared borders with land colonised by Germany, an economic and potentially a military rival. It was probably significant, too, that Crewe as head of the Colonial Office and responsible therefore for South African affairs, had always appreciated Herbert's qualities and often reminded Asquith of them.[122] From the prime minister's view, there was much to commend Herbert for South Africa, far more than the merely negative that he would divest himself of a man whose handling of the suffragette issue he did not care for. On the positive side, Herbert was a senior member of the cabinet which is what the South African premiers had requested. His name and reputation would commend themselves to all but the most ardent Dutch and British nationalists in the country. He had generally shown himself to be a quietly effective minister and he had significant personal attributes, above all a proven ability to hold together individuals of differing outlooks and opinions, essential in a country whose future internal stability was by no means certain.

In mid-October 1909 Asquith told the King of his wish that Gladstone should become South Africa's inaugural governor-general. The King, still smarting perhaps over the Catholic procession affair and doubtless mindful of the association between the Gladstone name and the perceived shame of Majuba, was not at all keen. Asquith, more secure in his own position than when he had last discussed Herbert with the Monarch, held his ground. By the end of the month he was able to tell Crewe that the King was now very good humoured about the appointment.[123] The governor-general designate was in equally good fettle. He had decided as early as 5 October to accept what he saw as a great opportunity to oversee the outworking of the South Africa Act. Personal considerations also weighed with him, for he believed that the climate might be better for Dolly's general health. Ever since their marriage she had suffered not only from difficulties relating to her throat but also from more intimate problems. Probing the euphemistically coy language beneath which such matters were conventionally hidden at the time, it appears that she suffered badly from fibroids. At the end of 1907 surgery had been recommended. This was a serious step but the doctors were reassuring that for a healthy person an operation under anaesthetic was not dangerous. That, however, could not have been particularly comforting for Herbert who knew the statistics all too well, the latest returns showing that in 1906 183 people had died under anaesthetic in England and Wales.[124] But the courageous Dolly had no desire, as she graphically put it, to carry the seeds of destruction about with her. It was arranged that Lady Paget should provide post-operative care for her daughter and Helen offered to step in if for any reason Lady Paget had to go home. Two operations were successfully performed early in 1908, although for two or three days Dolly's life hung in the balance and her recuperation was set back by the death of her father in February.

If Dolly's health influenced Herbert's decision about South Africa, his claim to Harry that he had completed or at least initiated all he had in mind for the Home Office was somewhat disingenuous. His own long illness at the start of the year might explain why the department's sole measure in the 1909 King's speech was the Cinematograph Bill, designed to enhance public safety at film showings. His enforced concentration on the suffragette issue had absorbed much of his attention and he missed Samuel, promoted to the cabinet in June. Masterman was an able enough replacement but he had been seconded for months working on the details of Lloyd George's budget, effectively leaving Herbert without his under-secretary. In a revealing initial interview with Masterman he had displayed his usual willingness to give a subordinate licence to exercise his own initiative. The departmental pigeon holes, he told his new colleague, were bunged full of overdue reforms. 'Take them and do what you can with them. I'll take all responsibility, but you are better at managing the House than I am. I don't care a scrap if people say how much better you do it than me – *only get it done.*'[125] That hardly tallied with his suggestion to Harry that he had run out of things to do and it might also be read as further confirming that for all the 38 bills he carried through parliament, he had never managed to get either himself or his officials comfortably on top of their work. By 1909 the Home Office registry was receiving over 71,000 items a year, a considerable increase since 1906 though the staff number had grown by only two. The number of parliamentary questions to be handled had risen enormously, especially after an autumn session became a permanent feature of the calendar. Freely admitting his own culpability Herbert told his successor that there had been a constant risk of breakdown in the department and that unless the volume and intensity of work decreased a failure was inevitable.[126]

Finally, there can be no doubt that Herbert's decision to accept Asquith's proposal was influenced by the escape it offered from the suffragette campaign, which he had now come to believe was not likely to subside in the near future.[127] The constant vigilance he felt bound to exercise over the treatment of hunger strikers and the endless barrage of propaganda and personal abuse had taken their toll, and his weariness was evident when he likened himself to 'a cab horse held up by the reins and shafts and bound to go on'.[128] Telling Harry of his intention to accept South Africa he admitted that his decision had been informed in part by his need for a long rest.[129] Even so, he took time to think things through in consultation with Dolly and it was not until 30 October that he replied formally to Asquith. In so doing he mentioned that his dominant consideration was his wife's health and that while he was not making any stipulation he might not complete the whole five-year term.[130] With the die cast and the suffragette burden about to pass from his hands his spirits soared, so much so that Harry told a Colonial Office official that escaping from the women had taken ten years off his brother.[131]

CHAPTER 6

South Africa

By the time Herbert's new appointment was officially announced it was clear that the impasse over the peers' rejection of the 1909 budget would necessitate a general election, the first for three decades that he would not contest. His mind, however, was already on other things. He prepared a long memo for his successor, which included his assessment of senior Home Office staff. Describing Troup as able and reliable, Herbert pretty well summarised his own approach in the department by adding that 'if you want to get the best out of him, give him his head.'[1] There was also the matter of finding for himself a reliable secretary. In the end he settled on H.J. Stanley but only after failing to lure away from Churchill the highly capable Edward Marsh, who found the prospect of exile in South Africa unappealing. Yet distance had some compensations, as Herbert discovered when he began to finalise the logistics of his move. The outgoing high commissioner, Selborne, offered to sell him not only his transport animals and wagons but also 1,200 cigars and almost a thousand bottles of wines, spirits and liqueurs, the remaining stock of his cellar. Herbert purchased the liquor and tobacco, but not all of the transport because he planned to ship out two motor cars. Conscious perhaps of his soaring overdraft and after discussion with Harry who was to look after his financial affairs while he was away, he sold his current Siddeley automobile and arranged to let out his house in Buckingham Gate.

Another matter to be resolved was the title which Herbert should take when, as expected, he was promoted to the peerage. The King wanted him to have a territorial designation but Herbert thought it wrong that he should adopt a title associated with land which he did not own, and he was also unwilling to abandon his father's family name. Harry's concerns were more prosaic, preferring a knighthood which would leave Herbert with the option of re-entering the House of Commons when he returned from South Africa. Herbert, however, was determined that he would not go back to the House, whereupon Henry advised him that if he was to have a peerage he should make sure it was a viscountcy. It was.[2]

The newly-minted Lord and Lady Gladstone finally sailed from Southampton on one of most recent additions to the Union Castle fleet, the *Walmer Castle*. The routine of a long journey, some 6,000 nautical miles taking over two weeks, was broken only when news of the King's unexpected death reached the ship on Dolly's birthday, 13 May. It compelled Herbert to amend the draft of his arrival speech but otherwise he had plenty of time to contemplate what lay ahead. Since his visit to Cape Colony in 1877 the European scramble for colonies and the Boer War had fundamentally changed the political environment and even the geography of Britain's South African territories. As high commissioner for the protectorates of Bechuanaland, Swaziland and Basutoland, Herbert was to govern almost 300,000 square miles, home to a handful of Europeans and some 625,000 Africans. Each territory had a resident commissioner but Herbert's was the ultimate responsibility for protecting natural resources, overseeing borders and land use, keeping the peace between rival tribes, suppressing witchcraft and pornography and controlling a wide range of human and animal diseases, none of which, in common with poachers and frequently the indigenous population itself, respected man-made territorial boundaries. He would also be the Crown's official representative in Southern Rhodesia where 24,000 settlers, overwhelmingly British, exercised largely unfettered oversight of some 746,000 Africans through a small legislative council effectively controlled by the British South Africa Company. Above all, Herbert had to hold the ring between the Colonial Office in London and South African politicians acutely aware of the economic potential of the protectorates whose eventual transfer to the Union had been provided for as part of the South Africa Act.

As in the other Dominions the role of governor-general was to act as the Crown's official representative, in this case in a new country of around six million inhabitants, at ceremonial and social functions and to deal with routine and mundane formalities such as recommendations for awards, requests to use the royal title and acknowledging the receipt of gifts. But other aspects of the South African posting were far more challenging, involving as it did the need to minimise the potential for conflict between the great powers colonising the continent, safeguarding the territorial waters of a new nation lacking its own navy, handling extradition and boundary incursions and seeking to ensure that Union Government policy threatened neither imperial interests nor its own internal stability. In particular, the governor-general was expected to refer to the Colonial Office any proposed legislation impinging on Britain's treaty obligations or South Africa's substantial Indian population. Furthermore, the job was bound to be more difficult and potentially far more influential than that of governors-general elsewhere simply because much of local political infrastructure was rudimentary. There was no national parliament and whoever led the first government was unlikely to have much accumulated knowledge of constitutional protocol or convention. Nor would the politicians be able easily to draw for advice on officials since the Union civil service was still being created out of the four constituent colonial bureaucracies and its predominantly British composition inevitably raised doubts in some minds about its impartiality. The new government in other words was likely to be unduly dependent on Herbert's familiarity with cabinet and parliamentary government procedures. Furthermore, it would have to operate in a racially charged environment: indeed, its own composition would have to reflect the main, still raw, division between Britons and Boers whose collaboration was essential if the Union was to work. Some accommodation would also be necessary with the large and economically important Indian community. Finally, and of particular interest to Herbert, there were the African tribes themselves. African labour, some of it recruited seasonally from the neighbouring colonies, was essential to mining and agriculture. Yet many deemed its sheer volume a potential threat to the social order and its culture a threat to the white man's civilisation. Consequently Africans had been excluded from the franchise under the terms of the South Africa Act. Patronising and demeaning as it appears in hindsight, Herbert shared that strong sense of paternalistic responsibility for indigenous populations which generally characterised the best of Britain's colonial rulers.

Whatever thoughts Herbert may have had about these various challenges, Selborne was not slow to pass on his own. Almost as the *Walmer Castle* docked in Cape Town he was striding up the gang-plank, taking the best part of a day to brief his successor. His surviving notes indicate a comprehensive discussion ranging over local politicians, broad strategic issues of imperial concern and relatively trivial matters such as wage levels for domestic staff and official travel allowances.[3] Doubtless Herbert found this meeting useful, or so he told Selborne. What he did not record, however, was his intense irritation at Selborne's continued interference in matters he should have dropped once he left South Africa the following day. Even before Herbert left England Francis Hopwood, permanent Under-Secretary at the Colonial Office, had warned him that Selborne would be 'anxious to pump a lot of stuff into you' and during their shipboard meeting Selborne strongly pressed on Herbert his ideas for reorganising the high commission.[4] By creating a section to deal exclusively with the protectorates and headed by three Imperial civil servants Selborne hoped to ensure the survival of embedded British principles and practices after the Union took them over. Herbert was not at all convinced. Apart from his doubts about the abilities of the individuals in question, he feared that such a move would not go down well either with the Union Government or with the Africans, who were by no means sold on the idea of the transfer and who might interpret such a reorganisation as a portent that it was imminent. Back in England, however, Selborne continued to lobby Crewe who as Colonial Secretary was initially supportive until Herbert set out his own opposition. Selborne was undeterred, urging Hopwood, who was on Herbert's side on this particular issue, to use his influence to push for the reconstruction as an insurance against any possible future maladministration by the Union Government. When Loulou Harcourt succeeded Crewe at the Colonial Office in the autumn of 1910, Herbert lost little time in reiterating, if anything even more trenchantly, his view that as far as these proposed moves were concerned Selborne needed to come to earth.[5]

But the former commissioner's interference did not end there. It had been agreed that legislation produced by the Union Parliament should be printed in both Dutch and English but Selborne claimed there had been a presumption that the formally signed and thus the authoritative version of measures would be the English one because a governor-general could hardly sanction a version he could not understand. Herbert dismissed this as absurd, telling Harcourt that the Dutch would most certainly see it as a contravention of the commitment to run Union affairs on a bi-lingual basis. He had therefore decided right from the start to sign roughly half and half, the English version when the subject affected mainly British interests or when the issues were so complex that they might lead to legal disputes. Harcourt approved, commenting that Selborne's mind was both small and ineffective, and his swans generally geese.[6] Small wonder though that when rumours circulated in 1912 that Selborne might be joining the government as colonial secretary, a dismayed Herbert described the prospect as flesh creeping.[7]

By this time, of course, the Gladstones were well established. After the opening ceremonials in Cape Town Herbert turned quickly to his first important official task, deciding who should be invited to form South Africa's inaugural government. This was easier said than done because while constitutional convention required that a prime minister be leader of the party enjoying the confidence of the lower house, there was as yet no parliament and indeed little in the way of nation-wide party organisation, apart from a very small Labour Party. Without even an outgoing prime minister to guide him, Herbert therefore had much wider discretion than was usually the case although he was not operating completely in the dark because there had been much press speculation and the colonial politicians themselves had been jockeying for position. As leader of South Africa's Unionists, Starr Jameson knew he could never win a national election outright and, anxious to pre-empt the extreme Boers, he had approached Louis Botha, the former Boer army commander who had subsequently become prime minister of the Transvaal, to see if he would be prepared to lead a ministry made up of the best men, but their discussions came to nothing. Neither Botha nor John Merriman, leader since 1908 of Cape Colony, the senior and most populous of the four joining the Union, was willing to serve under the other but they had indicated that they would serve under Martinus Steyn, last president of the independent Orange Free State (OFS). Steyn, however, was not well enough to consider taking office and for some time therefore Botha had been actively canvassing on his own behalf. Selborne's initial briefing with Herbert on 17 May had included his opinion that the Transvaaler was genuinely committed to reconciliation, a key consideration given Herbert's own aspirations for his new domain. Even without Selborne's input, however, Herbert had a fair idea of the way the wind was blowing long before he reached Cape Town. In February 1910 he had met the Transvaal's agent general in

London, Sir Richard Solomon, who told him that Botha was his colony's preferred choice. So it was, too, for Natal whose sometime prime minister, O'Grady Gubbins, was actively pressing Botha's name on the Colonial Office.[8] As for the OFS, Prime Minister Abraham Fischer believed Merriman to be more able than Botha but that the hostility of some of his own supporters in the Cape militated against his forming the Union's first government, leaving Botha as the pre-eminent national figure. Botha also had the advantage of strong personal links with leading members of the British Government including Crewe and Asquith, who had actually sounded him out informally as to who would be an acceptable choice as governor-general. Merriman, whose closest Liberal ally was Bryce, had not been so consulted. Crewe had also sought the views of Henry Scobell, the general officer in command of the Cape district and the man with whom the Gladstones stayed when they first arrived in South Africa. Crewe duly forwarded to Herbert Scobell's opinion that only Botha would be able to form a stable government. But if Botha was clearly the popular choice, Herbert certainly had not been ordered to nominate him.[9] No-one in government had authority to give any such instruction to the governor-general whose power to appoint was conferred directly by statute.

Between 12 and 20 May Herbert met with all the colonial premiers and several other leading figures, including J.W. Sauer from the Cape, Barry Hertzog, the attorney general and director of education in the OFS government, and Jan Smuts from the Transvaal. It was not an experience that he particularly savoured, as caginess prevailed with some declining to back men to whom privately or in other conversations they had offered support. Fischer would not commit himself one way or the other, and as Herbert told Crewe even John de Villiers, the Union's chief justice, did not run straight. But there was only ever likely to be one outcome.[10] For all his experience and status, Merriman simply could not command sufficient support and on 23 May, therefore, Herbert informed London that he had asked Louis Botha to form an administration. Crewe was satisfied. So, too, was the Unionist *Cape Times* which supported Herbert's choice and on the same grounds that Botha alone had backing from both the Dutch and British political communities.[11]

Herbert had rather mixed feelings, however, when Botha presented him with the details of his proposed cabinet, necessarily a juggling act to ensure that the four colonies and the interests of Dutch and British be as equitably represented as possible. The Transvaal had three representatives and the Cape four, while the OFS and Natal each had two. Herbert thought the Natal nominees, Moor and Gubbins, were weak and he did not think much either of Sauer. Francois Malan he felt was good, Henry Burton clever, and he liked Hertzog whom, in a remarkable piece of misjudgement, he described as level-headed. Smuts, he decided, was both clever and industrious but overall he was concerned that the cabinet lacked business experience, an appropriately high moral outlook and official training.[12] He might have been more confident had the ministers been supported by a well established civil service but the Union's initial administrative support structure was rudimentary. He had already concluded that Selborne's office had not been very businesslike and he was soon affected personally by operational hitches as the Union sought to merge four different colonial administrations, widely separated by distance and not particularly well equipped. Publication of the King's message to his newest Dominion was somehow held up and there were long delays and changes before Herbert's own financial arrangements were finalised. The inauguration of the Union was to take place in Pretoria but until he was formally sworn in he could not reclaim the travel costs from the Union Government. The Colonial Office, already paying him £3,000 a year, declined to pick up the bill for what it rightly regarded as Union business. But the local administration, responsible for the governor-general's annual salary of £10,000 a year, was so dilatory that it took well over a year to settle the matter. Arrangements to cover Herbert's general travel and other expenses proved equally problematic. Three times he thought the matter resolved and three times the details were amended. His annoyance perhaps owed something to the fact that his overdraft had reached well over £7,000 under the burden of his initial establishment costs. Harry encouraged him to remit regular payments to reduce it, but Herbert had resolved to devote his entire South African income to local purposes and eventually the Union Government agreed that he could use any surplus in his expense account to offset his initial outlays.

He may also have had cause to wonder about his choice of prime minister, who was no sooner in post than he was ready to abandon it. It had been determined that once the cabinet was chosen a general election would be held with the official opening of parliament to follow in November. The election, however, did not go as anticipated. Although his South African Party secured an overall majority Botha and two of his cabinet, F.R. Moor and H.C. Hull, were defeated at the polls. While it was easy enough to find an alternative constituency for himself, his confidence seems to have been dented and he told Herbert that he wished to resign. Herbert was horrified and set about putting some backbone into the defeated minister. Think, he urged Botha, of the disappointment in England and the implications for South Africa where his resignation would be misunderstood and ruin his career. When Botha threw his heart condition into the equation Herbert told him that he simply had to take the risk. They were all new to their posts, he affirmed, and they must stick to the boat they had launched. 'The idea of abandoning their majority!' he exclaimed to Crewe. 'It is unspeakable'[13]

His strong reaction perhaps also owed something to the rather lax manner in which the new administration was approaching the forthcoming visit of the King's brother, the Duke of Connaught, who was to open the inaugural session of parliament, a laxity which confirmed Herbert's doubts about the lack of professionalism among his new ministers. The delay in publicising the visit perturbed George V and in August Hopwood told Crewe they should get Herbert to expedite things. The reality was, however, that the Union politicians had wanted the new King himself to open parliament, the Duke, who had visited the country just two years earlier, not being considered much of an attraction. But in the event the whole thing passed off successfully and a pageant with 6,000 performers, half-a-dozen lunches and eight sizeable dinners were sufficient to satisfy the Duke. Connaught was also pleased with the ceremonials, which Herbert personally oversaw, rather giving the lie to Hopwood's fear that neither he nor his ministers were well versed in such things, the governor-general being 'still in the shadow of a curtsey'.[14]

This was an allusion to an unfortunate episode that clouded Herbert's early months in South Africa. At one of his first official dinners there had been some attempt to get Boer ladies to curtsey on being formally introduced, giving rise to reports that the Gladstones were pompous and overly concerned with protocol. Margot Asquith promptly dashed off a spiky letter warning Dolly against giving herself airs. Herbert was understandably annoyed. The incident had not involved Dolly but himself and as soon as he realised that the women resented the formality he had indicated that only a smile and nod were necessary. Writing to Crewe later about his visit to Natal, he remarked with heavy irony on the locals' astonishment at discovering he was an ordinary mortal, accessible and shaking hands.[15] Yet the story never entirely died and even when he was leaving for good in 1914 hostile elements within the local press were still contrasting the Gladstones' alleged stuffiness with the simplicity favoured by their successors, the Buxtons. But the charge was at once unfair and ill-founded. It was unfair because Herbert was anything but pompous. His whole public demeanour was an appealing combination of self-effacement and genial sociability. Former colleague Arthur Ponsonby commented tellingly in 1911 that when he saw photographs of Herbert performing official functions in South Africa, 'I cannot help feeling that there is a part of your duties which does not appeal to you very strongly', and Herbert was later to decline high office in Ireland partly because the associated pomp and ceremony held not the least appeal for him.[16] It was unfounded because the initial incident seems to have been the fault of overzealous officials trying, as Hopwood told Crewe, to fence the Gladstones in so as to invest them with 'almost royal seclusion'. While conceding that Herbert might welcome this as offering a chance to avoid bores, Hopwood shrewdly concluded that 'a bad staff may ruin a good Governor.'[17] He was able to see this for himself when he went to South Africa as part of Connaught's entourage in the autumn, finding the governor-general's officials variously very poor, incompetent, rude, brusque or diffident.[18] Crewe himself certainly did not put much store by the allegations of Herbert's regal pretensions. When he moved from the Colonial Office late in 1910 his parting message to Herbert stressed that he was doing a good job, especially in establishing good relations with the new government.

As Herbert's account of his visit to Natal suggests, it was his good-natured disposition that allowed him to win over most people as he threw himself wholeheartedly into familiarising himself with the country and taking full advantage of its wildness. He fished, rode a great deal and hunted whenever he could, although the local impala proved more adept than the Hawarden rabbits at evading his bullets. When time permitted he played a lot of tennis. Such recreations were squeezed into a hectic official schedule requiring him to be periodically present in all four provincial capitals and to play the patron at innumerable local and civic events. Some idea of what was involved can be found in his engagement diary for the three months between mid-December 1910 and March 1911. On 15 December he left Cape Town for Johannesburg where he attended the races, numerous concerts, two polo matches, a children's show, a garden party and a scouts' prize giving. After a busy Christmas and new year he was in Bloemfontein by 3 January watching cricket and on succeeding days he attended several political functions, visited the art gallery and presented the prizes at a local golf club competition. On 24 January he left for Cape Town where he opened the agricultural show, attended a degree ceremony at the university, met with the bishop's council, toured a local vineyard and sat in on a session of the local parliament before going on to the golf club and an Admiralty garden party. Playing tennis over-enthusiastically on 7 February and with his eye on the ball rather than his own whereabouts he collided with the net post, dislocating his shoulder so badly that he was out of action for two weeks. He was fit enough by 21 February to make the two-day boat trip to Port Elizabeth where he arrived, ready once more to jump, hamster-like, back into the ever-turning wheel of engagements. Such a level of activity was a normal expectation for any Dominion governor-general but in South Africa the whole process was made far more onerous by the sheer scale of the distances involved in a country whose transport infrastructure was still primitive. Herbert calculated that in his first year of office alone he passed 41 nights onboard trains travelling almost 10,000 miles, including one 200-mile journey which took 24 hours. Sea journeys added another 920 miles and involved four nights. He did 600 miles on horseback, spent 40 nights trekking and 31 under canvas. A later trip to the OFS, Rhodesia and the Congo border in 1911 took a full month during which he travelled over 17 nights, covering 4,500 miles by train, 200 miles on horseback and more by car on roads so bad that one 85-mile section of the route took 12 hours. Of course, there were servants to care for routine needs and officials to oversee the arrangements but it was still physically and mentally demanding, especially when the innumerable speeches, endless social pleasantries, political meetings and, when Dolly was with him concerns for her wellbeing, were taken into account. His energy was impressive as he maintained as public a presence for the Imperial Government in South Africa and the protectorates as time, distance and his constitutional duties allowed. Equally impressive was his courage, evident when he chose to visit the ailing Steyn in Bloemfontein in October 1910. Meeting with one of Britain's most implacable Boer War opponents was always likely to antagonise some sections of local British opinion and confirm the views of dyed-in-the-wool Unionists like the former provincial minister who wrote the new governor-general off within a few days of his arrival as a 'man without brains or ability'.[19] A quite contrary view was expressed by K.P. Apthorpe, sometime director of land settlement in the Orange River Colony, when he told Milner that Herbert was proving to be much stronger than he had anticipated.[20] Mental strength and physical courage alike were certainly needed when Herbert decided to go to Rhodesia in 1911 where the exercise of his prerogative of mercy in a notorious local legal case had outraged white sentiment.

The facts, which reached his desk in December 1910, were on the surface quite straightforward. In Umtali a black house boy had been sentenced to death for raping a white woman, his employer's wife. Herbert had no principled opposition to the death penalty. When Minister of Justice Herzog proposed releasing some of the 11 tribesmen sentenced to hang for murder in Zululand and commuting the sentences of the others, Herbert was appalled. It was he wrote, 'an absolute reversal of one of the most careful & deliberate judgements I have ever read'.[21] But it was precisely the absence of any such care and deliberation from the judicial process that so troubled him about the Umtali verdict. The prisoner had been provided with a very inexperienced defence lawyer and then only on the day before the trial opened, his statement had not been subjected to any examination in court even though it was adduced as evidence of his guilt, certain details of the prosecution case did not ring true and there was even some doubt that a rape had occurred. Herbert also knew that a few years earlier another Rhodesian court had sentenced an African to death for rape, only for Selborne to discover that the 'assault' had in fact involved a baboon which had leapt onto the alleged victim in the dark.[22] Suspicious, therefore, of the local legal process, Herbert was disinclined to let the Umtali sentence stand without fuller consideration. He wrote to the trial judge and Sir W. Milton, the British administrator in Rhodesia, for fuller details. His misgivings were not allayed when the judge provided new information not contained in the papers previously sent to him. Nor was he reassured by

Milton's comment that the actual facts had to be supplemented by the personal knowledge possessed by the residents of Umtali, code in Herbert's mind for prejudice. The judge did not help matters either by leaking part of Herbert's confidential letter to the press. Despite neither Milton nor his own legal adviser seeing any reason to change the verdict, Herbert persisted. Further investigation suggested that the woman in question was of dubious moral character, habitually allowing house boys to enter her bedroom whilst she was still in her nightwear and in her husband's absence from home failing to secure an unlocked bathroom window through which the alleged rapist had got into her house. Herbert was far too much the Edwardian gentleman to cast public aspersions on a lady's virtue or to allow doubts about it to influence his judgement but he was rightly puzzled by the fact that she had not once cried out during the several hours of her alleged ordeal. His doubts were finally vindicated when the woman's husband, who had not even appeared in court, admitted that his wife had actually permitted penetration. Herbert concluded that in the circumstances the boy could hardly be held guilty of rape and he had the sentence reduced to penal servitude for life on a charge of unpremeditated assault with intent to rape. Privately, he regarded even this as too harsh but Rhodesians and other whites both in South Africa and England were outraged both by his intervention and his decision. Petitions of protest poured into the Colonial Office and the high commission, questions were raised in Westminster and letters appeared in the press. Even the King was approached by Rhodesian residents and while he could not say so publicly, he clearly sympathised with them. Yet the outrage had little to do with the legal aspects of the case, owing far more to an underlying and persistent psychological fear of the threat thought to be posed to white women by sexually predatory tribesmen. Almost every subsequent assault by an African on a white woman was attributed to Herbert's judgement in the Umtali case which, it was claimed, had resulted in a rise in the number of such attacks. In fact, there was no such increase and in any case, the emotional ferment notwithstanding, they were always relatively few in number. But in South Africa, as Herbert was quickly learning, and indeed in London, facts were far less powerful than prejudice. Tory MPs took the matter up with Harcourt, querying whether Herbert had the power to commute a death sentence and reiterating the charge that the high commissioner's leniency had caused assaults by black men on white women to soar. Harcourt stuck loyally by his besieged colleague. Lord Gladstone, he told the House firmly, had acted quite legitimately on his own authority, his decisions could not be reversed and the government had the utmost confidence in his judgement.[23]

Superficially Herbert was quite unmoved by the furore. He thought about establishing a commission to look at whole issue of black-on-white rape but abandoned the idea because it could hardly ignore the converse and probably far more prevalent issue of white rape on black. At the back of his mind also, perhaps, was the memorandum he had earlier circulated to protectorate officers on the subject of imperial civil servants cohabiting with African women. A practice to which administrators tended to turn a blind eye, it rather disturbed Herbert's somewhat puritan expectations of public standards but his circular, actually quite consistent with official policy as laid down by Crewe in 1909, had been challenged by at least one official. In the end, therefore, he contented himself by telling Harry that the Umtali case determined him to destroy the Rhodesian jury system, a resolve further strengthened when another Rhodesian jury subsequently acquitted a white farmer who summarily shot an African for allegedly pestering his daughter.[24] Yet while he certainly faced his critics boldly enough when he went to Rhodesia, deep down the antagonism which he had provoked clearly troubled him and for several years references to Umtali surfaced in his letters. It was almost as if he was still trying to convince himself that he was right, even though his action had been strongly supported by some of South Africa's leading lawyers and also by Botha, although the latter could not comment publicly about a matter occurring in a British territory.

Far less in the public eye than the Umtali affair was the quiet work Herbert was doing behind the scenes to help Botha and his colleagues come to grips with the challenges inherent in forging a single nation from four different colonies and several contrasting cultures. Constitutionally Herbert's role in domestic affairs, like that of the sovereign in Britain, was restricted to offering advice and comment, as in 1911 for example, when provided a very detailed critique of Smuts's draft Defence Bill, much of which was incorporated into the measure before it went to parliament. But sometimes he was more pro-active, as when he recommended to the prime minister that he appoint a commission to examine the tricky problem of bi-lingual education or in September 1910 when he sent Botha a memo outlining how as home secretary he had dealt with imprisoned suffragettes and suggesting that a similar approach might be adopted in treating imprisoned Asiatics. Rather to the displeasure of Harcourt and other British ministers, Herbert also supported a proposal to transfer the contract for South Africa's overseas postal services from the Union Castle Line to the governor-general's office and in effect the Union Government. Harcourt thought the government's proposal to build its own fleet of mail ships quite foolish.

Herbert's backing for this measure may have contributed to the later assessments that he was effectively in Botha's pocket but this is to misread the dynamics of the contemporary political situation. Botha may have been the only man capable of holding South Africa together but he was not yet the powerful, dominant figure he was to become. Politically quite inexperienced and hampered by a cabinet constructed more on a basis of provincial equity rather than individual ability, he needed the governor-general's moral support and constitutional guidance. He received both, for instance in the immediate aftermath of the 1910 general election, and again in November 1911 when Herbert sent him a personal note after he had gone through a particularly testing time. It was good, Botha replied, to receive encouragement from such a man and to know that his own efforts for peace and harmony were valued.[25] Herbert offered practical help as well when he could, for example drafting a set of notes for Botha on cabinet practice and principles, stressing the need for ministers to consult colleagues before initiating action, the importance of collective responsibility and security, the requirement for bills to be circulated to ministers before being introduced and the need to consult the Treasury where proposals involved the expenditure of public money.[26]

The notes are undated but it seems quite possible that they were prepared in response to a minor cabinet crisis in the spring of 1912. Ignoring cabinet convention, Sauer brought in a railway bill involving financial appropriations that he had omitted to discuss with his colleagues. Hull, who felt Sauer's railway policy was benefitting the coastal regions at the expense of the interior, promptly resigned. Botha told Herbert that he, too, was contemplating resignation because Sauer was unwilling to accept a change in his portfolio. When Herbert intimated that this was far too drastic Botha asked what he would do in such a situation. Herbert advised him to draw up a document outlining the relationships which ought to exist between the various government departments and the Treasury. If Sauer accepted it, that would be a de facto admission of his error. If he did not, then Botha could reshuffle the cabinet leaving Sauer out and with no ground of complaint. In a follow-up letter he added a warning that in the general election that would follow a government resignation the Labour Party would probably increase its representation and cause more trouble than Sauer and Merriman combined. He further pointed out that if Botha went to the country he had no platform on which to fight since no programme had yet been formulated for the next session.[27] Botha followed Herbert's advice with regard to his own position but contented himself with simply moving Sauer to a different job. He also gave up his own ministerial responsibility for agriculture, a post he had held concurrent with his premiership. Herbert was pleased, believing that this would allow Botha time to concentrate on constitutional practice and improve the conduct of business which, he told Harcourt, had been 'terribly bad', with bills being abruptly dropped and parliament losing two days' business because of a member's death, never sitting on public holiday, and for half the session meeting only in the afternoons.[28] Botha was grateful for all the advice and with the reconstructed cabinet working well Herbert felt that he could contemplate his forthcoming absence from South Africa without undue worry.

It had always been his intention that Dolly should return to England periodically, with the first visit scheduled for the summer of 1912 after the completion of the parliamentary session. His plan was to accompany her for six weeks and then return to South Africa, leaving her in England for a further month or two. Herbert found the prospect of this separation 'beastly' but his gloom was soon to intensify.[29] Harcourt proved quite unsympathetic to his plan to take temporary leave and appoint Scobell as his deputy, telling him that he had no power to make any such appointment. Legally his replacement had to be the chief justice who would be Britain's only means of contact with the Union Government at a time when it was dealing with several critical issues and who would, furthermore, have access to all the confidential documents in the governor-general's office. It was, Harcourt concluded, impossible for Herbert to take leave.[30] Telling family and visitors alike that he intended to contest this, Herbert raised the matter again in September only to receive another firm rebuff. Dreading the thought of being separated from his wife for the long period that now seemed inevitable, he invited Harry to go out to keep him company.

At this point, however, fate intervened. Dolly had thrown herself wholeheartedly into the formal duties connected with her husband's role as well as managing a household which involved some 15 staff and a monthly expenditure of about £600. Visiting her brother in 1911, Mary Drew thought that Dolly's engagements entailed too many late nights and early mornings, though she admired 'the quiet unfussy way she gets through so much'.[31] Her niece, Evelyn, agreed, observing that Dolly was never too busy to attend to anyone who needed her, despite her many commitments and the fact that she had to put up with a good deal of domestic inefficiency in spite of which 'she never lets herself go in the way I know I should'.[32] This perhaps was a veiled reference to the Gladstones' housekeeper, who was less than competent, muddling arrangements, failing to communicate in a timely fashion, guessing at expenditures and mishandling her accounts – stupid with the brains of a rabbit was Herbert's verdict.[33] On top of all this, Dolly also had a project of her own. Based on similar schemes in India and other parts of the Empire, she planned to provide a centre in each of the Union's four provinces where registered staff would cater for what were believed to be the unique nursing needs of the Asian and African populations. It was a demanding undertaking. During Evelyn's visit, for example, Dolly was writing 300 letters soliciting support and also preparing to address meetings in Pretoria, Johannesburg and and Durban over the following weeks. That was a round-trip of just under 700 miles but thus far Dolly's rather fragile constitution had coped pretty well with the rather frenzied pace of her life. Since arriving in South Africa she had had not a single day's illness and was fit enough to play tennis quite regularly, although Herbert, forever worrying that she would overdo things, did try to restrain her somewhat, even taking on himself some of the administration involved in launching the nursing scheme.

However, on an overnight stay under canvas during one of their official trips in September 1911 Dolly contracted malaria. Whether in consequence or not, shortly afterwards she began to experience a recurrence of her previous gynaecological problems. There were even alarming rumours of malignant growths.[34] Local doctors agreed that a hysterectomy would probably be necessary while Dolly was in England, further adding to Herbert's dismay as the prospective separation would now be even longer. Both Mary and Harry tried to to raise his spirits. Dolly's previous surgery had in the end proved considerably more dangerous than expected but Mary was reassuringly confident that 'the removal of the womb, if found necessary, is quite an ordinary thing.'[35] Harry was equally positive if less direct. 'The main things are health & strength & even if there is an operation, under present marvellous surgical conditions, there is no reason why she should not get perfectly strong again.'[36] Armitstead joined in the chorus of consolation with the rather clumsy observation that things might not turn out as badly as Herbert feared, especially as such matters were now better understood and operations performed which 'nearly lack risk'. Rather more reassuring from Herbert's perspective was Armitstead's reminder that all things were in God's hands so he should put his trust in Him.[37] The one positive in the situation was that Dolly's condition provided a powerful argument to take back to Harcourt. It proved sufficient. The colonial secretary discussed the changed circumstances with Asquith and in mid-January let Herbert know that he could join his ailing wife in England.

Dolly left South Africa in February 1912 and, in a gesture which spoke much for their relationship, the Bothas sought to relieve Herbert's loneliness by sending various invitations for dinner, bridge and tennis. Armitstead took it upon himself to supply frequent updates on Dolly's progress though again his language was less comforting than he intended. On 4 March he wrote to say that he had met Dolly and was pained to see how she was anticipating her forthcoming surgery. When he saw her shortly after the operation, however, he was more positive, saying she looked well and cheery, before adding that he well understood Herbert's devotion to her.[38] Herbert was certainly committing expressions of that devotion to the mail frequently and effusively. 'Notwithstanding your 12 sides to her,' Armitstead reported in April, Dolly had still insisted that he show her his own latest letter from Herbert.[39] For her part, Dolly seems to have been equally bereft at their separation, telling Mary that marriage had quite unfitted her for the single life.[40]

In June Herbert was finally able to join his wife in England. Inevitably, though, there were imperial matters to attend to, including lengthy discussions with Harcourt about the future of the protectorates and Rhodesia. For the Colonial Office the prospect of Rhodesia joining the Union made a lot of sense, partly because its predominantly British population would help offset the Afrikaner majority in the Union, and partly because it would allow the exchequer to avoid buying out the rights of the BSA. Within Rhodesia itself, however, Herbert reported a strong undercurrent of hostility to the idea and certainly all of those elected to the legislative council in 1911 were against it. Nor was Rhodesia a priority for Botha who had no desire to take it on without the consent of its inhabitants, even had he had the necessary financial resources. It was agreed, therefore, that the only option was to renew the BSA charter and in line with Herbert's recommendations it was envisaged that by 1914 the company should disentangle its administrative and commercial functions, the legislative council be strengthened, a redistribution bill introduced and Milton pensioned off.[41]

The high commissioner and the colonial secretary also saw eye to eye on the future of the protectorates. Swaziland, a territory bitten out of the north-east corner of the Union and traversed by a rail connection running from Laurenco Marques in Portuguese Mozambique all the way to the Rand, had an obvious strategic and commercial interest for South Africans. Under some pressure from MPs in East Transvaal where the bulk of the population was Swazi, Botha had raised the matter of its incorporation early in 1911, though assuring Herbert that he himself was in no hurry. At that year's Imperial Conference Harcourt persuaded Botha not to pursue the matter, not least because the establishment of the commission required by the 1909 legislation would inevitably increase the pressure to complete the transfer of the other two protectorates. This, he feared, would run the risk of provoking unrest among the Basuto and and Bechuana, whose leaders were against any transfer. When Herbert mentioned Swaziland later in 1911 Harcourt commented rather tartly that he seemed to be under the misapprehension that it would transfer in 1912 with the other territories also following during his tenure. In fact Herbert had merely put in a request for additional staff to support a workload described by a tongue-in-cheek Harcourt as 'an appalling record of virtuous activity which leaves me tired and panting'.[42] He was absolutely at one with the colonial secretary, he wrote subsequently, on the need to retain Swaziland as long as possible.[43] Now face to face, the two agreed that while they would discuss with Botha the principle of its transfer, nothing would be implemented before June 1914 at the earliest.

Apart from political business, Herbert had relatives to visit, golf to play and private affairs to address. A meeting with Harry to consider his investment portfolio revealed that his shares in Russian coal and oil had declined, but other stocks had performed better, netting him an estimated income of some £3,500 for the year. This must have been welcome but Herbert actually seemed much more pleased when the King expressed the hope that the rest of his time in South Africa would be as successful as the past had been. He found this particularly gratifying because of the way defamatory allegations had 'been assiduously poured into his ears', a comment revealing just how personally he had taken the comments about his alleged snobbishness and criticism of his actions over Umtali and policy towards the protectorates.[44]

Herbert returned to South Africa in November 1912, much to the relief of de Villiers who as his stand-in had watched with growing dismay as relations between Botha and the outspoken Hertzog deteriorated. A champion of all things Afrikaner and a leading exponent of bi-lingual education, Hertzog's increasingly strident insistence that South Africa should determine its own own international destiny unhampered by ties to Britain, eventually prompted George Leuchars to resign as minister for trade and industry. Failing to get a resignation from Hertzog as well, Botha sent Herbert his own resignation in December. This time Herbert accepted it but indicated that at his next meeting with ministers he would read a statement on their constitutional position pending the appointment of a new administration.

It was intended to be deliberately critical of Hertzog by implying that he had ignored his oath of cabinet confidentiality. If Hertzog was willing to flout that, Herbert reasoned, then he might also be a threat to Imperial security. Hertzog sought to justify himself by insisting that he was a South African rather than an Imperial minister but he had taken an oath of loyalty to the crown. Liking Hertzog as a man, Herbert had little time for his histrionics and also thought him a dreadful administrator. He had found it frustrating that as Minister of Justice Hertzog had agreed that the African witch doctors' practice of 'smelling out' was evil, yet had done nothing to eliminate a tradition involved in about a third of all executions each year. Similarly, he had ignored Herbert's frequent complaints about the excessive delays in carrying out capital sentences. It was not to matter anymore, however, since Botha, invited by Herbert to form another government, omitted both Hertzog and Leuchars from it. Herbert's action raised hackles at the *Cape Times* which claimed that he ought to have asked either Merriman or Sir Thomas Smartt, leader of the Unionists, to form a new administration. For good measure, it dragged up again the Umtali rape case as another example of Lord Gladstone's blunders.[45]

These events could only have added to the vague sense of unease which Herbert's spell of leave seems to have stirred within him. Much as he enjoyed aspects of South Africa, the sport, the outdoor life, the flora and the work he and Dolly were undertaking to develop the gardens around Government House, he clearly missed England. His own household routine was very much that of the respectable Edwardian elite. He was aggrieved, for example, when his niece failed to turn up for morning prayers and then compounded the offence by absenting herself from Sunday church worship.[46] His domestic arrangements represented a little British island in the sea of a culture for which he did not much care and perhaps this was why he so often invited not only family but former colleagues to stay with him. He did not like Dutch cuisine, to which he necessarily had to submit on occasion, describing to Harry the appalling smell of sauerkraut, followed at one meal by coffee so strong that Dolly vomited.[47] Privately he missed the easy access to music, theatre and books, though his siblings tried to keep him well supplied with the latter. Compared with the sophisticated ambience of its English counterpart, he found South African society uninteresting and its standards unrefined.[48] These unsettled feelings were as yet vague and not often articulated, but they were evident in his correspondence, almost explicit in one letter penned to Harry in January 1913. Subject to Dolly's health, he wrote, he anticipated remaining in South Africa until August 1914 but 'I long to be at home again.'[49]

As this letter suggests, Dolly's physical condition was an ongoing worry to him. She was increasingly discomforted by the climate and a minor setback during her return voyage to South Africa prompted Herbert to arrange for her to undergo a thorough medical examination. It revealed scar tissue and other alarming anomalies developing around the site of her recent surgery. He promptly informed Harcourt that she would need to return again to England and that he could now not contemplate any prolonged stay in South Africa for her. Harcourt was astute enough to pick up the unwritten message. He replied immediately that both he and Asquith were keen that he remain as long as possible because he was doing so well in getting the Union established and they could not think who might succeed him. Icing the cake ever more thickly, he enclosed a note from his own permanent Under-Secretary, Sir John Anderson, expressing similar sentiments. If the Liberal Government was ousted and Herbert replaced by an imperialist, Anderson warned, the very existence of the Union would be at risk. Furthermore, it would be unfortunate if Herbert left before arrangements for Swaziland and Rhodesia were finalised. These, Anderson opined, rested largely on personal trust and because Herbert had the confidence of all parties he was more likely than anyone else to bring about their settlement.[50]

Herbert had never been susceptible to flattery and it was symptomatic of his underlying disquiet that in May 1913, after a brief and atypical spat with Botha, he told the prime minister that he intended to resign. It was a genuine misunderstanding. Herbert had secured from Botha a promise that the lavishly appointed railway carriage used by the Duke of Connaught would be made available to ensure optimum comfort for Dolly when travelling on official business. Somehow he got hold of the idea that the coach had been sent to a breaker's yard and in a fit of pique he told Botha that Dolly would not return to South Africa once she left for England on doctors' orders in July and that he himself would leave as soon as Rhodesia's future was settled. Botha ordered an immediate inquiry and apologised handsomely when it transpired that there had been a mix-up and that the Duke's carriage was still available for the Gladstones. A mollified Herbert did not carry out his threat but his reluctance to serve out his full term remained undiminished. When Harry in his usual solicitous way raised the question of what he might do if he did return, Herbert appeared indifferent, saying that he could always get committee work but the real attraction was the prospect of complete freedom. 'I just long for a free year when for the first time in my life I shall be master of my own time & can have 2 months of golf & fishing without interruption. Such a time I have never yet had'.[51]

Nor was it only Union affairs that were absorbing his energies, for when he penned these words to Harry he was in the middle of an ongoing disagreement with the Colonial Office about the protectorates. There had been a meeting of minds with Harcourt as far as Swaziland was concerned when they had discussed it over lunch the previous September. Now early in 1913 the BSA chairman asked the British Government to define the preferential rights his company held on currently unoccupied land in Bechuanaland, since he wished to start its development. Alarmed at the implications of this, Botha promptly opened the question of Bechuanaland's incorporation into the Union. With little appetite for defining the BSA's rather vague claims, the Colonial Office thought to fob Botha off with an assurance that that there was no intention of ceding any land to the company. Herbert had never thought it a good idea to encourage the BSA, fearing that its activities would be detrimental to the indigenous inhabitants. But he did not care either for prevarication, arguing instead that if Botha was happy to hold back, the high commission should be allowed to start a development scheme in Bechuanaland. He had first floated this idea with Harcourt shortly after returning to South Africa in 1912, arguing that the native reserves should be moved immediately in the interests of their current inhabitants and the development potential of the whole region. He was concerned that whenever the Union did take over the Africans would have no security of tenure in the 130,000 square miles they currently occupied. It was prime land that they could not develop themselves, while its location between the Union border and the Crown lands, would inhibit settlement in the latter.[52] The Colonial Office had been lukewarm, challenging his assumptions about the quality of the natives' land and querying how his proposals might be funded. Harcourt was equally dismissive when Herbert resurrected the idea in the spring of 1913, provoking the exasperated retort that the Union was not to take over, the BSA was to be kept out and the Imperial Government was to retain responsibility but do nothing. This, Herbert said, would leave Britain in the role of contractor for an indefinite period when Colonel Panzera, the resident commissioner, was scarcely competent to deal with cobwebs. It was 'neither dignified nor satisfactory'.[53] The officials thought this was too hard on Panzera but they were unaware that Herbert was actually considering charging him formally with maladministration. What perhaps made the Colonial Office position all the more galling to Herbert was that Harcourt had previously approved his development scheme for landlocked Basutoland involving mechanisation, afforestation and water conservation.

Herbert seems to have had a better grasp than the mandarins of the bigger picture. The Union's own small and scattered native reserves were overcrowded and suffering from a serious problem with squatters. He approved of Botha's aspirations to replace them with fewer, larger enclaves with fuller rights for the inhabitants. It therefore made little sense to him that the Union should try to to deal with its own territorial dispositions without taking into account the location and condition of the additional land which would be acquired with the transfer of Bechuanaland. But this longer-term strategic view did not go down well in the Colonial Office from whose standpoint, therefore, Herbert appeared almost cavalier and impulsive. The head of the Dominions department commented disparagingly that the high commissioner apparently thought of transfer as something to be prepared for rather than staved off, while Harcourt told Herbert that a Union request for Bechuanaland would not only be unfavourably received but would bring the whole missionary world down on his head.[54] When London officials suggested that he had failed to understand the objectives of Imperial policy in Bechuanaland, Herbert responded curtly that there was no misunderstanding on his part, he just thought that policy misconceived.[55] He had always agreed with the official view on the time scale for the transfers but not about how the intervening period should be used.

He disagreed with the Colonial Office, too, about the implications of the Union's 1913 Land Act. Civil service thinking was shaped, understandably enough, not by the Union's needs but by Westminster's unwillingness to accept the transfer of any protectorate without the agreement of the African inhabitants. There was little sign of any such consent but there were growing fears that the Land Act, which prevented tribesmen from buying land currently under white occupation, would also be applied to the protectorates when they did finally join the Union. This led to a restatement of Bechuana opposition to any transfer while in Swaziland local leaders set about acquiring as much land as possible outside the reserves before the law could be applied to them. Furthermore, the Colonial Office bureaucrats did not subscribe to the Land Act's underlying principle of segregated land holding and argued that ultimately it would force large numbers of natives off the land. Herbert believed that land segregation was a realistic approach that would allow each society in South Africa to develop at its own pace and in accord with its own traditions.[56] While this might suggest that he was condoning proto-apartheid it is important to stress that there was no hint in his thinking that separation also entailed subordination.[57] His whole wish to reorganise land holding in Bechuanaland in advance of transfer to the Union rested on a conviction that this would provide better protection for the Africans against future exploitation and expropriations by white settlers. For Herbert separate development was pragmatic, not ideological. His aspiration, as he later told the journalist, H.W. Massingham, was that South Africa should not be the white man's but the country of both black and white.[58] He was similarly concerned for the indigenous population in Rhodesia and in opposing the withdrawal of the British garrison from South Africa he averred that it would be tantamount to handing the protectorates over to the Union and abandoning Africans in Rhodesia to the administration, policies 'I will not consent to.'[59] In his final report to Harcourt Herbert re-affirmed his view that it was both right and necessary to encourage separate development, although affirming that this would be best achieved by weight of public opinion rather than the law and with most attention paid to social and economic conditions.[60] Nevertheless, by the time Herbert left South Africa, the Colonial Office had successfully stifled his development efforts and resisted the Union's overtures towards the protectorates, the latter helped perhaps by events in 1913 which underlined the extent to which the Union Government was still dependent on the Imperial power.

In May of that year management at the New Kleinfontein gold mine on the Rand unilaterally announced an alteration in employees' working hours. Claiming that any such change required a month's notice, some men walked out, the rest following suit when blackleg labour was introduced. Negotiations to settle the dispute collapsed when the company refused to reinstate all of the strikers, leaving about 40 out of a job as the specific issue became subsumed by the wider principle of trade union recognition. Unrest quickly spread and by the end of June 18,000 men had stopped work, leaving 63 mines idle. Wary of the potential threat to public order the Union Government drafted in extra police and men from the South African Mounted Rifles. The arrest of a number of the strike leaders further inflamed feelings and a mass meeting was announced for 29 June at Benoni. Notices appeared encouraging supporters to turn up armed and ready to defend themselves. As the responsible minister, Smuts found himself in something of a quandary. Police resources in South Africa were thin on the ground. In an area roughly eight times larger, the ratio of officers to population was about two-thirds of that in England and Wales.[61] The domestic military, the South African Defence Force, had only just been established, authorised by parliamentary act the previous year. New and untested, its effectiveness was uncertain since it contained men speaking different languages and from different military traditions operating under a divided command structure as a safeguard for sectional interests and against a military coup. It would take six days, far too long in the deteriorating circumstances on the Rand, to mobilise 2,500 men, an inadequate number anyway to guard the main population centres in the Transvaal and protect the mines, railways and public buildings. The only other readily available force in the country was the British garrison and it was to its commanding officer, General Hart, that Smuts appealed for assistance on 29 June. Hart immediately ordered 500 men to Johannesburg and readied a further 500 as a reserve. Only then was the governor-general's approval sought.

There was a precedent from Selborne's time for using Imperial troops in support of the civil authority but Herbert was effectively presented with a fait accompli by his chief military officer and a Dominion minister. As with the suffragettes he was torn between his responsibility (albeit in South Africa at one remove) for law and order on the one hand and, on the other, sympathy for the protesters' cause tempered by an intense dislike for extremists whose activities he feared would undermine it. In the rhetoric of some of the

Rand strikers he detected echoes of the syndicalism then widely thought to be behind an international upsurge of industrial unrest, while he had an innate distaste for a trade unionism whose concept of working-class solidarity excluded native workers. But torn or not, he was fully alert to the danger of clashes between strikers and the authorities as well as the possible spread of disaffection to the 250,000 Africans working in the Rand. He also realised that if the railwaymen joined the strike then the deployment of any substantial body of troops would become virtually impossible. He was certainly not minded, therefore, to counter Hart's orders, although he had a low opinion of him and had protested strongly but fruitlessly at the War Office's choice of such an elderly and in his view incompetent officer as Lord Methuen's replacement earlier in 1912. What he did do, however, in sanctioning the use of the British troops was to stress that they must be kept under the control of the civilian authority and avoid confrontation with the public.

But this was not to be. By the time Smuts' instruction to ban another mass meeting planned for Johannesburg on 4 July reached the city's chief magistrate, the crowds were already gathered in Market Square. An appeal to disperse fell on predictably deaf ears and prompted a rather disorganised intervention by the police before the British troops were sent in to clear the area. At this juncture serious rioting, arson and shooting began. The offices of the *Star* newspaper went up in flames, the main railway station was burned and two people died after the soldiers opened fire. Next day even more serious disturbances erupted when strikers assembled outside the Rand Club, a favourite haunt of the mine owners. Numerous casualties, mainly from gunfire, finally acted as the spur to more peaceable counsels and on 7 July Smuts and Botha met the strike leaders and with some reluctance reached a settlement. By 2 August they felt sufficiently confident to recommend that the Imperial forces be withdrawn at the earliest convenience.

When the telegram first requesting their deployment arrived on 30 June, Herbert was virtually alone in Durban apart from his household staff. His ministers were widely dispersed over the country and Hart 'useless except for fighting', leaving Dolly as his only confidante, although he found her advice invaluable.[62] Having telegraphed his agreement to Smuts he left the next morning for Pretoria intending to speak directly with ministers. He maintained constant telegraphic contact with the Colonial Office, explaining his decisions, sending vivid descriptions of the mayhem in Johannesburg, and outlining his own efforts to bring about a resolution which included allowing a deputation of strikers into Government House, a typically courageous act which alarmed his officials because the soldiers guarding the building had no ammunition in their rifles.[63] Herbert did not let his low opinion of Hart be deflected by the soldier's old-world charm but it was the government which earned his severest censure. Perhaps more aware than most South Africans of recent events at Tonypandy in Wales which demonstrated all too vividly what industrial disputes could lead to when the military was utilised, he found it frustrating that the Union ministers were so slow to appreciate the seriousness of what was happening, so apparently unwilling to accept that the men might have a case and so inclined to react to events rather than intervening in a proactive way. Furthermore, he felt that Smuts had blundered in trying to ban the Johannesburg meeting on 4 July. There was, he told Harcourt on 5 July, an

> extraordinary absence of method in facing & dealing with the situation & events as they arise. I have spent hours in urging ministers to be more active & resourceful & to make the public realise they had a Gov't in being wh. is looking not only for the suppression of disorder but for settlement.[64]

The same day he contacted Botha, urging him to press the men and owners alike to accept the help of a third party to settle the dispute and offering to help in any way he could because the government did not seem to have any policies other than repression.[65]

Despite this, in the eyes of organised labour both in South Africa and Britain it was Herbert who emerged as the villain of the piece. He did not doubt that he had done the right thing but he knew his actions would expose him to criticism. As he told Harry

> What has happened here cannot fail to have a distinct effect on my position here & so far as I can see the end will understandably be hastened. A Constitutional GG who is pursued by the bitter & active hostility of a considerable section of the community must lose authority.[66]

From labour's perspective the use of Imperial troops was bad enough but the fatalities provoked uproar. The relevant South African archives contain resolutions from workers' meetings all over the country demanding his recall, although few were as abusive as the attack delivered by a member of the original strike committee.[67] Gladstone, he sneered, was getting a fat living on his father's reputation and was still as thick-headed as he was as a boy. It had, he went on, taken 17 people to design his uniform but still nobody could tell if he were an admiral or a postman. Inevitably, Umtali was resurrected once again, the speaker crudely reminding his listeners that the governor-general had reprieved 'a nigger' convicted of raping a white woman.[68]

Ultimately, the criticism in Britain also descended to personal abuse. In wrongly blaming him for banning the Johannesburg meeting on 4 July, Horatio Bottomley liberally sprinkled the columns of *John Bull* with terms such as 'incredible ineptitude', 'hideous mistake' and 'ghastly blunder', although Herbert's remonstrance did extract an apology of sorts.[69] At the Colonial Office Harcourt was anxious to avoid any impression that British troops had been used to suppress freedom of expression and assembly but neither he nor his officials doubted the propriety or legality of what Herbert had authorised and at Westminster Harcourt defended him as the man on the spot and thus best placed to act. The parliamentary attack was fronted by Hardie and R.B. Outhwaite, recent

Liberal winner of a by-election at Hanley. Neither was deterred by their ignorance of where Herbert's own sympathies lay or of what he had done to encourage a more constructive approach from the Union ministers. Focussing on the issue of the authority by which British forces had been deployed, they suggested, erroneously, that Harcourt had the legal power to overrule the governor-general. In reply he pointed out that the soldiers had been called out under an old and unrepealed Transvaal law which provided the legal basis for the governor-general's action.[70] When Hardie raised the issue again Harcourt delivered a blunt riposte.

> I had no legal, and I am sure that I had no moral right to interfere with the decision of the Union Ministers who are the responsible Government of the country, and of the Governor-General, the principal Imperial officer on the spot.[71]

The Speaker repeatedly disallowed attempts to censure Herbert and when Outhwaite asked the prime minister on 16 July about those rulings Asquith indicated that the House had every right to discuss the use of Imperial troops but only when it had the full information which Gladstone would provide. A week later Herbert's critics were once again rebuffed when they asked if the Transvaal Labour Federation might supply its account of events. Told that only the governor-general's report would be considered, Outhwaite asked if Asquith ever thought 'that Lord Gladstone is deceiving him as to the position on the Rand?' This earned him another reprimand from the Speaker.[72] Hardie returned to the attack on 31 July. Seconding a proposal to reduce the Colonial Office estimates, he noted that the soldiers were entrained before Herbert was asked for their deployment, surely proof that 'it was taken for granted, either from his lack of character, or from an easy-going disposition, that his assent might be assumed.' Herbert's assertion that the strike was unexpected, he concluded, showed how out of touch he was with South African life, for he had acted without making any inquiry and with no knowledge.[73] In fact it was Hardie who was out of touch, and not just with

South Africa. It was all very well to sit securely in the safety of Westminster and pontificate about points of constitutional practice or quasi-philosophical issues about the maintenance of civil order, but Hardie had not been the one facing an immediate and potentially explosive emergency, with very limited forces at his disposal and a quarter of a million Africans looking on. He had not been caught up in the atmosphere of uncertainty and fear that Herbert portrayed so graphically in his daily dispatches. But Harcourt and even a number of Tories pitched in on Herbert's behalf and further vindication came when the official report appeared in October 1913. Colonial Office officials agreed that it fully justified the use of British troops, one adding that the Union ministers had not come out of the affair well, particularly in failing to deal more promptly with the original mines dispute.[74]

That was precisely the view which Herbert himself had taken from the very start. He had been shocked by the ministers' failure to appreciate the imminence of a confrontation, never understanding how it was that the two senior officials in the mines department had both been allowed to take leave just before the crisis broke, and dismayed by the dilatory nature of the official reaction once the strike began. As soon as the immediate emergency was over, therefore, he urged Botha to redress the grievances leading to the dispute. When he had allowed the strikers' deputation into Government House, Herbert had pointed out that wages in the industry were relatively high. But he had readily conceded the validity of the retort that few men lived long enough to enjoy them since the death rate from phthisis was so high. Almost a third of underground workers suffered from the condition and the recently established Phthisis Board had not been able to cope with the number of applications for compensation, even though the levels set were regarded as too low by the men. Herbert had no doubt that failure to address this had contributed significantly to the rapid escalation of the original dispute and his view was that the mine owners should be handled without mercy. The strike had also highlighted the strategic significance of the railways where, Herbert stressed, the mutual lack of trust between men and management also posed a threat to industrial peace. Here, too, he was clear that the owners were culpable, critical of their tendency to manage by threats to wages or pension rights. In the same note he raised doubts about the competence of the relevant ministers, Sauer because he had a tendency to say the wrong things, Malan because he lacked any sense of urgency. Botha did not act on his advice to place the mines under the jurisdiction of a new department of industry but he did move Sauer. He also took up Herbert's recommendation to establish a commission of inquiry into the strike, but ignored his suggested members, instead handing the responsibility to two judges.[75]

Following the 7 July settlement it was agreed that the South African Industrial Federation should draw up a composite list of trade union concerns for government consideration. The list ranged widely, including demands for a minimum wage, indentured apprenticeships, the abolition of piecework in government establishments and the recognition of the railway workers' union. It actually complemented quite neatly the framework Herbert presented to Botha for a more constructive approach to industrial relations, including the establishment of joint committees of employers and workers in all leading industries, an act to make factory inspections more effective, and the creation of a conciliation authority with an arbitration court.[76] Whether it was a sign of growing confidence or an acknowledgement of weakness, the government's actual response to the July strike was to bring forward a number of proposals so harsh that Herbert felt compelled to recommend wholesale changes, especially to the draconian restrictions proposed on the freedom of assembly and expression. He was equally alarmed by Malan's draft factory legislation, suggesting that the inclusion of some clauses taken from equivalent English measures would diminish the likelihood of trouble. Proposals covering industrial disputes he found similarly vexing and he warned the minister that they were unworkable, especially if forced through parliament against the wishes of the majority of working men.[77] As a consequence, the original drafts of measures dealing with industrial disputes, factories and trade unions were all considerably modified. H. Warington Smyth, the senior mines department official primarily responsible for the drafting, was grudging in his acknowledgement of Herbert's input but his sourness probably reflected Herbert's refusal to recommend him for a civil honour. That in turn might reflect Herbert's awareness that Smyth was one of the senior officials who had taken leave just before the Rand strike without giving any intimation to anyone that trouble was brewing.

> Lord Gladstone has really helped with some useful suggestions. I don't like to be ungracious [...] but he has a curious strain of conceit which you bump up against just when you think he is forgetting himself & getting interested. The trouble is his brain does not allow him to become interested in anything – I fear he is the most superficial thinker & he has dreadfully little influence on the Ministers [...] Anyhow I am grateful that Lord Gladstone has really helped us in this case a bit & Ministers have been prepared to listen.[78]

Even with Herbert's moderating influence the legislative proposals still struck Harcourt as too severe although he abandoned his initial thought of having them disallowed, impressed perhaps by his Under-Secretary's scribbled reference on Herbert's dispatch to 'the extraordinary itch to interfere with S. Afr. in regard to purely internal affairs', an indication of how little people understood either of self-government or the peculiar condition of South Africa.[79]

Yet despite his obvious engagement with the Union Government in its efforts to build a viable industrial relations infrastructure and despite the strong official backing he had received both in South Africa and Britain, the inner restlessness was still apparent, if usually concealed beneath a cheery outward demeanour. By the late summer of 1913 Herbert had decided that he definitely did not wish to stay much longer in South Africa. He made this known to Harcourt and in November the colonial secretary wrote to say that he had discussed the matter with Asquith and they had agreed he could leave his post in June 1914 with Sidney Buxton going out as his replacement.[80] Contrary to what was sometimes claimed, therefore, Herbert's decision to leave was his own, not the result of any official censure of his handling of the Rand strike. Nobody in authority in England thought he had acted inappropriately and Herbert himself had made it clear from the outset that his wife's health might prevent him from completing his full five year term. In July she had sailed again for England where London doctors confirmed the local diagnosis of an excitable heart and an over-demanding life in South Africa.

Further confirmation that Herbert's departure owed nothing to any perceived failure in South Africa is provided by the fact that Harcourt raised with him in August the possibility of another appointment, in Ireland. With home rule once more on the government agenda, who better to be the first viceroy under the proposed arrangements than a Gladstone, particularly one with Herbert's sympathies and practical experience of a divided society? But it was not a particularly appealing proposition. Herbert disliked the ceremonial and formalities associated with the role but more off-putting still was the hostility between Orange and Green in Ireland, at the time perhaps more deadly and implacable than the ethnic frictions he encountered in South Africa. Herbert's innate loyalty and his particular sense of duty to the prime minister pulled in the opposite direction so strongly that 'if Asquith asks me to go & wants me to go well I suppose I must go.'[81] It says much for his relationship with Dolly, the trust he placed in her and the priority he accorded to her needs and preferences, that he explored every angle of the move in an extensive but now lost correspondence with her, 40 letters over the five months of her absence, before asking her to thrash the whole thing out with Harcourt and let him know her conclusions. She hardly needed such a volume of writing to know the way her husband was thinking. When she saw Harcourt for tea in September 1913 she made it very clear that he was set on leaving South Africa by the following June.

Harcourt did not press for any further stay and moved the conversation on to Ireland. Dolly was as noncommittal as Herbert but gave Harcourt the impression that she was not totally opposed to the idea, a view subsequently confirmed by a letter from Herbert himself. On that basis the Colonial Secretary told Asquith that a little more prime-ministerial pressure would probably secure Herbert's compliance. Ultimately, however, Herbert's reluctance proved decisive and after further discussions with Asquith, Harcourt told him that he should consider the Irish offer withdrawn as it clearly did not appeal to him.[82] 'It is a relief', was Herbert's comment to Harry.[83]

Relief it may have been but it was short-lived, for the volatile state of local industrial relations, simmering in the background ever since July, soon boiled over into another crisis. The government response to the 1913 strike had included the establishment of an inquiry into working conditions on the railways. But even as the investigation was in progress the railway management board announced a programme of retrenchment. Aware perhaps that Herbert had a low opinion of the industry's managers and frustrated by the slowness of the proceedings, the workers first petitioned the governor-general and then called a strike on 8 January 1914. Minister of Defence Smuts was in no mood to risk a re-run of the previous July and authorised his generals to mobilise the army. On 10 January two union leaders and a Labour Party official were arrested. Following a ballot on 11 January strike action spread and a general stoppage was called for 14 January. Troops had already been manning railway facilities but Smuts now asked Herbert to authorise the declaration of martial law from midnight. This he approved willingly enough, subsequently stressing to Harcourt by way of justification that in the rioting of 4 July, the first fatality had been a photographer killed by a striker's bullet and the second an African stranded in a building burned by rioters, while 88 of the 95 total casualties had been policemen.[84] Whatever the veracity of these statistics, Herbert certainly believed them accurate. Furthermore, he himself had no responsibility for the government's actions following the declaration of martial law in January, the deployment of even more soldiers together with measures banning strikes in public utilities, forcible recruitment by unions and meetings deemed a threat to public peace. More immediately there were widespread arrests, culminating in the deportation of nine strike leaders. Botha did consult about this latter action but all Herbert could constitutionally do was ensure that ministers submitted their deeds to parliament, which they did in the form of an Indemnity Bill endorsing their behaviour, necessary because the deportees had not appeared before a court.

Herbert had suspected syndicalist influence the previous July and this time round, like Smuts, he discerned the same extremism at work in the call for a general strike, a key element in syndicalist ideology. Yet there was a certain ambivalence in his whole attitude. He believed that deportation was justified, but he had doubts as to whether due process had been observed:[85] he was sympathetic to the railwaymen's cause and believed that management was culpable, but he was careful in his official communications to exclude his personal views: he decried what he believed to be a politically motivated strike, but stressed that the men's leaders had been careful in public to discourage violence.[86] Furthermore, he may have told Botha that it was up to the Union forces to deal with any violence that might occur, but that did not prevent him from offering to supply spare rifles to the government forces. Nor did it deter him from ordering Hart on 10 January to prepare to assist with escorting tribesmen back to their homelands. Objecting that his force was too small and that the long distances involved made speedy logistical arrangements impossible, the unimaginative Hart asked that Herbert's orders and his own objections be submitted to the Imperial Government. Herbert refused, replying that the Union Government had already prepared water and food supplies as part of its emergency plan and that his soldiers would be required only if Union troops had to be diverted from the escort duty. But if this made it appear that he was hand in glove with the government, it is important to note what Herbert had told Harcourt but not Botha, that if 'crisis progresses [...] I must reserve my discretion.'[87] What precisely he meant by 'crisis' and 'discretion' in this context is uncertain but in all the discussions which had taken place since 1910 about reducing the size of the Imperial garrison in South Africa, Herbert had always insisted on the need to maintain some military presence in case civil unrest threatened British interests. He was as determined in January 1914 as he had been six months earlier to minimise any threat to civil society and in reserving his discretion he may simply have been keeping open the option of using the British troops quite independently of the Union Government in the event of some major catastrophe.

No such catastrophe occurred. There was no bloodshed and the government's draconian measures effectively and quickly crushed the strike, although the declaration of martial law and the deportations ignited an anger amongst some South Africans that did not quickly subside and which brought electoral benefits for the Labour Party. In Britain there was an equally hostile reaction and much sympathy for the deportees, who received an enthusiastic reception from organised labour when they arrived in Britain. In February, the matter was raised in parliament as well, Ramsay MacDonald seeking an amendment to the King's speech calling for the Indemnity Bill then being discussed by the Union Parliament to be reversed pending a judicial inquiry into the circumstances leading to the declaration of martial law. Once again Herbert came in for some ill-informed criticism but once again Harcourt, despite his own considerable misgivings about the deportations, was supportive. A refusal to sign the declaration of martial law would have led, he said, to Botha's resignation and no other government could have been formed. This was a telling point, given that Hertzog, having resigned from the administration, was threatening the very survival of the Union in its current form by working to establish an Afrikaner National Party. A governor-general, Harcourt further pointed out, was bound to take the advice of his ministers and Gladstone had neither the need nor the time to refer to the colonial secretary, who was in any case in no position to judge the gravity of the situation. Finally, he stressed that constitutionally the role of governor-general was analogous to that of the sovereign and he doubted that any member of the House would want the King to ignore the advice of ministers commanding the confidence of parliament. Hardie was almost apoplectic. If a governor-general was not responsible to Westminster, he demanded to know, then what purpose did he serve? If Gladstone represented the British constitution, he thundered, he should have opposed a government which had violated its every principle. Piling up the conditionals he added that if Gladstone had disagreed with what was being done he should have resigned. He had not done so and thus the House of Commons was being asked to condone one of the greatest violations of British liberty in modern times. His overblown rhetoric did not go down well and the amendment was heavily defeated.[88] Most members seem to have taken the view put, not in the House but in a nutshell, by Lord Methuen. The South African Government had certainly gone too far, he thought, but the outcry in Britain was equally ill-considered because 'in granting self-government to South Africa, we accepted the inevitable consequences of Boer Government, and cannot complain if Boer ideas of dealing with industrial disputes belong to the past.'[89]

Herbert thought Harcourt's speech had reduced the debate to 'a fizzle', but he was acutely aware that Labour might have raised more searching questions about his knowledge of the Union Government's intentions.[90] His official narrative of events, sent to the Colonial Office on 22 January with an insistence that it be published, contained no reference at all to the matter of deportation.[91] Strictly speaking, that was appropriate, for he was not informed officially until 26 January, by which time the men were practically on the ship, which sailed the following day.[92] It is possible that he was ignorant of Smuts's indication to his generals as early as 8 January that deportations were a possibility, but Herbert himself had written to Harcourt the day before saying that H.J. Poutsma, the strikers' main leader, was a bad fellow and ought to be deported.[93] He was also curiously and probably deliberately vague about a discussion with Botha, stressing to Harcourt that in so far as the prime minister had mentioned deportation at all, as governor-general he entered a caveat to the effect that there would be trouble if any such step was taken purely on the grounds that the men were inconvenient to the government, it being be essential to show that they had incited others to violence or had themselves committed criminal acts.[94] His failure to put a precise date to this discussion suggests strongly that when he authorised the declaration of martial law he did know, if not officially, that deportations were in the wind. Although he was not altogether happy, he still signed because he believed they were necessary. Later, when the recriminations had somewhat died down, he reiterated to Harcourt his support for the deportations, adding, however, that had he been in England he would probably have subscribed to the general Liberal view even though it did not at all comprehend the South African perspective.[95] Viewed in one light this might appear to support Hardie's assertion that Herbert had been too weak to oppose the Union Government's actions. Viewed in another, it might suggest that Herbert, ever the pragmatist, fully understood the need to suppress his liberal instincts in the interests of resolving industrial conflict in a unique society which still had the potential to fragment along several different racial fault lines.

If his reputation took another battering, he was content that the strike had ended without bloodshed. But he was furious that in the midst of it news of his impending departure from South Africa leaked out. Harry suggested that the source might have been Margot Asquith (an inveterate gossip) or George Buckle, once of *The Times* and now at work on a biography of Disraeli that was never going to show the Gladstones' father in a favourable light. Discussing the official wording of the announcement with Harcourt, Herbert had been particularly concerned to avoid giving any impression that he was leaving because of the Rand strike. Now he feared that the breaking of the news at this particular moment when he was again at the centre of a labour controversy, might also be interpreted as a sign of official disapproval. Harry thought this unlikely because there existed ample and long-standing documentary support for the official explanation.[96] That may have been so, but Herbert had no wish to see Dolly's medical details exposed to public scrutiny. In the event the agreed formal explanation, 'private and personal reasons', was still open to any number of interpretations.

In the midst of worrying about this and the aftermath of the latest industrial upheaval Herbert was still 'toiling away', as he put it to Harry, 'at the Indian business'. [97] This referred to the government's attempts to deal with tensions arising from the presence in South Africa of migrants from the other side of the Indian Ocean. By the time of the Union Indians were long settled in all four provinces although most heavily concentrated in Natal. Most had entered as indentured labourers to work in the coastal sugar fields and then further north on the coalfields and railways, usually remaining after their indentures expired. From the 1870s onwards their numbers had been further supplemented by an influx of merchants and traders from Gujarat who so flourished that by 1908 they had established their own chamber of commerce in Durban. Outnumbered ten to one, Natal's white community, a third of which was British-born, viewed the Indians as a serious commercial threat and tried to reinforce their own sense of identity both symbolically and administratively. Thus even Durban's new town hall, opened in 1910, was a near-replica of Sir Alfred Thomas's recently completed and rather magnificent building in Belfast. Natal's administration discouraged Indians from remaining, partly by refusing to renew trading licences and partly by imposing a £3 tax on those who failed to leave when their indentures expired. Notwithstanding some dilution under pressure from London and India itself, the colony's laws and culture both remained highly discriminatory against Indians when the Union was established.

Given that Botha had had to form an administration representative of all four constituent colonies, there was always the potential within his cabinet for tension over racial issues between ministers from Natal and those from the relatively liberal Cape, while the more extreme Boers like Hertzog also had strong views on the Indian issue. His main press outlet, the *Friend*, warned in 1911, for example, that there could be no compromise over the £3 tax.

> The Asiatic demand is for full rights, political and otherwise with the European. It is a demand that South Africa cannot concede [...] It would be a thousand times better for South Africa to secede from the British empire at once than to permit the country to be handed over to an alien and coloured race.[98]

Clearly, the government could not ignore an issue about which so many citizens felt so strongly and which had the potential to provoke civil disorder and political friction. It was also under pressure from an anxious London government, in principle at least committed to protect non-white races in its empire and wary of the growing nationalism which threatened to tarnish the imperial crown jewel that was India. Constantly lobbied by the South African British Indian Committee, the Colonial Office was keen to influence South African policy towards the Indian migrants, fearing that if it did not get its say in first, its wishes would be ignored.

In November 1910 Herbert suggested to Smuts that the best way to defuse the issue in South Africa would be to get the Indian Government itself to ban migration to Natal. He reported this conversation to London and the following month he received notification that the Indian Government would introduce such a measure from 1 July 1911 if in return the Union Government would produce standardised and colour-blind entry regulations for the whole of South Africa. In the early months of 1911, therefore, Herbert was keeping London well posted with drafts of the proposed Immigration Bill. It was a minefield of conflicting interests with the OFS demanding safeguards to stop the Indians moving into its territory and Indians in the Cape concerned that their relatively privileged status might disappear. Although he wisely and quite properly avoided getting involved in the detail, Herbert was on constant tenterhooks lest the Indian Government make things worse by commenting on the measure. Eventually the Union Government did manage to get a second reading of the bill but it was far in advance of South African public opinion. Herbert was probably quietly relieved when in April Harcourt accepted that it would be dropped because it had no chance of getting through in the current parliament.

When the government resumed its deliberations the following session, Herbert told Harcourt that the whole business was highly disagreeable, dogged not only by special pleading from individual provinces but also by the general consensus in South Africa that Asiatics should be kept out as far as possible. He did think, however, that the government's latest draft represented a slight improvement, although his optimism was not shared in the Colonial Office where one official likened it to an infant in feeble health which neither the India office nor the Union Government really wanted.[99] London was pressing for the abolition of the £3 tax and a relaxation of proposed rules on polygamous marriages, but Herbert, very much caught in the middle, warned that to push the Union ministers too hard could be counter-productive.[100] In South Africa itself, Labour was opposed on principle to any immigration control, nationalists wanted all Asiatics banned, and hostility to the bill was further stoked up by the fact that as currently drafted there was a possibility that white immigrants might also be excluded. Nevertheless, in compliance with London's wishes Herbert kept nagging away, securing minor changes and warning ministers of the likelihood of unrest in both India and South Africa if no measure was enacted. Yet Botha's colleagues remained as divided as their countrymen and none was particularly enthusiastic. In June he told Herbert that he could not even get wholehearted backing from his own party and that the bill was effectively dead. Smuts was equally pessimistic and while he expressed a hope that the British might now help find a solution, his own ambivalence was all too clear when he made it clear that he was unwilling to hold a November session of parliament for the purpose. A few days later Herbert departed to England on leave.

While Herbert was meeting Harcourt in London, Gopal Krishna Gokhale, a moderate leader in the Indian National Congress, was in South Africa discussing the concerns of the local Indian communities with a number of leading figures. In the process he secured, as he thought, a direct promise from Botha that the laws pertaining to Indians would be more humanely administered and the £3 tax abolished. But Botha was unlikely to have gone that far, fearing that Hertzog would use it as further evidence that the government was too deferential to the British at the expense of Dutch interests. Gokhale's claims therefore alarmed him and when Herbert returned from his extensive leave in November Botha warned him that the Indian leader had been saying foolish things.[101] But as far as the Indian community was concerned, events did not seem to bear out Gokhale's claims anyway because in March 1913 the courts decided that Indian marriages conducted under Islamic or Hindu rites could not be recognised in South Africa because both allowed polygamy. Against this background Fischer produced the latest version of the Immigration Bill.

Herbert met with him early in 1913 and recommended a number of changes which Fischer accepted. In particular, Herbert was disturbed to find that the bill proposed to give the governor-general power to ban the entry into any province of any individual deemed unsuitable to its specific needs. Realising immediately that this would potentially involve direct conflict with the many Indians who were de facto British subjects, Herbert urged Fischer to adopt the mechanism used in the 1905 British Aliens Act by giving such powers to local officials. For the rest, Fischer's draft, instead of merely stating that appeal boards would be set up, fully set out their functions and jurisdictions, removed the requirement for immigrants to complete a dictation test in English, and also omitted direct references to particular racial groups. The Colonial Office thought these changes a

considerable improvement on earlier versions, and readily
agreed to Hebert's request for a telegram of support to
strengthen Fischer's hand. Within South Africa itself,
however, the response remained mixed. It is possible that
some Indians might have accepted the proposed controls had
their own rights to stay been protected, but the absence of any
appeal mechanism in this particular respect gave rise to fears
that ultimately the bill might be used to deprive even
established residents of the right of return if they left the
country. The survival of the £3 tax was also contentious and
behind the scenes Herbert again pushed Botha for its abolition,
warning that its retention might lead to unrest. As for the white
communities, nationalists were unlikely to accept anything but
the most stringent of measures and Herbert conveyed to
Harcourt the views of one parliamentary opponent that the bill
had been 'designed to meet the sentiments of benevolent
people who live somewhere in the neighbourhood of Downing
Street.'[102] But enough of the moderates had been won over to
see the bill through and it received royal assent just before the
Rand strike erupted in July.

It soon became clear, however, that the Union Government, whether intentionally or not, was playing a crafty game.
In August appeal boards were set up for Cape Town, Durban
and Pretoria, each including the provincial chief immigration
officer as one of its three members. Herbert's protest that this
effectively allowed officials to review their own decisions was
in vain. He proved equally impotent when the chair of the
Durban appeal board read a statement from Fischer to
the effect that every Asiatic was undesirable under the test of
the new law. The Indian Government reacted angrily and
while the Colonial Office backed Herbert's protest to his
ministers against what was widely seen as a breach of faith,
the limitations of British influence in the internal affairs of
what was now an independent state were once more all too
apparent and there was little choice but to acquiesce. Botha
claimed, again somewhat disingenuously from Herbert's
perspective, that his government had committed itself to
avoid differentiating between Indians and others only in law

South Africa 203

or in any proclamation issued under the law.[103] His own commitment to racial equality extended only to the white inhabitants of South Africa but even had it been more inclusive he could not in a democracy ignore the strongly held views of the electorate, however limited, on the issue of immigration. Herbert understood this political reality and always felt constrained by his belief that, even yet, no other political leader in South Africa could hold together a stable government. Nor was he entirely devoid himself of the same patronising view that his political peers in London often took towards Indians, and while promising Whitehall that he would do his best for them he also opined that the local Indians were inconsiderate and their demands exorbitant. Perhaps he had in mind here Gokhale's request that a high official from the Indian Government be allowed to go to South Africa to make representations about the administration of the new legislation. Certainly when the Colonial Office raised this possibility with him he opposed it on the grounds that it would be resented by his ministers who had had enough trouble with their own supporters in getting the bill through. The actions of Mohandas Gandhi, the Indian lawyer who had boosted his previously rather localised profile in 1912 by accompanying Gokhale wherever he went, were rather more direct. He accused the government of a breach of trust and started a campaign of passive resistance demanding the abolition of the £3 tax.

In October, when Herbert was still mulling over the possibilities of Ireland, Indian miners in Natal struck work and began trekking into Transvaal. In the following month Indian agricultural workers went on strike, threatening the sugar harvest. Arrests followed and Herbert felt it necessary to apologise to Botha when the British press began to circulate allegations about atrocities perpetrated on imprisoned Indians. In reporting Gandhi's campaign to Harcourt, he stressed that in his view the Union's attempts to maintain order had been very considerate, not perhaps a very powerful endorsement but one prompted by his perpetual fear that the loss of Botha would destabilise government and result in far

more inflamed inter-racial tensions. As one local paper
pointed out, if the government gave in to the Indians there
was always a danger that 'coloureds' would be encouraged to
adopt the same tactics.[104] At this point Herbert received an
unwelcome communication. Sir Charles Hardinge, Viceroy
of India, defied all diplomatic convention by writing to
complain that the imprisoned strikers had been subject to
floggings and incarcerated in the mines, treatment which had
sparked off mass protests in India itself. He demanded that
Herbert urge the South African Government to use civilised
methods in dealing with the strikers.[105] Herbert was so angry
that he replied by return, claiming that statements about
flogging were untrue and strongly deprecating the allegations
being circulated in India. He was still simmering when he
dashed off a further missive the following day. The whole
thing, he protested, was being orchestrated by agitators in
India who were inventing bogus atrocities which the British
press had taken up without bothering to ascertain their
veracity. Certainly, a few mine compounds had been used as
gaols but that was to prevent the Indians being put into
ordinary prisons where the consequential overcrowding
would have made their conditions even worse. As for the £3
tax, it was effectively dead in the water since little effort had
been made to collect it.[106]

Paradoxically Hardinge's claims did provide Herbert with a
legitimate excuse for taking a stronger line with his ministers
than he had hitherto thought advisable. He did not
immediately show Hardinge's communication to them but
he did ask Smuts for a full account of how the Indian prisoners
were being treated. Doubtless mindful of his experience with
the suffragettes when subordinates had sometimes ignored or
misapplied official guidelines, he pressed the minister to see
personally all those who alleged that they had suffered or
knew of ill treatment. In a telegram of 24 November he told
Harcourt that he would resign if the Union Government did
not now formally concede on the £3 tax and also appoint
an impartial commission to investigate the allegations of
mistreatment.[107] Fearing that this might be interpreted as

evidence of differences between the Imperial and Union Governments and bring under public scrutiny an argument that had hitherto been privately conducted, Harcourt warned Herbert off but encouraged the idea of an inquiry. Two days later Hardinge went public in Madras about the South African Indians' treatment, ignoring both the content and the confidentiality of Herbert's telegrams. Botha had to measure his own response carefully, not least to avoid giving Hertzog further cause to claim that his government deferred to Imperial interests. Herbert, however, was on this occasion both decisive and firm. He persuaded the prime minister not to make any public response to Hardinge, told Smuts that his idea of a judicial review was useless and then on 27 November he revealed to the executive council the full contents of his communications with both Hardinge and the Colonial Office, before convincing the ministers to accept a full commission of inquiry chaired by Sir Richard Solomon. Reading the report of all this in the less-frenetic atmosphere of his London office, Harcourt's Under-Secretary, Lord Emmott, thought that the governor-general deserved congratulations for his handling of the situation.[108]

Hardinge, on the other hand, had been very reluctant to accept anything that Herbert told him about affairs in South Africa, claiming as late as December that he was mistaken in thinking the agitation was sourced in India. It was South Africa's Indians who were protesting, demanding only fair treatment, not unrestricted immigration, and they would be satisfied with the abolition of the poll tax and the recognition of de facto monogamous marriages.[109] Whatever the truth of the claims and counter claims about the Indians' treatment, and doubtless there was the usual gap between official accounts and realities on the ground, Herbert's anger was largely driven by Hardinge's impropriety in interfering in the affairs of an independent Dominion. If in a more charitable moment he wondered if Hardinge's equilibrium had been upset by an assassination attempt 12 months earlier, he was still resolved to protest formally if he did not get support from London. He need not have worried, for Hardinge's action

had severely disturbed the smooth waters of imperial
diplomatic convention. Governors-general were in effect
civil servants and not therefore expected to comment publicly
on political matters, certainly not those involving other
countries. The King conveyed his annoyance to Hardinge in a
personal note, influenced possibly by his consort's opinion
that Sir Charles was absurdly pompous with pretensions to
absolutism.[110] The India Office's rebuke to Hardinge was
comparatively mild and for the Colonial Office Harcourt
indicated to Herbert that his reprimand to Hardinge both for
the content and nature of his communications, might be
made known to Botha but not made public.[111]

After further exchanges it was agreed that the Indian
Government should be represented on the commission of
inquiry by Sir Benjamin Robertson, Chief Commissioner of
Central Provinces. Gandhi, whose capacity for changing his
mind and thereby confusing opponents generally exasperated
Smuts, threatened to boycott its meetings and to dissuade
Indian witnesses from giving evidence. Herbert helped Smuts
out, drafting replies to the effect that unless the Indians did
present evidence to support their allegations of mistreatment
the government would conclude that no further action was
necessary. Smuts gratefully adopted this line.[112] Robertson
also proved helpful, not least in conveying to Hardinge the
strength of feeling which existed in South Africa on racial
issues and in proving adept at pinning Gandhi down.
Difficulties over the marriage issue were resolved when Smuts
persuaded himself that South Africa's monogamy laws were
not incompatible with Gandhi's suggestion that where Indians
had plural wives, the status of one be legally recognised with
Muslims not barred from marrying other women. Hardinge
was satisfied with the commission's final report which also went
down relatively well in South Africa where its recommendations were incorporated into draft legislation. The proposed
bill did not give total satisfaction to British Indians but the
key thing from an Imperial point of view was that immigration
would now appear to be controlled but without any
discrimination against British Indians or Asiatics.

It was a pleasing enough outcome but the controversies which surrounded the immigration question certainly added to the trials, both personal and public, which marked the final months of Herbert's time in South Africa. Mary, who had originally gone out to keep him company during Dolly's absence, seems to have rather outstayed her welcome. Herbert was apparently exasperated by her complaint that she had not been appreciated or asked to remain so that they could return to England together in the summer. She was even threatening to stay with the Buxtons so that she could compare establishments.[113] There was also something of a contretemps with Hart who in February received an official intimation that he should retire concurrently with Herbert's departure. Hart interpreted the sudden and unexpected arrival of this as evidence that he was somehow in disgrace. The only explanation he could think of was official dissatisfaction with the part he had played in deploying the troops during the Rand strike. Herbert, too, professed puzzlement since Harcourt had never mentioned Hart's future to him but he must have realised that his offhand criticisms of the soldier's abilities would get around Whitehall. Hart certainly had his suspicions and his correspondence with Herbert dragged on for months, growing every more tetchy on both sides. On top of these personal aggravations, Harcourt decided to publish Herbert's dispatches relating to the 1913 strike. Herbert's initial response was one of weary resignation, although his anticipation that it could mean the end of his active political life did not trouble him unduly because that was what he had been hankering after for some time. He tried to dress things up in rather grander terms for Harry, however. He did not object to publication, he said, since his name was black with labour in South Africa and could not be any blacker at home. 'As to active party work I don't mind at all if I am virtually out of it. But I will not keep in it at the price of hiding away the principles & opinions which have guided my actions here.'[114]

By this time he and Dolly were well into the round of formal events marking his imminent departure. Dinner followed dinner and while much of what was said was little more than the conventional pleasantry of such occasions, there is no reason to doubt the genuineness of Botha's sentiments, for only nine months earlier he had pressed Herbert to take a second term. Privately, both he and Smuts had already expressed gratitude for Herbert's work and regret that their cordial relationships were to cease.[115] At the government's official farewell banquet the prime minister acknowledged that the governor-general had handled difficulties with tact, wisdom, discretion and impartiality. Labour supporters might have quibbled at the last epithet but they had not been privy to Herbert's offstage efforts to improve the measures in which they were particularly interested. Even in the midst of making arrangements to leave, he found time to compile a lengthy commentary on the flaws in the management structure of Africa's railways.

Of course, much else remained to be addressed, as Herbert acknowledged in his final report to Harcourt, particularly with respect to the law and education, but on the whole he thought the government had done well. 'I doubt whether any four years in the records of any Dominion can show any approximation to the politics and material advance of South Africa since Union.'[116] Within the limitations imposed by his own constitutional position, the political reality that only one man could hold the infant country together and without much precedent to guide him, Herbert's actions, advice to ministers, encouragement of Botha and his backstage contributions to legislation did much to ensure that in those first vital years after its establishment the new Union avoided open racial conflict, remained intact within the sphere of British influence and began to build the necessary infrastructure for future economic and social development. That was the legacy Herbert and Dolly left when on 11 July 1914 they once again boarded ship to leave South Africa. They were not to return.

CHAPTER 7

Wars to the Death

When the Gladstones returned to England their expectations did not extend much beyond the private and domestic, although Herbert admitted to a lurking fear that Asquith might still try to entice him to Ireland as Viceroy.[1] The Home Rule Act passed in May had still to receive royal assent and was then suspended when war broke out but in September the prime minister told his confidante, Venetia Stanley, that the idea of appointing Herbert was still in some official minds.[2] After 30 years of public work, however, all Herbert wanted was a house with space for a library and music, enough land for gardening, easy access to a golf course and fishing, with some nearby shooting, a few company director-ships and perhaps a royal commission or two. But like so much else in the summer of 1914 these aspirations perished as part of the collateral damage caused by an assassin's bullet in Sarajevo.

Although as governor-general Herbert had often rep-resented his ministers' concerns to the Foreign Office whenever international treaties bearing on South Africa were being negotiated, his priority had always been the Empire and he had generally discouraged anything that might strengthen Germany's position in the region. As high commissioner he had dealt with occasional flare-ups on the borders between British and German territory, not to mention some rather amateurish efforts by German colonial officials to gather military intelligence. Now as a private citizen he believed that a similarly firm line with the Kaiser offered the best hope of averting war.[3] But by the time he shared this opinion with Almeric Fitzroy the Austrians were already shelling Belgrade. Three days later Germany declared war on France and attacked through neutral Belgium. Within days a flood of tired and frightened Belgians began to wash into Britain's south-eastern ports.

Their plight stirred up philanthropic sympathies among Britain's higher orders including Lady Lugard, wife of the prominent colonial administrator, who immediately set about organising relief and enlisting helpers from among her friends. One of the first to respond was Edith Lyttelton, widow of the Gladstones' cousin Alfred. In turn she brought in others, among them Dolly who immediately offered her husband's services to what soon became the War Refugees Committee (WRC). Its general committee read like a *Who's Who*, with Margot Asquith, Austen and Mrs Chamberlain, the Earl and Countess Grey, Loulou Harcourt's wife, the Labour MP Arthur Henderson and the Salisburys all providing the social clout without which few charitable enterprises could flourish. The actual work was to be undertaken by an executive committee chaired initially by the Tory MP, Hugh Cecil, although it was Herbert who soon emerged as the dominant figure. His prominence owed much to the administrative and political experience which he brought to the table but it also rested on sheer tenacity, for he remained actively involved in the work throughout the war. His long absence from Britain had perhaps left him somewhat disconnected from mainstream public life but here was an obvious outlet when the national emergency roused his always powerful sense of duty.

On 24 August the WRC appealed publicly for help with the Belgian women and children currently arriving in Britain. It was premature and the outcome was mayhem. It resulted in a flood both of refugees and well-meaning volunteers at the committee's Aldwych offices where lack of preparation and the absence of a secretariat rendered it virtually impossible to impose order or accountability. But somehow the committee got on top of the chaos, arranging for refugees to be met from trains, opening a reception centre in premises lent by the India Office, establishing a clothing warehouse, and equipping makeshift residences in Earl's Court and Alexandra Palace, no mean feat when the military was commandeering most large buildings. Given the committee's dependence on voluntary financial donations, Herbert's initial role as treasurer was crucial and by bringing in a professional team he ensured some financial probity and accountability. He was also able to exploit his political connections to secure official help although in the upheavals following the outbreak of war it took almost daily approaches to officials and then a strong letter to the prime minister himself.[4] Eventually the president of the Local Government Board (LGB), now Herbert Samuel, agreed to take responsibility for the refugees' initial reception and temporary shelter with the WRC then providing maintenance and clothing before allocating individuals to accommodation arranged by the numerous local committees spontaneously springing up for the purpose. Herbert promptly closed the committee's offices for a week, hired clerks to sort the files and organised the various activities into separate departments, the most important headed by paid workers and reporting directly to him as chairman of the managing committee. Volunteers remained responsible for clothing and miscellaneous activities such as the education of refugee children with which Dolly became particularly involved. There was nothing of self-aggrandisement in any of this. Herbert had encountered first-hand in South Africa the problems caused by inadequate administrative infrastructures and did not want similar problems hampering the WRC. His often inexperienced amateur colleagues were probably relieved to allow him to assume authority in a process perhaps best described as one of consensual osmosis.

Both the LGB's involvement and Herbert's subsequent reorganisation of the WRC were timely because the German capture of Antwerp and Ostend in October resulted in a massive upsurge in the numbers fleeing the continent. Herbert later reckoned that by the end of 1914 the committee had registered almost 150,000 individuals at Aldwych and allocated 130,000 of them to billets across the country whilst itself leasing residential property and paying £47,000 to hotels in room rentals.[5] As in his other public roles, the minute books show his considerable personal engagement even in quite minor matters concerning individual refugees, over and above the chairing of thrice-weekly management meetings. A brief letter dashed off to Agnes at the end of October indicates that both he and Dolly had been hard at it for ten weeks and had had only three Sundays off in that time.[6] Nor did the pressure show much sign of easing. With gifts of clothing tailing off he arranged for the post office and the railway companies to make up the shortfall by supplying appropriate items from uncollected parcels, but this, too, soon proved inadequate. Even more serious was the decline in cash donations as the war began to squeeze disposable incomes, leaving the numerous relief charities to chase a shrinking resource pool. Herbert was particularly exercised that money intended for the WRC's work in Britain was often misdirected to the Belgian Relief Committee established to provide relief *within* Belgium itself and relations between the two bodies remained strained for some time. With the coffers almost empty Herbert asked for another meeting with Samuel. In January 1915 the LGB itself took on the subsistence costs of the refugees processed by the WRC although Samuel required this fact, in an arrangement referred to as the screen, to be kept confidential so as to preserve the public belief that the WRC was financially responsible. In this way he hoped to minimise any further drop in voluntary contributions and also to prevent the rush of funding applications from local refugee committees that would inevitably follow if it was known that the state was paying. It had the further advantage that any criticism of refugee relief would be directed at a private body rather than government. The agreement also sanctioned the establishment of a Private Relief Fund (PRF) for refugees hitherto living off their own resources but which were now exhausted. Herbert himself sorted out the necessary organisational arrangements for the PRF which eventually occupied almost a quarter of the WRC's total staff, but again it proved impossible to sustain this work from voluntary donations. Samuel agreed to pick up this bill as well, at about the same time also authorising a clothing subsidy for the refugees. With its commitment mushrooming, the LGB deemed it prudent to install one of its own officials in Aldwych to oversee the WRC's financial affairs. Setting all this in place was so time-consuming that in February Herbert calculated that he had been absent from the office for only eight working days since 23 August, adding that Dolly was finding the work very tiring.[7] Even so, he was more than content. The new arrangements gave his committee access to public funds whilst the LGB's insistence on secrecy actually handed him a powerful bargaining tool in any future negotiation.

As the flow of incomers began to ease after its initial surge, so the emphasis of WRC work shifted progressively towards the education of children and jobs for the adults. A new employment department was set up in the spring of 1915, although the LGB once again insisted on having representation in order to satisfy the Treasury that expenditure was appropriately supervised. It was not always easy to convince the WRC's volunteers, all unaccountable and in a few cases dishonest, of the need to observe civil service standards and protocols. Lady Lugard proved particularly difficult. Determined to cater primarily for wealthier refugees by providing hostels with all the trappings of gentrification, including servants, she eventually broke away to establish her own committee and later attempts by the LGB to reintegrate her organisation into the WRC caused endless problems for Herbert in trying to impose some financial discipline upon her activities.

But Lady Lugard at least realised the value of a good press. Herbert took longer to catch on with the result that the WRC initially did not always deal very effectively with the popular newspapers' sensationalist claims about deserting soldiers and spies disguising themselves as refugees, WRC residential facilities attracting prostitutes and other criminals, overly generous relief scales and donated clothing being pawned. Such stories were clearly damaging to an organisation dependent, if to a diminishing degree, upon charitable giving. On top of this, the initial goodwill shown to the refugees by their hosts began to evaporate. Walloon and Flemish differences sometimes created unwelcome tensions within refugee communities while both were often separated from their hosts by a language barrier. Religious and cultural diversities also became apparent, especially in overcrowded private homes, Cecil Harmsworth noting that while his own family had been lucky with their refugee, many of those 'taken hospitably into English homes were terrors'.[8] As the Belgians became more settled, there were also growing complaints about their taking British jobs or simply malingering, the latter arising mainly because for some time the minimum call-up age for Belgian men remained higher than that for their British peers. Instances of localised rioting further encouraged elements in the yellow press to pander to populist anti-foreign sentiment.

Herbert found all this irritating but generally manageable: his over-riding concern remained finance. Samuel was replaced at the LGB by Walter Long in May 1915, but he was briefly allowed to retain responsibility for refugees. It was to him, therefore, that Herbert turned again for help the following October. Herbert's progressive replacement of volunteers with paid staff had by now resulted in a weekly wage bill of some £425, in addition to which the committee had to find a substantial sum for rents. After consulting the Treasury, Samuel agreed to fund the WRC's staffing and general organisational expenses from 1 November 1915. The price was a further tightening of control on the scales of relief the committee was able to provide. An unanticipated consequence was that the WRC's paid workers were now deemed to be government employees and as such entitled to receive the war

bonus supplement. Herbert fought tenaciously and successfully with the Treasury to get it. He agitated equally vigorously
to secure equal pay for his female workers, although on this
issue he had to concede defeat.

He fared rather better when he went back to the LGB with
his begging bowl in January 1916, this time securing a
commitment to cover all the office expenses apart from rent,
rates and taxes. But having by now assumed virtually the
entire cost of the WRC, the government's natural expectation
that in return it should have more control led to friction.
Herbert believed the politicians realised that only his
committee had the appropriate experience and skill to care
for refugees but he disliked the bureaucratic mindset and
feared its growing influence. 'I am not going to be run by the
LGB but they know *they* cannot run Aldwych', he told Harry
in October 1915.[9] Yet Walter Long appeared determined to
try. Initially appearing content to leave well alone, in the
spring of 1916 he set up a committee of inquiry headed by the
Duke of Norfolk and aware that the government's financial
support for the WRC was by now widely known, he proposed
to abandon the screen and establish an alternative management structure which he could control. He wanted all
financial affairs to be handled by LGB officials and a
reorganisation into four departments whose heads would co-
ordinate policy through regular meetings with Basil Peto, his
own newly appointed commissioner for refugees. Much to
Herbert's disgust Algy Maudslay, who had been the WRC's
chief officer almost from the start, was to be demoted to lead
one of the four proposed departments. Nor did Herbert
welcome Peto's involvement, fearing that a man who had
served on the Norfolk Committee and who lacked any
personal experience of dealing with refugees would be unduly
influenced by the ethos of the LGB which held that recipients
of government aid were the dregs of society and thus treated
them meanly and uniformly. Herbert thought such an
approach entirely inappropriate to foreign refugees who
deserved generous and individual consideration. With some
feeling he complained to Harry that the essence of hospitality

had gone, the committee's work now simply reduced to business maintenance.[10] He had no intention of giving in meekly, however, but rather than oppose Long outright he suggested that the minister's objectives could be more easily attained by simply adding Peto to the existing management committee. The less than astute Long agreed. Once in place, however, Peto, an inexperienced lightweight and lacking tact, proved no match for Herbert. His responsibilities were somewhat ill-defined anyway and although the minute books suggest that he tried to assume many of the duties Herbert had been undertaking since 1914, Herbert was still in the chair and had the backing of his colleagues. The somewhat uneven contest lasted until early the following year by which time Long had gone from the LGB as part of government restructuring when Lloyd George replaced Asquith as prime minister. Long's replacement, Lord Rhondda, initially proposed that Peto chair a new committee to replace the existing management structure. Confident of his ground Herbert told him that this was just unacceptable and shortly afterwards it was announced that Peto had resigned. Herbert derived considerable satisfaction from this victory, and it certainly appeared to confirm that both he and the WRC were viewed as indispensable when it came to refugee relief. When a critical official report on the committee's work appeared in February 1918 he was haughtily dismissive. 'We who are familiar with the intricacy of Belgian Refugee affairs and who have been in it up to the neck from the first reject this not very formidable and really paltry attack on our work.'[11] In slightly less pompous tones he later conceded that the LGB officials had been excellent but still stressed that they had come in only after 'the main troubles & responsibility had been worried through'.[12]

With external bureaucratic intervention effectively if somewhat frostily contained, routines well established and structures generally working smoothly, Herbert reduced the frequency of the committee's regular meetings in 1917 and even began to consider what might happen after the war. He envisaged that having dealt with the initial emergency and then overseen the generally successful settlement of almost a quarter of a million Belgians, the WRC would be central in the repatriation process. Officialdom, however, did not share that view. Only belatedly did the government add a WRC representative to the committee it established in October 1916 to plan for repatriation, adding insult to injury by later appointing Peto as the repatriation commissioner. Tactless as ever, Peto issued a press notice to all refugees in October 1918 without even consulting Aldwych, prompting a sharp and decisive reaction from Herbert. 'It is quite clear that the little man wishes to run repatriation exclusively', he told Maudslay. 'That being so it wd. be bad policy to continue our existence & seek for crumbs of work.'[13] On 31 December 1918, therefore, the WRC formally ceased to exist. A final executive meeting was held the following May at which Herbert's unstinting contribution was unanimously acknowledged in word and more tangibly in a book of illuminated pages. As he pointed out, however, he had not worked alone, a remark which sparked off such a round of mutual back-patting that eventually it was agreed to terminate the meeting before everyone had thanked and congratulated everybody else. But the self-satisfaction was not unwarranted. Government eventually provided most of the money but it was Herbert's indefatigable leadership, strong sense of patriotism and underlying humanity that continually energised and inspired the committee in finding and organising staff, devising processes and offering assistance to those caught up in the largest and most urgent immigration crisis in the country's history. Government acknowledgement duly came in the form of civic honours, typically for four members of the committee and only one of its workers.

Four years of the WRC proved physically and mentally demanding for Herbert and if Dolly's was a lesser role she had also been looking after South African nurses in England and France. The Gladstones' work required a regular presence in London but their main residence in Cleveland Square cost £600 a year to run, and in the absence of either a salary or a pension it proved difficult to maintain their life style without eating into capital. Disposing of Cleveland Square never crossed Herbert's mind simply because his wife loved it so much but other assets had to go. He sold his car, his seaside cottage at Littlestone and in 1916 his other London property in Buckingham Gate. Added to a handsome cheque from Harry the proceeds financed a move to Dane End, a Hertfordshire property owned by Dolly's widowed mother. Five or so miles from the nearest station at Ware, it was then something of a rural fastness but not too far from a golf course, while a nearby tributary of the River Lea offered good fishing. The restoration of the long-neglected gardens and house and the acquisition of appropriate furniture afforded some occasional respite from the WRC but would not have been possible without Harry. He had always intended to help Herbert when his official duties in South Africa ended and another generous cheque, the first, he said, of what would be an annual gift left his brother 'all of a heap'.[14] But rising prices and higher taxes almost doubled Dane End's running costs by the time the war ended, leaving Herbert to contemplate attending only shoots which were accessible on foot and abandoning golf altogether. He had not benefitted financially from his time in South Africa where, as his record of sustained and generous giving to a variety of good causes suggests, he had fully honoured his intention to devote his official income to local benefit.[15] While the odd company directorship did come his way after the war, it was again Harry who provided the financial lifeline, his £500 Christmas gift in 1920 enabling Herbert to create his library and to begin developing his land. Over the next few years he and Dolly gave themselves with obvious enjoyment to installing poultry pens, putting in a well and pump, planting trees and building walls and apple racks. The regular and substantial gifts from Harry also helped him acquire a new car and in 1925 reversion on the Dane End property from Lady Paget.

Business success allowed Harry to be generous to all his siblings but he felt a special affinity for Herbert, believing that he should not lose out for having maintained their father's legacy by following him into a financially unrewarding public

career. Arguably, Harry's was the most powerful voice among
the trustees of the Gladstone Memorial Fund, the energy
behind the memorials in Hawarden village and the parish
church, and the inspiration behind the Gladstone Library at
St Deiniol's and the Gladstone studentship, all vehicles for
preserving the father's memory and values. But Herbert
certainly shared that same desire and by helping to relieve him
of financial anxiety Harry hoped to free him to concentrate on
another important means of achieving it. As the refugee work
became less time-consuming, so he began urging Herbert to
sort through their father's vast collection of papers with the dual
purpose of deciding what could safely be put into the public
domain and then preparing it for publication.

When W.E. Gladstone died in 1898 his oldest son, who
had inherited Hawarden Castle from Sir Stephen Glynne,
had predeceased him. Responsibility for the estate and the old
man's papers passed to his grandson, Will, whose uncles
Stephen, Herbert and Harry, had jointly acted as trustees
until he reached his majority in 1906. Five years later he
became the fourth generation of the family to enter
parliament where, it was widely assumed, he would pick up
the family mantle. Despite his very vocal opposition to
Britain's involvement he refused the offer of a non-
combatant role at the War Office when war broke out in
1914 and opted for the battlefield instead. He was hardly
in the front line before a bullet from a German sniper hit him
in the head. Apart from a badly shot-up brother-in-law, Will's
death in 1915 was Herbert's closest personal encounter with
the terrible realities of the conflict. Although Stephen also was
later to lose a son, Will's loss was particularly cruel for
Herbert who had perhaps found in his nephew a surrogate for
the child Dolly had been unable to bear. At his sister-in-law's
request he willingly undertook to write a memoir although
pressure of work delayed its completion for three years. It was
a well-constructed volume, neither maudlin nor piteous
although tending to suggest that its subject's every trait was
exemplary and his every action duty-driven.[16] Virtually the
whole print run of 1590 sold within a year and it was well

received by the reviewers, although only one was perceptive enough to notice that in demonstrating how Will's character had compensated for a lack of intellect and energy, something of Herbert himself had crept into the text.[17] In agreeing to Harry's suggestion with respect to their father's papers Herbert certainly conceded that while he could write rubbish quickly, complex matters took longer because he was no intellectual.[18] Either way, Harry's promptings assumed a greater urgency in the light of Will's death, which had effectively put the chief responsibility for preserving the family legacy back into his uncles' hands.

After discussing a number of options the brothers agreed that the best starting point was their father's diaries. Herbert started working on them in March 1917 and by August his working day had fallen into a steady rhythm, five to six hours each on business, writing and physical labour. Over the following 18 months he read more than half the 41 volumes. As he progressed, however, he began to appreciate that publicising them would be problematic. Introspective and self-accusatory passages, accounts of spiritual misgivings and confessions of human weakness so often connected to the opposite sex constituted what Herbert described somewhat enigmatically as a 'difficulty which will continue increasingly'.[19] He censored them so heavily that his typescript version reduced the bulk by about a third. Whether or not he understood the precise meaning of the symbols his father generally used to denote instances of sexual temptation or self-flagellation is not clear but he certainly grasped their significance. For this reason the brothers ultimately decided that the diaries should not be put into the public domain but handed for safe-keeping to the Archbishop of Canterbury.

There is no doubt that Herbert's long engagement with his father's private reflections on both political and personal matters served to point up for him the contrast between past and present moralities, in particular the integrity of his father's private anguish in struggling with his own humanity as against the apparently shameless philandering and the dubious political practices of the current prime minister.

His growing distaste for Lloyd George had little to do with the controversial circumstances of his accession to the premiership, which Herbert was inclined to attribute to Asquith's inadequacies rather than his successor's ambition. It rested both on the latter's subsequent policies and behaviour, Herbert believing Lloyd George's shameless use of the honours list for political purposes to be the very antithesis of his father's principles and integrity.[20] His antipathy ran deep. When a filmmaker asked in 1918 to use Hawarden Castle as the backdrop for a shot of Lloyd George purportedly talking to W.E. Gladstone in the 1890s, Herbert refused partly because it imputed to Lloyd George an importance he did not then have, partly because it would imply that he was Gladstone's political heir, but mainly because to his father the prime minister's 'methods and the absence of principle in his changing and most adaptable views would have been Anathema Maranatha'.[21] 'The Welsh goat', he commented on another occasion, 'only has principles when it suits him & this makes his really great qualities the more dangerous.'[22]

By the time Herbert made this judgement the country was in the throes of a postwar general election which produced a massive majority for Lloyd George's Liberal-Unionist coalition. Lacking the coalition's 'coupon' of endorsement, Asquith's remaining supporters were almost annihilated, forming themselves into a small Independent Liberal Party, led in parliament by Donald Maclean because Asquith himself lost his seat. Although Herbert accepted that his old leader's lack of enthusiasm and energy compared unfavourably with Lloyd George's dynamism, he attributed his electoral defeat primarily to the fact that he had been outwitted by less scrupulous people.

LG I utterly distrust so far as his methods are concerned but he has the eye of a leader with unbounded energy & the power to sacrifice his own comfort & to make people feel he is a real live man bent on action. I have a good affection for HHA but if he cd.not hold the party when in Gov't. power how can he pick up the remnants from the dust?[23]

Harry was equally disturbed by Lloyd George's triumph and suggested more than once that Herbert consider returning to active politics to provide the Independents, who still controlled the official party organisation, with some much-needed experience. Although Herbert's invitation to join the Speaker's Conference on Devolution was already drawing him back into public life, he was unsure of how exactly he might re-engage with party politics. 'So you want me to emerge again into active fighting politics!', he wrote to Harry. 'We will talk it over. If I had a quick clear brain it wd be simple enough so far as the effort is concerned. But bitter experience has taught me that for parliamentary effect I am of no use.'[24] Following this exchange both added their signatures to those of other leading Liberals on a public statement supporting Asquith's candidacy at the Paisley by-election in February 1920. At a pre-election party Herbert did his best to give Harry credit for this document since it had been his idea, but some of the guests thought they detected the hand of the former whip. Margot Asquith, whose views on Lloyd George's 'indescribably corrupt & wrong' financial goings on tallied exactly with those of both the Gladstones, was both enthusiastic and grateful.[25]

But if Herbert was willing to test the political water again he was cautious and determined to stay within his depth. His only politics, he told Harry in the summer of 1920, were those of practical administration and 'if I take any new line it will be in the L(eague) of N(ations) to wh. I am devoted.'[26] His enthusiasm for the League was shared by many other Liberals but inevitably also drew him towards one of its main architects, the Unionist free-trader, Lord Robert Cecil, especially as Dolly, herself emerging as a central figure in the League of Nations Union, had Cecil's confidence. Harry, too, had high hopes for the League and believed that Cecil also shared the values championed by W.E. Gladstone. With Lloyd George's repressive policy in Ireland, his foreign policy and his extravagance all seeming to discard fundamental Liberal principles, Harry suggested in March 1920 and not for the first time that an alliance of Asquith, Cecil and

Edward Grey, together with moderate Labour leaders like
J.R. Clynes, might represent a viable alternative to the
government.[27] So it might but it would need effective
organisational underpinning and the Independent Liberals'
election machinery was far too run-down to provide it. In July
Maclean asked Herbert to join the committee responsible for
its operation but after consulting with Hudson, still at party
headquarters, Herbert came to the conclusion that it was a
hopeless vehicle for political regeneration. In his opinion a
successful party needed two things. The first was a strong
leader in the House of Commons and although Asquith had
won Paisley Herbert worried about his apparent disinclina-
tion to assert himself or take command. The second was a
capable organiser and he believed that Geoffrey Howard,
currently responsible for fund raising and the constituencies,
was simply not up to the task.[28] Hudson himself had not been
particularly happy with the rather ramshackle arrangements
made after the debacle of the 1918 election and following
his discussion with Herbert he put another proposition to
Maclean.[29] After a long delay Herbert, Hudson, Howard,
Maclean, Harcourt and others met at Crewe's house on 15
December to consider this, subsequently going on to discuss
what Herbert rather coyly described as central things 'not to
be committed to paper', by which he meant an approach to
Grey and Cecil.[30]

Maclean had in fact already approached Cecil, reporting
that he probably outdid many Liberals in his dislike of Lloyd
George but did not consider Asquith a viable alternative.
Encouragingly, he did agree that it was desirable to involve
Grey although subsequently he expressed doubts about his
willingness to resume active political life.[31] Nevertheless, in
April 1921 Herbert dined with Arthur Murray, formerly
Grey's private parliamentary secretary, Hudson and Lord
Cowdray, one of the party's most generous financial backers,
to consider how best to bring Grey in. Conscious that in 1906
Grey had initially resisted efforts to get him into government,
Herbert readily accepted Murray's point that any approach
had to be made with great delicacy and could come only from

Asquith as current leader. This was conveyed to Asquith by one of his own close allies, the scholar Gilbert Murray another enthusiastic supporter of the League of Nations.[32] Murray duly reported back that Asquith had particularly stressed the importance of cooperating with Labour and rejected all suggestions except Grey as a potential prime minister.[33] Asquith, however, hesitated in making the desired approach to Grey perhaps because at a meeting the previous October Grey had told him that he did not want to re-enter politics. Apparently unaware of that meeting and fretting at the hiatus, Herbert blamed it on Howard's lukewarm support for the plan. By mid-June he was pressing the need for urgency on Gilbert Murray, while Cowdray was threatening to withhold further financial support unless the desired developments occurred. Finally, on 29 June, Asquith met privately with Grey. They discussed potential collaboration with Cecil and Grey's health problems. That done, Asquith indicated that he would arrange a further meeting with other colleagues.

Two days later Cecil drafted a letter for Asquith to sign, formally inviting Grey back into public life. Herbert thought this a positive step but having read the draft, Asquith told Crewe that he did not think Grey would accept and that he doubted whether the party rank and file would welcome the plan anyway. Certainly, those who thought the unacceptable policies of the existing government arose from the very fact that it was a coalition could see little point in an alliance with Cecil and Labour which merely offered the country an alternative coalition. Crewe thought that if Grey did come back it would be more out of duty than inclination and Grey certainly appeared less than wholehearted. In August he first told the Liberal leaders that his failing eyesight would not allow him to take up the work for any length of time and when it was indicated that this could be made clear to the public from the outset, he shifted tack, saying that his main reason for considering any involvement at all had been the current situation in Ireland, but that it was now on the verge of resolution.[34]

Lacking any official position, Herbert was not involved in any of the meetings organised by Asquith in early August, and although Maclean kept him posted the lack of progress rankled and he told Harry that the Asquith-Howard menage was beneath contempt for wasting months of valuable time.[35] He was rather more tactful when he decided to acquaint Asquith directly with his views on the current state of the party. Howard, he opined, was a good man but self-centered, lacking imagination and not understanding man-management. Having talked things over with Maclean, he went on, he believed the headquarters situation was quite impossible and that a triumvirate of Asquith himself, Grey and Cecil, backed by a drastically revamped party organisation, could best provide the unity needed with an election pending.[36] Apparently unaware of the extent of Herbert's background involvement, Asquith replied that he had already met with Cecil and other Liberal leaders including Grey. But Herbert's doubts about Asquith's appetite for the struggle ahead only increased when he learned that he had also met with Hudson but had signally failed to discuss party organisation with him. Harry was equally astonished, suggesting that Asquith must be mad not to have had that conversation.[37]

Nevertheless, on 6 December 1921, Asquith joined Herbert, Maclean and Hudson to discuss organisational matters and over dinner it seems that Asquith was now made aware of the scheme which the others had already discussed 12 months ago. The outcome was an agreement that Herbert should take sole charge of Liberal organisation, now in Abingdon Street, until the next election. As the talk shifted onto the matter of leadership Herbert concluded that while Asquith appeared willing to work in the triumvirate he would still not commit to it either publicly or privately until he was certain it would lead to the desired result, hence his continued prevarication in extending any formal invitation to Grey.[38] Yet such a gesture was essential, Herbert believed, first because Cecil would serve only under Grey, second because Grey himself was anxious to avoid any hint of disloyalty to the party's current leader and third because it was the only way to avoid the impression of an intrigue against Asquith. Asquith still seemed to believe that Grey's health would prevent him becoming involved but this did not tally with what Herbert had gleaned from Grey's friends or indeed from Grey himself when he dined with the Gladstones on 15 December. Cowdray, Hudson, Maclean and Walter Runciman were also present and Grey agreed to cooperate on condition that Asquith pressed him in the right terms. Herbert was commissioned to inform Asquith immediately, reiterating that he was to remain as party leader whilst guiding the country to make the proper inference that Grey would ultimately be the next prime minister.[39] Cowdray thought this a very positive step and attributed it to Herbert's skill in handling things. He backed his words with cash too, offering £20,000 to Abingdon Street, and £5,000 for Cecil to establish some organisation of his own.[40]

Maclean reckoned that the whole party was fired up by the news of Herbert's return to Liberal headquarters and John Simon, viewed by some as a future leader, was among those who wrote supportively. Herbert even allowed himself the conceit that his return might do some good. As for the leadership, he thought that while the proposed combination might not galvanise party supporters or voters it was the best that could be achieved. Among Liberals he detected an almost universal opposition to Asquith becoming prime minister again and felt that the party's electoral appeal could best be enhanced by indicating that the next prime minister would be a trusted man with an unsullied reputation and who could appeal to the country on great principles.[41] But to offer this as a viable alternative to Lloyd George, candidates and money were essential and these were his priorities as he picked up the reins at Abingdon Street again. But in demanding and getting sole control of affairs and the resumption of regular meetings of the party leaders, he had committed himself to spending half a week in London. That effectively scuppered his intention to let out his London house which would in any case be needed for private meetings. Reluctant to ask Maclean for party money to compensate for the forfeited rent, he turned to Harry who promptly obliged by providing £500 and offering to throw in an additional £100 for entertainment expenses.

For Herbert the whole situation must have seemed akin to that of 20 years before. He was back at the heart of party organisation, in harness with Hudson, meeting with potential candidates and negotiating to bring in a reluctant Edward Grey. The context was not dissimilar either in that the loyalties of party supporters were torn between two rival leaders and a note Herbert sent to Runciman in January 1922 might equally well have been written in 1905. In pointing out that he held too many strings to speak his own mind he stressed that his main tasks were stirring up the electorate and getting the leading men into harmony.[42] True, Rosebery had been no Lloyd George as far as political ambition was concerned but his manoeuvrings had been as baffling and random as Lloyd George's now sometimes appeared, while Asquith's apparent diffidence in the 1920s mirrored that of Campbell-Bannerman before 1906 and annoyed Herbert in equal measure. Thanking Harry for his latest financial help he confessed that he was not looking forward to his next meeting with the party leader because he intended to press him for the public statement about Grey and Cecil.[43] To prepare his ground he wrote to Asquith setting out the plan's rationale, stressing that its main objective was to defeat Lloyd George. Conceding that an attack by Asquith on the prime minister might be seen as personally motivated, he reiterated his conviction that the Independents would rally to Grey, that Cecil's involvement would attract the League of Nations enthusiasts, and that both men would broaden the party's appeal to Labour. The key thing, however, was that the inclusion of Grey and Cecil must be proposed by Asquith himself.[44] Asquith, however, had already confided in Maclean that he thought Herbert was 'entrenched' and after a tough 90 minutes Herbert noted mysteriously that he had not got all he hoped for.[45]

Nevertheless he presided at the public meeting on 23 January 1922 which saw Grey and Asquith share a platform to announce their collaboration, an event which Gilbert Murray attributed solely to Herbert's backstage manoeuvrings. Herbert himself was so encouraged that he responded bullishly to calls for a new Lib-Lab electoral alliance, suggesting that it was up to Labour to take the initiative since it was now no longer a matter of Asquith and a rump: rather there was a genuine prospect of a Liberal Government led by Grey and supported by Cecil.[46] His optimism that Lloyd George could be ousted was further boosted when in February an Asquithite won the Bodmin by-election. Herbert found it difficult to see how the prime minister or his supporters, rebranded in January as National Liberals, could return with any honour to the official Liberal camp. Not only did he dislike Lloyd George's current policies but he thought his use of the 'coupon' in the 1918 election a contravention of Liberal principles of free speech and private judgement.[47] He was also disgusted by the prime minister's abuse of the honours system, as he made clear to the royal commission on the matter which the growing weight of public concern forced Lloyd George to set up in the summer. 'If a Prime Minister cannot be trusted to act upon his responsibility in this connection, can he be trusted at all?', was Herbert's question.[48] Yet his determination to remove Lloyd George seems to have blinded him to flaws in the Independent Liberal plan which over the next few months began to unravel.

For one thing, while even Lloyd George himself admitted to a sneaking admiration for Grey, there lingered, especially among those Liberals who had actually served in the war, a suspicion about the former foreign secretary's secret pre-war diplomacy which had committed Britain to the fight. Herbert certainly thought this a plausible explanation for his own difficulty in attracting young people into the party.[49] Christopher Addison, a sometime Liberal minister in the Coalition Government, made a similar sort of point in observing that the postwar generation would not want to return to the methods associated with Asquith.[50] Also, while the Independent Liberals might protest that Lloyd George had effectively purchased much of his political support, they overlooked the fact that his radical policies had a genuine popular appeal. C.P. Scott was quite right in reminding Herbert that not all party members were enthused by the developments outlined at the 23 January public meeting and that the advanced section needed to be won over as well.[51] This might have been less compelling had the Independents themselves had a distinct policy platform from which to work but apart from commitments to free trade and the League of Nations their ideas were generally ill-defined. A meeting in July 1922 to thrash out policy made little progress, Herbert noting that nothing was agreed about significant issues such as nationalisation, rent restrictions, housing, House of Lords reform or a whole host of labour-related matters.[52]

Then there were the difficulties involved in revitalising a party machine that had atrophied over the years and was markedly inferior to those of other parties. Relationships between the NLF and the LCA were vague and their competition for personnel and funds wasteful. What money there was in the party coffers was dribbling away and needed to be replenished. Yet some of the wealthy individuals on whom the party had previously depended had been impoverished by the war while others had thrown in their lot with Lloyd George. Harry and a few others like Cowdray and the Runcimans could still be relied upon but times had changed. As Mckenna pointed out, Herbert's proposed general appeal for money was unlikely to succeed, partly because few saw much prospect of a Liberal election victory, but mainly because Lloyd George's exploitation of the honours system had produced a culture in which most potential donors now expected a reward.[53] Finally, Herbert's own absence from domestic politics since 1910 meant that he knew relatively little about many sitting or potential members, though he rapidly concluded that good candidates were in short supply because Howard's judgements had been so unsound. A further complication was that despite the January meeting, there still remained a general uncertainty as to who might be prime minister in any future Liberal administration.

These underlying problems were abruptly compounded in March 1922 when Grey was diagnosed with a kidney stone, for which the prescribed treatment was surgery with a second operation to follow eight months later, or radio-active water in May. Either way, he was effectively out of action. This was a severe setback, for while Asquith was friendly enough and certainly doing his share of public speaking Herbert thought him lacking in both energy and ideas. It took half-a-dozen letters to get him to do anything, he told Harry, and phrases like 'we have to carry him', 'a dead weight' and 'the negation of victory' punctuated his private correspondence at this time.[54] Grey's incapacity also underlined the urgency of bringing Cecil fully on board as the only big personality capable of matching Lloyd George on the platform. Yet precisely how was that to be achieved? The previous year Cecil had cited Asquith's leadership as his reason for rejecting Herbert's suggestion that he join the Liberal Party.[55] At one stage he appeared to be thinking of setting up a new independent party, an idea for which Herbert really had little sympathy although he had raised it for consideration at the 6 December meeting in 1921. Probably to his relief the others had rejected it on the grounds that it would lead to competition for funds. The prospect of a more informal arrangement involving liberal Conservatives under Cecil and Independent Liberals under Grey vanished as far as Cecil was concerned when Grey joined Asquith on the Liberal platform at the 23 January meeting.[56] Now with Grey effectively out of the picture Herbert resumed his exhortations to Cecil to make a clean break and join the Liberals. But for the scion of one of the country's great Conservative families this was tantamount to political and social suicide and in any case Cecil did not share Herbert's view that he could revitalise Liberalism from within, though he did suggest that it might be different if Grey were leader.[57] For his part Herbert could not understand why if duty could call Cecil into a Liberal Party led by Grey, antipathy towards Asquith's leadership should stop him joining. Herein lay the unbridgeable gap between the two, for throughout Herbert's life duty had

generally triumphed over personal opinions. This was
certainly the case now, for while he consistently re-iterated
that Asquith was the leader he had strong reservations about
the man himself, having no qualms in telling Cecil frankly
that he was past his prime and that it would be for the country
and the party to decide at the appropriate moment who would
be the prime minister. 'In strict confidence, our stroke oar
neither sets the time nor rows his weight. And the worst of it is
he does not know it.'[58] Herbert even tried indirect pressure,
asking Gilbert Murray to write to *The Times* pleading for Cecil
to come over, adding with an uncharacteristic cynicism that
the great thing was 'to make his own people anxious to
remove him'.[59] The exchanges continued fitfully through the
summer of 1922 with Herbert constantly re-affirming
Asquith's leadership but unwilling to say what he really
thought for fear of appearing disloyal, and Cecil repeating
that Asquith as leader 'repels me' while the thought of finding
himself in the same party as Lloyd George 'disgusts me'.[60]

Yet Herbert may have thought to detect a faint glimmer of
hope when Cecil inquired if he could be found a safe seat in
case he had to give up his current one in Hitchin. Herbert's
suggestion of Warrington did not strike Cecil as a good bet
when Labour was expected to sweep Lancashire in the next
election and at the end of September he made it clear that he
remained unmoved.[61] Stressing that it would have been
different had Asquith been willing to retire in favour of Grey
as Herbert wished, he added rather tactlessly that Herbert
clearly had not been able to achieve very much.[62] Cecil then
made one final appeal of his own to Asquith for a public
indication of his willingness to serve under Grey. Perhaps
Cowdray was right in suspecting that at bottom Cecil could
not bring himself to abandon his Tory roots. Perhaps Herbert
might have been more forceful with Asquith but his loyalty to
a man whose faults he freely acknowledged, in private at least,
pre-empted any possibility that he would press him to stand
down, still less that he would emulate Lloyd George by
plotting against him. But if his negotiations with Cecil
misfired his position was a principled one from which he

never wavered and throughout the correspondence he displayed considerable patience and a personally dangerous candour.[63] It might also be relevant that throughout the summer of 1922 while he was working on Cecil, he was not only trying to come to terms with his new responsibilities at Abingdon Street, but of far greater import to him, he was having to cope with another of his wife's medical emergencies.

In 1915 Dolly had experienced a recurrence of some familiar symptoms but examination revealed that adhesions from her 1912 surgery had developed around her intestines, a complication which had had to be addressed before the underlying condition could be tackled. Now after returning from a visit to Poland in June 1922 she fell ill again. Herbert admitted to being 'much disturbed' when Dolly's medical consultants advised that the cyst they had now found might be malignant.[64] As so often in the past, he felt some inner reassurance that things would turn out safely, despite one of the doctors being so anxious that he was unable to eat on the morning of the prescribed operation. The surgeon, who had carried out well over 4,000 abdominal operations, confirmed after the event that Dolly's condition presented new features and the procedure took far longer than anticipated since it revealed a large lump and produced significant haemorrhaging. Pronounced out of danger after a couple of days Dolly then suffered a relapse when an unsterilised stitch caused a potentially fatal infection. 'Oh, the thankfulness' was all Herbert could manage when letting Harry know that the crisis was finally over, adding that it was the worst scare he had had since 1912 and that he could just not be happy away from his wife.[65] By early September Dolly was able to get downstairs again but the threat of phlebitis kept her bedridden until the end of the month. Not until the end of October was Herbert convinced that she was finally at the end of her troubles. He was distraught, however, when the doctors recommended that she take three months recuperation abroad: political developments had finally precipitated a general election which ruled out any possibility that he could accompany her.

His only small comfort perhaps was the portrait of Dolly which he had recently commissioned and which now adorned the house at Dane End.

Lloyd George's Government had been in trouble for some time as the postwar economic boom faltered, the promised homes for heroes failed to materialise, the proposed Irish settlement threatened to disappear beneath a tide of blood and an international conference convened in April on his personal initiative failed to resolve the issues it discussed. The prime minister then made a strange miscalculation. Attempting the forcible reclamation of territories ceded to Greece by treaty in 1920, Turkish forces swept aside Greek forces before confronting a British outpost at Chanak in the neutral Straits. Lloyd George ordered military action but General Harington wisely overlooked his instructions while the Turks, with equal sense, did not attack. On 11 October the Pact of Mudania ended the crisis and in the subsequent euphoria Lloyd George's cabinet decided to hold a general election. Many Tories, however, had been unhappy at his militant posturing and after a meeting at the Carlton Club on 19 October, they proceeded to ditch him. He resigned the same afternoon, Bonar Law formed a Conservative administration and an election was called for 15 November.

Herbert was instinctively sympathetic to the Greek cause and his lifelong distrust of the Turks had been exacerbated by their massacre of Armenians during the war. He had actively encouraged Armenian sympathisers in Britain and argued that the postwar settlement should clear the Turks out of all Christian territory. 'The Turk', he declaimed early in 1919, 'has snapped his blood-stained fingers in the face of Europe.'[66] But such was his dislike of Lloyd George's policies and morality that even these strong sentiments did not dispose him more favourably towards the deposed prime minister. Even had they done so, reciprocation was unlikely since Lloyd George thought that both Asquith and Gladstone were 'hopeless'.[67] With his agile mind already contemplating a reunion of the Liberal factions, Lloyd George was aware of Herbert's antipathy and also of the influence he could still exert within the party and the country. Accordingly when Herbert publicly criticised the cabinet's handling of the Chanak crisis he responded with a savage and vitriolic personal attack. In a hastily arranged speech at the Manchester Reform Club, he accused Herbert of being offensive, sneering at a 'man without adequate gifts' who gave himself airs and who was 'the best living embodiment of the Liberal doctrine that quality is not hereditary [...] There is no more ridiculous spectacle on a stage than a dwarf strutting before the footlights in garments he has inherited from a giant.'[68] It was typical Lloyd George, clever and spiteful, and if the sentiment was hardly novel, Harry thought its expression took the cake for offensiveness.[69]

By polling day Herbert had managed to raise just over £45,000 for the campaign, a creditable enough total perhaps, given the failure to establish a more appealing leadership, the distraction of Dolly's illness, and his very recent return to an Abingdon Street organisation still reliant on paper systems or, worse still, Geoffrey Howard's memory. The money enabled the Independents to put up just over 330 candidates, roughly twice as many as Lloyd George fielded. Ominously for the future, though, all but £7,000 of it had been given by 12 individuals and almost half was from Cowdray and Runciman. Although he told Harry that he expected to win or hold over 100 seats and had strong hopes of a further 50, these were little more than guesses and not very good ones. Freed of the incubus of Lloyd George the Tories won 345 seats while Labour secured about four million votes and 142 MPs. The Liberals received slightly more votes but the vagaries of the electoral system translated them into only 117 seats with Maclean among the casualties. Asquith's supporters took comfort from the defeat of all the National Liberal leaders save Lloyd George himself and from the swing in the balance of power within Liberalism towards them, manifest in 2.5 million votes against 1.6 million and a slight advantage in the number of seats over Lloyd George's men. Cowdray donated a further £20,000 to the party, telling Herbert that no one could have pulled things around as he had done in such a

short time and that he was as much needed now as ever
before.[70]

But Herbert's return to Abingdon Street was meant to
terminate with the election. On the eve of polling he had told
Maclean that Lloyd George was already pushing for reunion
and that most of their own supporters would probably favour
it as well.[71] The election's outcome certainly strengthened
the case for unity but Herbert feared that the difficulties were
being underestimated. The Independents might now be
stronger in parliament but they had only a single organisation
compared with Lloyd George's four, not to mention his
effective publicity department and strong press support.
While Herbert anticipated little difficulty in actually
arranging and co-ordinating the work of two sets of offices,
he understood that because Lloyd George had the greater
financial resources he would want control. Monetary clout
would also be influential at constituency level since the
official party would find it hard to raise cash for elections.

> The power of money in these matters is decisive no matter
> how corruptly accumulated. It is all this that I am asked to
> encounter. As a minor matter they will make a dead set
> against me & our little lot. At my age the prospect is rather
> deadly & I am a good deal worried about it.[72]

Having agreed to stay on, however, he seemed a little more
hopeful in the new year, telling Maclean that he thought
Lloyd George would come to terms and suggesting that he be
asked to put up £200,000 towards the next election and
£50,000 into a pooled account to be used jointly by their
respective organisations.[73]

At the same time he pressed ahead with plans to
reinvigorate the NLF by giving the local federations more
defined responsibilities and empowering them rather than the
annual general meeting to elect the management committee.
Asquith gave his backing in March and while the
NLF followed suit at its annual general meeting in
May, others were unconvinced. J.M. Hogge, an Independent

Liberal growing increasingly disillusioned with the party establishment, was disparaging. Gladstone's remedy for Liberal disaffection was machinery, he wrote. They had asked for bread but he had given them a steam engine.[74] He was right in the sense that no amount of organisational tinkering could achieve the genuine reunion that rank and file Liberals seemed to want until the party's main leaders came to some accommodation. Effective reunion had to be a matter of minds as well as structures but as far as Herbert was concerned (and he was by no means alone among the Independents), issues of principle and conduct had to be resolved if there was ever to be a formal reconnection with the gifted but morally flawed Lloyd George. Discussing the prospects with C.P. Scott in July, Herbert remarked that personally he was resolved never to accept Lloyd George as a colleague again, adding that he did not see how he could take money from him even if it was offered. He appeared content, Scott noted, to let things drift.[75] Perhaps that was all Herbert could do, given the uncertainties surrounding Lloyd George's own intentions. In the immediate aftermath of his abandonment by the Conservatives and the subsequent election defeat he had appeared to one of his best friends to be somewhat lost.[76] Despite his apparent willingness to work with Asquith there were always suspicions that he was keeping other options open, perhaps another coalition with the Conservatives or a new one with Labour, or perhaps an entirely new centre party. Furthermore, he was convinced that in consort with Howard, Herbert and what one Lloyd Georgite described as a small group of 'embittered men who have not hesitated to use Lord Oxford as a stalking horse', were using every endeavour to persuade party members against reunification.[77] Nor were such claims totally without foundation, for the previous January Herbert had certainly opposed a suggestion that the National Liberals be asked to select a deputy to Grey when he succeeded Crewe as the Liberal leader in the Lords.

With the key players apparently so far apart, it was hardly surprising that little progress had been made towards reunion when out of the blue another general election was called in 1923. Stanley Baldwin, keen to make his mark after succeeding the dying Bonar Law as prime minister, announced that he could deal with rising unemployment only by introducing protection. Since Law had made precisely the contrary pledge, an election to secure the popular mandate was deemed necessary. Any call for protection tended to rally Liberals around the free-trade flag, in the process boosting rank and file sentiment for organisational reunion, although Asquith was lukewarm even about the Liberals' agreement to fight as a united party, referring to the rapprochement with Lloyd George as 'le baiser de Lamourette', something with no consequence.[78] Herbert's concern as he contemplated another election, however, was still cash. Dolly helped to entice another generous donation from Cowdray who also enclosed £20,000 from Lord Inchcape, scraped together he said by the skin of his teeth, but Herbert's hopes of a contribution from Lloyd George to the pooled account had not materialised and he had no real expectation of the £100,000 allegedly promised for an election fund.[79] Given that he had committed £135,000 to 337 candidates it is not surprising that he was worried, even more so perhaps as Lloyd George had provided £80,000 to support 123 National Liberals. As in the previous campaign, Herbert's estimates of Liberal results (between 170 and 220 seats and more than Labour) proved unduly optimistic. Labour 's numbers rose to 191 and the Liberals to 159, though Herbert seemed more bucked by the fact that the National Liberals were reduced to a mere 26. The Conservatives remained as the largest party overall but the loss of more than 90 seats meant that when parliament re-assembled Baldwin was promptly outvoted. The King was advised to invite Labour to form its first ever government.

However, as a minority administration its days were likely to be numbered, leading Herbert to entertain serious hopes that within 18 months the Liberals might once again be in power.[80] That of course could happen only after another election but two in quick succession had drained his resources and the party was now effectively broke. To obviate this he proposed to reorganise headquarters, creating a dedicated department headed by himself to concentrate on election finance. But a financial arrangement with Lloyd George remained the priority, for while the last election had further shifted the parliamentary balance of power within Liberalism to the Independents the weaker Nationals still had most of the money in the form of Lloyd George's infamous fund. In the urgency of the need and with another election possible at any time pragmatism seems to have trumped the scruple which Herbert had expressed to Scott six months before, although his reservations were still evident when he set out for Maclean possible ways of getting their hands on Lloyd George's cash. Dismissing both a complete amalgamation of resources or an arrangement akin to what he thought he had secured but which had not materialised in the recent election, he proposed a merger of the two funds, less what Lloyd George wanted to retain for his personal expenditure, but with control vested in Maclean, Hudson, himself and a Lloyd George nominee.[81] This would certainly have allowed Herbert to maintain what he had laid on the line to Asquith, that he would countenance no adoption of Lloyd George's financial methods, because as he told Harry, the Welshman's supporters were bounders and they could not have them in.[82]

But it was wildly optimistic to expect Lloyd George to surrender control of his fund and he showed no inclination to abandon the bargaining power it gave him when negotiations got underway early in 1924. Furthermore, as Herbert frequently conceded, he was easily Liberalism's most dynamic personality and a dominant figure whose rhetorical force made him an invaluable electoral asset. The Independents were further disadvantaged in that they had no idea of exactly how much Lloyd George had at his disposal and the discussions, in which Herbert was not involved, soon dissolved into what he described as all manoeuvring for position.[83] Lloyd George proved his usual inventive self in justifying his reluctance to hand over control of his fund, the money had been given to him personally rather than to the

Liberal Party, legally it was controlled by trustees not him, he had committed it to policy projects. More likely he had invested much of it in newspapers and there were also rumours that he was having to make refunds to keep some of those he had honoured out of the bankruptcy courts. But whatever the truth Herbert, who suspected the latter, found his slipperiness irritating, not least because he did not want to place candidates without having the necessary resources to support them. He was encouraged when Lloyd George wound up his own separate organisation in February and raised the question of funding a joint operation, but he grew increasingly frustrated at the subsequent lack of progress. In July his patience finally ran out. He had been able to fix only half of the 500 candidates he thought necessary to give the Liberals credibility as an alternative government and he told Maclean that Lloyd George must be presented with an ultimatum to resolve the financial position. Lloyd George then raised another difficulty, suggesting that headquarters organisation was rotten and needed drastic restructuring if he was to provide financial help. Perhaps more in desperation than real hope of getting the money he wanted for the election, Herbert pressed Asquith to deal directly with Lloyd George. Lloyd George may well have believed that putting up 500 candidates was tactically wrong but his prevarication seems to have been fuelled in part at least by a personal animus towards Herbert. If he genuinely did believe that headquarters organisation was defective it was strange both that he should have disbanded his own agencies six months before and that he did not raise it as an issue during a joint meeting held with the organisers of the NLF district federations on 23 July. All he did on that occasion was to glance briefly at a proposed scheme of reorganisation circulated by a member of the Manchester Federation before declaring it to be on the right lines. Now he dismissed Herbert's letter to Asquith as misleading and proposed that he and Alfred Mond should meet directly with Asquith and Maclean.[84] As that meeting on 14 September broke up, Mond almost appears to have confirmed that organisation had been raised as another red herring when he privately told Maclean that Lloyd George had no understanding of it all. But that had not stopped the National Liberal leader from demanding during the meeting itself that the personnel at Abingdon Street be completely changed. When Maclean replied that he had no intention of dispossessing Herbert or any of his colleagues, Lloyd George countered by suggesting a committee to inquire into the structure.[85] Herbert himself had been consistently critical of his own organisation but he rightly saw this as a personal attack. Perhaps wearying of the endless uncertainty, he indicated that if this inquiry did recommend change then he would go, although adding darkly that he would have to spell out his reasons which would not help the cause of unity. It was all down to Asquith's slackness, he complained. He had invited him to Abingdon Street but now it was up to Lloyd George to determine whether he stayed. 'Humiliation may reach a point my dear Donald as things are going wh. I cannot face.'[86] With Dorothy away cruising in the Gulf he turned for consolation to Harry, claiming with unusual vituperation that 'the little Welsh devil' was trying to undermine him.[87] He perhaps felt vindicated when the reorganisation inquiry recommended that change be delayed in order to give priority to election arrangements and that he should chair a special campaign team comprised of both National and Independent Liberals. Lloyd George, however, rejected both suggestions and offered just £50,000 for the campaign.

The failure to find a modus vivendi dealt a fatal blow to Liberal hopes when the contest finally came. In October Simon drafted a motion of censure on the government over its handling of an incitement case but Asquith proposed a select committee instead. The government rejected this attempted compromise but the Conservatives supported it and MacDonald's administration was outvoted. The Liberals thus appeared to be divided in the House of Commons and also to have been directly responsible for the government's defeat. Asquith had not intended this outcome and Herbert's fury that a dissolution had been engineered without anyone inquiring if the party was in suitable shape to fight an election was misdirected. But in the absence of any arrangement with Lloyd George, he was totally strapped for funds, short of candidates and locked into wasteful three-cornered fights. 'What you can do for us I cannot guess', he wrote to Harry, 'but the position is pretty desperate.'[88] Even his most generous backers disappointed. Cowdray's contribution was half what it had been the year before while Inchcape declined to give anything, pointing out that he had given £22,000 in the last twelve months and had therefore done his bit.[89] With inadequate resources and denied even the unifying slogan of free trade by Baldwin's recent repudiation of his call for protection, the Liberals were annihilated, securing a paltry 43 seats. Asquith's own defeat left Lloyd George as the undisputed leader in the Commons, further adding to the awkwardness of Herbert's personal position as the recriminations started, directed chiefly at himself and Howard.

Given Lloyd George's own funding practices, his supporters' charge that the party was 'antiquated, undemocratic, supported by rich men's money, run by well-meaning but superannuated persons who should be replaced' was somewhat ironic, even more so since Lloyd George himself had denied the cash which might have funded the necessary modernisation.[90] As it was, Herbert had more than once acknowledged the party's organisational deficiencies and within his limited means had done his best to redress them, even though his proposed remedies had not always been very enthusiastically acted upon at grass-roots level. This was true of his efforts to get local associations to establish separate organisations for women, for example, and personally he blamed local apathy for the failure of his NLF reforms to have much impact. At heart he felt justifiably aggrieved, given that his involvement had not been primarily of his volition, had only ever been intended to be temporary and had entailed no personal gain. Both his disappointment at the election result and his bruised feelings coloured the detailed and occasionally rather self-righteous account he subsequently prepared of the negotiations with Lloyd George, a document he insisted on having formally approved by Maclean, Hudson and Howard.

Maclean at least was sympathetic and wanted Herbert to stay on but the fact that Lloyd George was now firmly in the driving seat made that impossible. Herbert's spirits were already low when he wrote to Harry shortly after the election.

> What is to happen to me I can't say at present. My job terminated with the election. I just have to wind up finance. But then? Reorganisation must of course start again at once. Who is there to do it? Every whip is out. There's not a soul left of any experience except the old aged gang [...] Theoretically it sounds well after this catastrophe to put in new blood at A St. But where the deuce is it?[91]

As the volume of criticism mounted he became even more despondent. Overall, he thought, the party position was hopeless, Asquith too old, Lloyd George untrustworthy. He was just glad to be out of things.[92]

Yet if his organic connection with the party was ending his emotional and intellectual ties meant that he could never fully disengage, for Liberals continued to seek his advice and even involvement. In the aftermath of the election Maclean pressed him to meet with the newly established reorganisation committee. With Lloyd George's grip on the party tightening as he removed opponents from key positions, Maclean was similarly insistent that Herbert meet with the Asquithite leaders in December 1925 to discuss the situation, if only because he himself wanted 'a chance of being buried with a Gladstone'.[93] Herbert was unable to attend because he was nursing Dolly from concussion sustained in a motoring accident but he expressed his doubts that Asquith had sufficient stomach for the fight with Lloyd George, although he said it did not bother him.

> It has been hard enough wrestling with Georgian intrigues without the support of the leader for which one was looking. But if the leader refuses to part company with L.G. chunks of

fat will hurtle freely into the fire [...] So I make my bow
though always ready to serve the Party if I have the chance.[94]

In the main, however, his service was henceforth confined to
words. He was unmoved by an invitation from Samuel
to return to active politics and by Cowdray's similar appeal to
him as the only one with the sufficient knowledge, experience
and vision to resolve the party's ongoing difficulties, which
worsened when after a very public falling-out with Lloyd
George over the 1926 general strike, Asquith resigned the
party leadership. Believing that this would strengthen Lloyd
George's grass-roots support, Herbert recommended caution
when Maclean sought his counsel. The idea of unity, he
suggested, had to be protected to avoid schism between 'us
and the party in the country which accepts what we refuse'.
Paradoxically he then suggested that they should establish
their own organisation.[95] But when this came into existence
as the Liberal Council he rejected Maclean's request to serve
as chairman, only offering support in less public ways.[96]
These included fundraising but even with Dolly's help he
managed to garner only about £8,000 to sponsor some
30 anti-Lloyd George Liberals in the 1929 general election
and he found it dispiriting that his advances frequently
elicited little more than good wishes. Discussing party
organisation with Ramsay Muir, who found the task no easier
in the second half of the decade than Herbert had in the first
half, he said that the current decadence of Liberalism
depressed him. Unity depended on a leader whom everyone
could trust and while he conceded that Lloyd George
possessed many of the essential qualities that final issue of
personal credibility still remained.[97]

After 1925, therefore, Herbert's efforts to contain Lloyd
George's influence within Liberalism changed from that of an
active player at Abingdon Street to that of a vocal and
occasionally demonstrative spectator. A consistent theme
throughout, however, was his determination, matched
equally by Harry's, to ensure that their father's reputation
and principles were not only kept well in the public eye but

preserved unsullied by association with Lloyd George. Once Grey and Cecil were out of the picture and with Asquith a spent force, it appeared to the brothers even more important to highlight the contrast between the characters of the party's most eminent leader and the most plausible claimant to his succession. In this respect they had to lean hard on Mary who was growing progressively more idiosyncratic with the passing of the years. She had already upset the family first by criticising Herbert's portrayal of Will and then by coming out in favour of Lloyd George. But it was too much when she proposed to write a biography of Catherine Gladstone to expose that the main business of her own life had been 'to hide the state of things and act as a buffer at home'. She wanted, she said, to write frankly about the fractious relationships between Catherine and her daughters, her coolness towards her sons' wives and her willingness to overlook her three elder sons' romantic indiscretions.[98] In the face of strong remonstrances from Herbert and Harry, who feared the damage to the family image, Mary backed off and much to their relief concentrated on Catherine's many positive attributes.

But if they were able to head off Mary, they could not do the same with Peter Wright, a maverick character who had turned to freelance journalism after his brief attachment to the Supreme War Council Staff had been terminated on security grounds. He had already tried to destroy the reputation of Godfrey Isaacs before turning his attention to W.E. Gladstone, describing him in 1925 as an immoral hypocrite and a man who in public spoke the language of morality and principle whilst seeking 'to pursue and possess every sort of woman'.[99] Fearing that if these charges went uncontested their truth would be assumed, Herbert, displaying a capacity for invective unsuspected even by Harry, wrote to Wright deliberately libelling him as a fool, a liar and a coward. Wright sent Herbert's letter together with his own indignant rebuttal, written on the Bath Club's headed notepaper, to the *Daily Mail*. As a member of the club's committee, Herbert promptly protested strongly, referring to Wright as 'a foul fellow'. The club first asked Wright to refrain from using its address, then invited his resignation and finally expelled him. When his complaint that he been given no opportunity to explain himself received merely an acknowledgement, Wright sued the club. In the course of that action his barrister argued that his expulsion had been engineered from behind the scenes by 'the Great Lord Gladstone', a man who also 'writes letters behind my client's back', a reference to Herbert's grievance about Wright's use of club notepaper.[100] Although the case was not about the validity of Wright's claims about W.E. Gladstone, the club's counsel was Herbert's political ally Sir John Simon, and he knew what was wanted. Accordingly, he effectively conceded Wright's claim that he had been expelled from the Bath Club without being given a chance to defend himself. This allowed him to be the last to address the court and he used the opportunity to provoke Wright into making repeated interruptions asserting that his allegations were true and that Herbert was as big a humbug as his father. In the end Wright was awarded paltry sums for the loss of club amenities and the damage to his reputation. With that out of the way he now sued Herbert for his original libel and use of the term 'foul fellow'. The Gladstones hired Norman Birkett KC, a former Liberal MP and one of the outstanding legal figures of his generation. One by one he examined Wright's various 'proofs' that especially in the latter stages of his life Gladstone had been a sex maniac and perhaps a criminal, that he had an illegitimate son living in Eastbourne, that Lily Langtry, Olga Novikoff, Laura Bell and a French actress had been his mistresses, and that he had made explicit overtures to several others. It emerged from Birkett's relentless cross-examination that 11 of the individuals from whom Wright claimed to have these stories were dead and that he had made no attempt to verify the reliability of those still alive. Birkett then pondered why so many people so long ago should have confided to a young and unknown individual like Wright information about the alleged sexual peccadilloes of the prime minister. As his case crumbled under this ruthless dissection, Wright went to pieces, insulting any whose evidence contradicted his own, shouting and interrupting from the witness box so frequently that the judge formally warned him. In the end he was awarded nominal damages of one farthing. Costs were awarded to the Gladstones, although in 1928 Herbert abandoned his efforts to get them when he discovered that Wright was being pursued for bankruptcy. He was pleased enough with the widespread welcome for the case's outcome.

Whilst their pursuit of Wright was thus vindicated in law and validated by the evidence, both Herbert and Henry were all too well aware that their father's well-publicised work with prostitutes did make him highly vulnerable to charges of sexual impropriety. Herbert had been aware of scurrilous allegations about it even in the 1880s and was never convinced that the good his father intended was commensurate with the reputational risk it entailed. Gladstone himself had also realised the risks and tried to cover himself and the family by leaving with Stephen a written declaration of marital fidelity to be opened on his death, a document Herbert briefly considered putting into court as evidence during the Wright case before deciding it was unnecessary. He came to the same conclusion with respect to the diaries. He knew from his own intensive study of them that *in toto* they recorded the inner turmoil of an individual whose drive to do good was marred by all-too-human weaknesses. But removed from that context, individual entries might be made to read very differently by a clever lawyer, especially in what Maud Gladstone described in her court submission as a vicious and scandal loving world.[101] Yet if Herbert decided not to use the diaries in court he also understood that everyone knew about the prostitutes anyway. Better therefore to make open acknowledgement of the facts and emphasise the purity of motive. Thus while Morley's three volumes of Gladstone's life had omitted all reference to it Herbert over-ruled the editor's desire to follow suit in the abridged version which appeared in 1927. He insisted that it be mentioned to show that Gladstone had been struck at Oxford by the horror of the business and the heavy responsibility of men in relation to it.[102] An appropriate passage was duly inserted.

It had always been understood that Morley himself would produce the single-volume abridgement of his original work, sales of which reached almost 141,000 by 1924.[103] When asked about it in 1921, however, Morley first demurred, then agreed and finally mislaid his manuscript so effectively that it could not be found after his death in 1923. With Harry's encouragement a somewhat reluctant Herbert then made a start but found the work of compression too demanding, given his commitments at Abingdon Street – and his preference for gardening. Nevertheless, the brothers were set on keeping their father accessible to a younger and a wider audience, and after some consultation agreed to approach Charles Masterman. Herbert's former under-secretary was already a successful writer and shared their aspiration to publish something that might encourage a Liberal revival by revealing that successful leadership was not about making cheap electoral promises but about stirring up enthusiasm for righteous causes. But if he shared their motivation Masterman was rather more perceptive than either of his patrons. In accepting the commission he pointed out that success could not be guaranteed, intuitively sensing perhaps that an appeal to principle and disinterestedness represented a type of politics whose day was disappearing.[104] But Herbert was pleased to have found another scribe, although he vetted everything Masterman wrote and whenever he thought necessary exercised a firm editorial oversight. Frustratingly from his point of view, when the book finally appeared the papers were generally reluctant to review it on the reasonable grounds that it was essentially a re-jigged version of an existing work.

If Masterman's work disappointed in keeping the older Gladstone in the public mind, Herbert's own writing did work in the desired direction, though perhaps with mixed results as far as the paternal reputation was concerned. Between 1910 and 1920 the sometime editor of *The Times*, George Buckle, had collaborated with W.F. Monypenny to produce a multi-volumed biography of Disraeli which in Herbert's opinion had given a highly distorted impression of Gladstone senior. Knowing that any response must inevitably involve a critical assessment of Queen Victoria's relationship with his father and wishing to honour the latter's explicit instruction that she was not to be criticised, Herbert kept silent.[105] But then the King invited Buckle to edit and publish the Queen's correspondence and early in 1922 Lord Stamfordham, the court official responsible for the royal archives, asked the Gladstones if they would make her letters to their father available. Herbert did not trust Buckle and stalled for time, trying to persuade the King to replace him with Sir Sidney Lee. When that failed he proposed that Buckle be asked for a guarantee not to comment on certain matters and that some letters highly critical of government policy between 1880 and 1885 be withheld because they raised awkward constitutional questions. Stamfordham was not a royal official for nothing and replied glibly that adverse comment might arise if some correspondence were to be withheld. Herbert seemed resigned to losing this battle but the 1928 appearance of Buckle's first two volumes, 'a positive cataract of aspersion and disparage-ment', proved too much.[106] He had long been contemplating a book of his own covering particular episodes in his father's political career and aspects of family life overlooked by Morley. But Buckle's work so outraged him that Harry had to tone down his proposed protest to Stamfordham. By the time the royal court learned that Herbert's own work included a critical analysis of Buckle's highly selective and partial use of Victoria's letters it was already at the proof stage, thanks in no small part to Dolly's help with the research. Stamfordham was left in no doubt as to Herbert's displeasure with Buckle's portrayal of his father as a discredited and even contemptible figure. For his part Buckle hotly refuted Herbert's charges of partisanship and of deliberately omitting or suppressing relevant letters. Neither was inclined to emollience and in November Stamfordham somewhat lamely told Herbert that he expected further thrusts in the duel between them.[107] He was right.

With Herbert's book scheduled for publication in mid-December, Buckle changed tack and threatened to sue the publisher. Herbert re-assured Macmillan that this was nothing more than 'woolly bluff' from a bully.[108] He did, however, agree to insert into his book a slip explaining that he had not meant to accuse Buckle of suppressing documents. This did nothing to mollify his antagonist who now complained to *The Times* that Herbert had still not withdrawn the charge of partisanship.[109] But Herbert would make no further substantive concession and minor changes in the second impression of *After Thirty Years* failed to quell Buckle's apparent determination to act as Herbert's editor. Predictably the reviews concentrated mainly on their dispute. *John O'London* thought Herbert had entirely vindicated his father as did the *Manchester Guardian*, although Buckle's version convinced the *Glasgow Herald*.[110] *The Saturday Review* went further, describing Herbert as a child in Buckle's hands and suggesting that he had written only because his father's reputation had been waning since 1900 while Disraeli's had risen. The Gladstones might be irritated by this, the reviewer went on, but to expose their annoyance 'by reviving an extinct enthusiasm for their illustrious sire is pure folly'.[111]

Far less controversial or historically significant was another, slighter work which Herbert had ready for publication by the start of 1930, having worked on it intermittently for some time. His history of the Catch Club was essentially descriptive and lacked much sense of organisation or theme, but like his memoir it was equally a work of love.[112] First it was a testimony to his lifelong passion for music, especially singing. He had been the club president since 1919, finding in its dinners, less opulent than they had once been, and its concerts a welcome relief from the gloom of postwar politics. Even more importantly, it was music that had brought Dolly into his life. He had joined the club in the very year that he married, and their common interest remained always an important bond between them.

That bond, however, was about to be broken. Herbert's robust constitution had allowed him regular tennis and golf well into his 70s, although failing sight and neuritis prompted his doctor to suggest in 1928 that he take things more easily. The asthmatic tendencies he had occasionally exhibited in childhood had never developed into anything more serious but in January 1930 he took a severe cold which he could not shake off. By mid-February and after several weeks of what Dolly described as 'acute anxiety' the doctors were optimistic but she herself suspected that her husband was not yet out of the wood.[113] Her intuition proved accurate as his condition deteriorated into pneumonia. She was constantly at his bedside but few of his siblings remained to visit. Stephen had suffered a fatal heart attack in 1920, Helen and Mary had died respectively in 1925 and 1927, while the long-widowed Agnes was in her late 80s. That left only Harry who rushed immediately to Dane End as Herbert's condition worsened. Twice Harry thought him sufficiently restored to risk his own return to Hawarden. Twice he was summoned back. On 6 March, weakened by heart failure, Herbert's eyes closed for the final time. Four days later he was buried in the churchyard at Little Munden near Dane End where he had lived out his final years in such domestic contentment. Dolly wrote movingly to Gilbert Murray of their three decades of 'cloudless love and companionship', adding that she felt 'utterly lost & bewildered & desolate without him'.[114] Her personal tributes included a memorial tablet in Herbert's alma mater, University College, and an offer to fund a scholarship in his memory. Her deepest wish, however, was that his life be recorded in print. She felt it a sacred duty, she told Murray, who was her preferred author, that 'Herbert should live and all the more acutely because I did not give him a son who might have inherited some of his character and carried on the tradition.'[115] Stressing his courage, selflessness and self-effacement, she forwarded a few of Herbert's own biographical notes to Murray but he felt able to offer only a character sketch which despite Dolly's initial enthusiasm, did not materialise and eventually she looked elsewhere for a biographer.

Nationally, Herbert was accorded a well-attended memorial service at Westminster Abbey, a fitting location for a Gladstone and a deserved acknowledgement of a long life of public service. Two years later Harry dedicated his own personal memorial to a remarkable and enduring sibling relationship. That Herbert was able to leave an estate worth slightly more than £64,000 was due in no small part to Harry's enduring generosity in providing both a regular income and the occasional windfall. As recently as 1928 he had increased his annual gift from £500 to £1250 and thrown in a lump sum of £15,000. Now his bronze tablet in the remote and rural setting of St Deiniol's Church at Hawarden seemed just as appropriate as Westminster Abbey for a brother who had never sought the limelight.

Epilogue

Herbert's funeral service at Little Munden was conducted by the Bishop of St Albans, who as Bishop of Pretoria from 1909, had become a close family friend. It would be easy to dismiss the prelate's closing remarks as little more than conventional funeral oratory but they were clearly heartfelt.

> Few men – if any in our time – inherited a finer or higher tradition of public service or of genuine Christian faith and service than he did – and no man was more loyal to it [...] all through his life he showed that loyalty, in being ready to put at the service of his country whatever he had to give and that at a far greater cost than most people ever realized, for naturally [...] he was a man to whom public life offered few attractions but to whom a country life with the peace of its pursuits was always an absorbing interest [...] He never pretended to be anything but himself [...] a wise counsellor [...] a fearless champion of any whom he thought were not having a fair deal (for he always had a tender spot in his heart for the under-dog); a delightful host, a very human companion and a Christian gentleman to whom his religion was a living reality and no mere tradition of the past.[1]

It was a remarkably accurate portrait. Loyalty, for example, had certainly characterised Herbert's career, not least in South Africa where Louis Botha was the main beneficiary of his consistent support and advice. By no means blind to their failings and indeed often irritated by them, Herbert was similarly faithful to both Campbell-Bannerman and Asquith, in the latter's case well beyond his political sell-by date: it was Herbert who organised financial help when Asquith fell on hard times, subsequently describing him as a true friend to whom he owed a great deal.[2] Loyalty also meant not using others as pegs on which to hang his own career, as Herbert demonstrated in sticking by Commissioner Henry in 1908 and in being prepared to resign after his intervention in the Rand strike in 1913. Not surprisingly, therefore, he made lifelong friendships outside his natural social circle, with constituency officers like Kitson and Joseph Henry, Hudson at Liberal headquarters, his private secretary at the Home Office and several imperial officials from his time in South Africa.

Above all Herbert remained true to his version of Liberalism and the father from whom he had imbibed it and for whom he always retained the deepest filial affection. Herbert was neither particularly intellectual nor ideological in outlook and if Liberalism for him was largely a matter of principle, albeit sometimes rather vaguely defined, it was, like his father's, tempered with pragmatism with respect to details or timing, as in the case of licensing reform and even home rule. He was certainly more open than his father to the idea of state intervention in daily life, for what the bishop described as his soft spot for the underdog was actually a profound compassion for the underprivileged, be they exploited wage earners, harshly treated convicts, the immigrants whose reception he oversaw both as home secretary and later as chair of the War Refugees Committee, or the indigenous Africans for whom as governor-general and high commissioner he sought justice and long-term security. For the Irish, in his opinion the victims of uncaring landlords and indifferent Dublin Castle rule, he had an enduring and underlying sympathy, moderated in the face of violence by his strongest value of all, belief in the rule of law. The suffragettes and the South African strikers both confronted him with a similar dilemma between public order and private compassion. Formally upholding the law as he was constitutionally bound to do anyway, he worked quietly behind the scenes, largely unnoticed and certainly unsung, to humanise the imprisoned suffragettes' custodial experience and to create a more favourable industrial relations framework in South Africa.

But Herbert's version of Liberalism and thus the man himself appeared increasingly dated in the light of the urgent international and domestic questions thrown up by World War I. He had few answers of his own other than the League of Nations and structural reorganisation but he was certain that those offered by Lloyd George as prime minister were anything but Liberal. The Welshman's political and financial methods were arguably more relevant to the mass male electorate created by the postwar extension of the franchise, but they contrasted starkly with the sense of public propriety and integrity inherent in the Liberalism Herbert inherited from his father. There is no doubt either that he strongly disapproved of Lloyd George's private life, although awareness of his own father's vulnerability in that respect prevented him from making much of it in public. But he stoutly resisted any suggestion that Lloyd George was a worthy inheritor of the Gladstonian political legacy and it is misleading to suggest that his antipathy to Lloyd George in the 1920s was based on fear for his own position.[3] Indeed, as the bishop implied in his funeral eulogy, there was not an ambitious bone in Herbert's body. He never consciously sought office and was often reluctant to accept it. Even in 1905 his priority was the overall composition of the cabinet rather than his own position within it. As a minister he never tried to take from colleagues the credit which was rightly theirs for important departmental initiatives, content to give them their heads and encourage them from the sidelines. It is worth pointing out, too, that Herbert re-engaged with Liberal politics in the 1920s only at the invitation of others and in an offstage role. Lloyd George's jibe about him being a dwarf strutting around in giant's clothes was entirely misconceived. Herbert was not interested in the limelight for himself. He knew better than anyone that he lacked the oratory, the cunning or the intellect to fill his father's boots: his concern was to keep Lloyd George's feet out of the boots.

In its own way, Lloyd George's vituperativeness was an acknowledgement of the influence Herbert still exerted in the 1920s, even though his role at Abingdon Street was essentially a backstage one. But that was always where he had preferred to be. 'I like this business', he told Donald Maclean in 1923, 'because it allows me to prune roses with my wife.'[4] Certainly he was often at his most effective behind the scenes, particularly in his unstinting and unheralded efforts to hold the party together during the Boer War and its havering between Campbell-Bannerman and Rosebery. His work as chief whip in organising the Liberals' parliamentary forces to exhaust the Tories in parliament throughout 1905 was similarly unobtrusive and overshadowed by his mastermind-ing of the very public electoral triumph of 1906. Significantly, he once said that he had never been happier than during his time at party headquarters between 1899 and 1906.[5] But even before that, extended private discussions and the information he provided influenced his father's thinking on home rule. In South Africa his official communications, together with informal conversations and notes provided valuable modifications of legislative proposals, guided cabinet tactics or smoothed relationships between the Imperial and Union Governments. Later, in 1920–1, he was so much in the wings that his pivotal role in the ultimately unsuccessful effort to draw Grey, Asquith and Cecil together also went largely unrecognised.

Offstage was perhaps a strange preference for a man of well-attested charm and social ease but Herbert had his preferences and well understood his own capabilities. The bishop was quite right in emphasising his love of country life, marked by his delight in being out-of-doors, whether building lakes at Hawarden, tending the gardens of Govern-ment House in Cape Town or cultivating his orchards and chickens at Dane End, not to mention his lifelong enjoyment of field sports and a passion for dogs, which he himself once described as 'terrifying'.[6] As for his limitations, he had neither the vision nor the charisma to be anything more politically than he was. He may have been a good platform speaker but he struggled in parliament, save perhaps on Irish matters, where his passions most readily sometimes overcame his inhibitions. Although he did try in 1905 and again in the 1920s to encourage party colleagues to think about broad policy, in cabinet between 1906 and 1910 he showed little interest in matters outside his own ministerial brief and made no contribution to discussions on government strategy or issues of principle. Some attributed this to laziness, a trait to which Herbert himself sometimes admitted. Yet he was unjustly hard on himself, for while he did not often enjoy hard work he could certainly embrace it, for example as an election organiser and as chairman of the WRC. It is true that at the Home Office he failed to energise his officials and sometimes appeared overwhelmed but personally he undertook a great deal and without his department's contributions the reforming credentials of the Liberal Government, certainly prior to 1908, would have been sparse.

The perception of idleness was perhaps fostered by Herbert's reticence, which made him a reluctant self-publicist. This in turn reflected a certain lack of inner confidence, surprising perhaps in one who never lacked courage: personally, as he showed in his teens when alone he chased armed poachers out of the Hawarden woods; morally, when he refused to sanction the execution of the alleged Umtali rapist; and politically when he chose to swim against the tide of Lloyd George's popularity in the 1920s. By then, however, age and experience had perhaps tempered his self-doubt. Yet it had inhibited his parliamentary performances from the very first and thereafter showed itself in his habit of writing summary reports or private letters recapitulating and justifying his actions during particularly controversial episodes, such as the Eucharistic procession, the suffragette campaign, the Umtali rape case, the Rand strikes and the extended negotiations with Lloyd George in the early 1920s.

Herbert, it seems, needed constant affirmation. Politically, this was provided by his father and, after his death, by Harry. Emotionally, Dolly similarly filled the gap left by Catherine Gladstone, providing the constant comfort and reassurance of human affection. Herbert's reciprocal devotion to her was transparent in his dread of their being apart and consistent willingness to allow her needs to influence his own decisions.

Above all, as the bishop asserted, Herbert was a Christian gentleman. He was a devoted churchman, conscientious in the ritual observances of his Anglicanism and a generous supporter of numerous Christian charities. If his faith did not often find overt expression outside of these conventional channels or, except at times of particular personal stress, in emotional language, it was none the less sincere and he never lost the sense of a benign Divinity watching over him, just as he believed his father to have been the Almighty's instrument for good. This certainty came through in the letters he sent to Harry from Sofia 1927, when he took part in celebrations marking his father's support for the Christian Armenians against the Turks, 'a hectic time but I would not have missed it for the world.'[7] It was evident as well when the Wright case was settled, a literal trial which Herbert found physically and emotionally draining but during which he derived great comfort from the thought that 'God was watching over our efforts for his great servant on earth.'[8] In this matter of faith, as in his approach to the practice of politics and his concept of Liberalism, Herbert Gladstone was essentially a Victorian. Yet for all that, he still deserves to be brought out from the shadow of his father.

Notes

Chapter 1   Hawarden to Westminster

1. Herbert J. Gladstone, *After Thirty Years* (1928).
2. See Eric Hopkins, *Charles Masterman 1873–1927. Politician and Journalist. Splendid Failure* (1999); Anthony J.A. Morris, *C.P. Trevelyan. Portrait of a Radical* (1977); Kenneth D. Brown, *John Burns* (1977); Daniel Waley, *A Liberal Life. Sidney Earl Buxton, 1853–1934* (1999).
3. Charles Mallet, *Herbert Gladstone: A Memoir* (1932).
4. FRO. GG MSS 975. A. Wickham to HJG, 6 January 1874.
5. Colin Matthew (ed.), *The Gladstone Diaries with Cabinet Minutes and Prime Ministerial Correspondence* (fourteen vols, 1968–94), 7 January 1857. Hereafter cited as Gladstone Diary.
6. Ibid., 7 January 1862.
7. Ibid., 8 November 1862.
8. Gladstone, *After Thirty Years*, p. 7.
9. Quoted in Georgina Battiscombe, *Mrs Gladstone: The Portrait of a Marriage* (1956), p. 118.
10. See Christopher Stray, *Contribution towards a Glossary of the Glynne Language* (2005).
11. Quoted in Mary Drew, *Catherine Gladstone* (1919), p. 210.
12. Quoted in ibid., p. 213.
13. Battiscombe, *Mrs Gladstone*, p. 123.
14. Quoted in Drew, *Catherine Gladstone*, p. 92.
15. Gladstone Diary, 10 April 1863.
16. FRO. GG MSS 635. HJG to W.E. Gladstone, 17 October 1863.
17. Ibid., 838. HNG to W. Gladstone, 4 February 1864.
18. Ibid., 765. HJG to C. Gladstone, 9 April 1864.
19. Gladstone Diary, 8 September 1864.

20. FRO. GG MSS 948. M. Gladstone to HJG, 9 September 1864.
21. Ibid., 971. S. Gladstone to HJG, 12 September 1864.
22. Ibid., S. Gladstone to HJG, 25 May 1867.
23. Ibid., 948. M. Gladstone to HJG, 14 September 1869; ibid., 957. Helen Gladstone to HJG, 14 September 1869.
24. Ibid., 872. HJG to HNG, 26 September 1870.
25. Ibid., HJG to HNG, 9 January 1871.
26. Ibid., HJG to HNG, 25 January 1871.
27. Ibid., 971. S. Gladstone to HJG, 12 February 1872.
28. Gladstone Diary, 21 April 1872.
29. Cited in Shane Leslie, *Sir Evelyn Ruggles Brise* (1938), p. 19.
30. FRO. GG MSS 971. S. Gladstone to HJG, 14 May 1872.
31. Ibid., 873. HJG to HNG, 23 May 1872.
32. Ibid., 958. HNG to HJG, 25 May 1872.
33. Ibid., HNG to HJG, 10 November 1872.
34. Ibid., 873. HJG to HNG, 11 November 1872.
35. Ibid., HJG to HNG, 25 May 1873.
36. Ibid., 958. HNG to HJG, 5 February 1873.
37. See for example Gladstone Diary, 13 September 1871, 7 January 1872, 14 January 1872.
38. FRO. GG MSS 971. S. Gladstone to HJG, 17 November 1873.
39. Lucy Masterman, *Mary Gladstone. Her Diaries and Letters* (1930), p. 303.
40. FRO. GG MSS 873. HJG to HNG, 1 June 1874.
41. Quoted in Mallet, *Gladstone*, p. 49. Herbert's father suggested this change. See Gladstone Diary, 19 October 1873.
42. FRO. GG MSS 874. HJG to HNG, 11 March 1875. The incidents referred to here are described in numerous letters written by Herbert to members of his family in 1875.
43. Ibid., HJG to HNG, 29 July 1875.
44. Ibid., HJG to HNG, 5 November 1875.
45. Ibid., 975. A. Wickham to HJG, 2 June 1876.
46. Ibid., 874. HJG to HNG, 7 June 1876.
47. UCO. P218/C1/13. D. Gladstone to G. Murray, 26 June 1930.
48. Gladstone Diary, 19 June 1876.
49. Cited in Masterman, *Mary Gladstone*, p. 106.
50. Gladstone Diary, 17 October 1874.
51. FRO. GG MSS 874. HJG to HNG, 20 June 1876.
52. Ibid., 873. HJG to HNG, 29 January 1873.
53. Ibid., 874. HJG to HNG, 3 October 1879.
54. Gladstone Diary, 29 September 1879.
55. HJG Papers. BL Add Mss 46475, f 252. HJG to R. Hudson, 11 November 1927.
56. FRO. GG MSS 765. HJG to C. Gladstone, 17 February 1880.

57. Gladstone Diary, 29 December 1879.
58. FRO. GG MSS 1019. S. Gladstone to C. Gladstone, 12 March 1880.
59. Cited in Masterman, *Mary Gladstone*, p. 189.
60. FRO. GG MSS 1867. HJG Political Diary, 12 March 1880.
61. Mary's descriptions of Herbert's campaign are cited in Masterman, *Mary Gladstone*, pp. 189–91.
62. *Letters of Lord Acton to Mary, Daughter of the Right Hon. W. E. Gladstone* (1913), pp. 8–9.
63. Dudley R. Bahlman (ed.), *Diary of Sir Edward Walter Hamilton* (two vols, 1972), I, p. 6.
64. BLO. MSS Bryce 70, f 14. C. Gladstone to J. Bryce, 3 April 1880.
65. W.E. Gladstone Papers. BL Add Mss 46043, f 23. W.E. Gladstone to J. Kitson, 14 April 1880.

Chapter 2   Ireland and Back

1. FRO. GG MSS 1867. HJG Political Diary, 26 January 1881.
2. After hearing Herbert's maiden speech, his aunt declared that he spoke very like his father. See Elsa Richmond, *The Earlier Letters of Gertrude Bell* (1937), p. 14.
3. FRO. GG MSS 1867. HJG Political Diary, 23 March 1881.
4. Ibid., 875. HJG to HNG, 8 April 1881.
5. Ibid., 1867 HJG Political Diary, 28 March 1881.
6. Ibid., The prime minister also told Harry that everyone had been delighted. See Gladstone Diary, 21 April 1881.
7. Bahlman (ed.), *Diary of Edward Hamilton*, p. 120.
8. Mallet, *Gladstone*, p. 84.
9. *Hansard*, 3rd series, c 1583. 4 August 1883.
10. Constance Battersea, *Reminiscences* (1922), p. 207. Stuart J. Reid (ed.), *Memoirs of Sir Wemyss Reid, 1842–1885* (1905), p. 291.
11. FRO. GG MSS 1867. HJG Political Diary, 30 April 1881, 21 June 1881.
12. Ibid., 875. HJG to HNG, 11 March 1881. Mary certainly thought Herbert was attracted to Laura. See Sheila Gooddie, *Mary Gladstone. A Gentle Rebel* (2003), p. 160.
13. FRO. GG MSS 1867. HJG Political Diary 1881, summary entry, August–October 1881.
14. Masterman, *Mary Gladstone*, p. 267.
15. Noted in Gladstone Diary, 3 October 1881.
16. Gladstone, *After Thirty Years*, p. 185.
17. FRO. GG MSS 968. HNG to HJG, 20 October 1880.
18. Ibid., 1867. HJG Political Diary, summary entry 19–30 April 1881.
19. Gladstone, *After Thirty Years*, p. 264.
20. FRO. GG MSS 875. HJG to HNG, 22 September 1881.

21. Ibid., HJG to HNG, 26 Oct 1881.
22. Ibid., 1867. HJG Political Diary, 14 October 1881.
23. Ibid., 31 October 1881.
24. Ibid., 7 November 1881.
25. Ibid., 738. HJG to H. Seymour, 9 December 1881.
26. Ibid., 635. HJG to C. Gladstone, nd 1881.
27. Ibid., 1867. HJG Political Diary, summary entry February 1882.
28. Ibid.
29. Ibid., 6 April 1882.
30. Ibid., 22 April 1882.
31. Ibid., 24 April 1882.
32. Ibid., 875. HJG to HNG, 21 April 1882.
33. Ibid., 1867. HJG Political Diary, 11 May 1882.
34. Ibid., 983. HJG to M. Gladstone, 31 May 1882.
35. Ibid., 1867. HJG Political Diary, 8 May 1882.
36. Ibid., 875. HJG to HNG, 24 May 1882.
37. Ibid., 1867. HJG Political Diary, 31 December 1882.
38. Ibid., 10 January 1883. For a similar contemporary use of the term 'interview' see Anthony Trollope, *Barchester Towers* (Penguin edn, 1987), p. 448.
39. FRO. GG MSS 948. M. Gladstone to HJG, n.d.
40. *The Times*, 13 February 1883.
41. *Freeman's Journal*, 30 November 1882.
42. HJG Papers. BL Add Mss 46050, f 26. G.O. Trevelyan to HJG, 22 February 1883.
43. Bahlman (ed.), *Diary of Edward Hamilton*, 15 February 1883.
44. FRO. GG MSS 1867. HJG Political Diary, 27 January 1883.
45. *Freeman's Journal*, 8 January 1883.
46. Bahlman (ed.), *Diary of Edward Hamilton*, 6 July 1883.
47. FRO. GG MSS 1875. HJG Political Diary, 15 December 1885. He resumed his diary again on this date with a summary of the past months.
48. Ibid., 4 August 1885.
49. Ibid.
50. Ibid., 974. W.E. Gladstone to HJG, October 1885.
51. HJG Papers. BL Add Mss 46015, f 43. HJG to H. Labouchere, 18 October 1885.
52. FRO. GG MSS 875. HJG to HNG, 12 November 1885.
53. Ibid., 958. HNG to HJG, 13 November 1885.
54. Ibid., 974. W.E. Gladstone to HJG, 14 November 1885.
55. NLS. Rosebery Papers, MS 10041, f 26. W.E. Gladstone to HJG, 10 December 1885.
56. FRO. GG MSS 1875. HJG Political Diary, 15 December 1885.
57. Ibid., 17 December 1885.

58. Ibid., 18 December 1885.
59. Hamilton Papers. BL Add Mss 48611, f 180. HJG to E. Hamilton, 5 January 1886.
60. HJG Papers. BL Add Mss 56445, f 144. HJG to L. Cavendish, 31 December 1885.
61. Cited in Michael Barker, *Gladstone and Radicalism: The Reconstruction of Liberal Policy in Britain, 1885–94* (1975), p. 158.
62. Hamilton Papers. BL Add Mss 46811, ff 198–9. HNG to E. Hamilton, 14 December 1885.
63. Algar L. Thorold, *The Life of Henry Labouchere* (1913), p. 253.
64. HJG Papers. BL Add Mss 56445, f 144. HJG to L. Cavendish, 31 December 1885. My italics.
65. BUL. Chamberlain Papers, 5/38/41. W. Harcourt to J. Chamberlain, 4 January 1886.
66. FRO. GG MSS 875. HJG to HNG, 29 January 1886.
67. Ibid., HJG to HNG, 21 May 1886.
68. Ibid., 765. HJG to C. Gladstone, 23 July 1886.
69. Ibid., 875. HJG to HNG, 30 July 1886.
70. Noting that she liked Alfred Lyttelton 'immensely', Laura added that Herbert was a 'really fine good character [...] of whom I think better every day.' Mary Drew, *Acton, Gladstone and Others* (1924), p. 128.
71. SRO. Tennant Papers, GD510/1/66. HJG to E. Tennant, 22 August 1886.

Chapter 3   Into the Wilderness

1. FRO. GG MSS 876. HJG to HNG, 26 March 1887.
2. SRO. Tennant Papers, GD510/1/70. HJG to E. Tennant, July 1887.
3. *Hansard*, 3rd series, 322, cc 511–22, 5 February 1888.
4. FRO. GG MSS 876. HJG to HNG, 29 November 1888.
5. Ridley's comment was reported *The Times*, 6 December 1886, Herbert's in ibid., 30 October 1888.
6. Mary later said that she could not believe he knew anything about it but Herbert admitted in court in 1927 that he had. FRO. GG MSS 951. M. Drew to HJG, 19 May 1914.
7. *Hansard*, 3rd series, 346, cc 941–1030. 7 July 1890.
8. Ibid., cc 1401–6. 10 July 1890.
9. Ibid., 4th series, 4, c 1403. 19 May 1892.
10. HJG, 'Ireland blocks the way', *Nineteenth Century*, XXXI (June 1892), pp. 899–904.
11. HJG, 'Obstructionism: what is it?', *New Review*, 8 (April 1893), p. 391.
12. *The Times*, 6 October 1890.
13. *Speaker*, 8 August 1891.

14. HJG, 'Physical training' in Freeman C. Wills (ed.), *Lay Sermons for Practical People* (1890), pp. 61–76.
15. *The Times*, 1 July 1891.
16. See HJG Papers. BL Add Mss 46020, f 10. HJG to R. Hudson, 9 March 1898; ibid., f 15. HJG to R. Hudson, 10 March 1898.
17. Ibid., 46022, f 185. J. Bryce to HJG, 15 March 1892; ibid., 46019, f 28. J. Bryce to HJG, 24 March 1892. The paper was drafted for the *Albemarle Review*.
18. Gladstone Diary, 30 January 1892.
19. FRO. GG MSS 765. HJG to C. Gladstone, 9 July 1892.
20. Ibid., HJG to C. Gladstone, 16 July 1892.
21. HJG Papers. BL Add Mss 46036, f 17. J. Henry to HJG, 20 July 1892.
22. M. Drew papers. BL Add Mss 46224, f 157. Copy of HJG to W.E. Gladstone, 3 April 1894.
23. NA. HO 45/9857/B12432. Building Societies Bill (1892–3).
24. *Leeds Mercury*, 9 August 1893.
25. NA. HO 45/9865/B13816; HO 45/9866/B13816; HO 45/9866/B13816A; HO 45/9866/13816E. Workmen's Compensation and Employers' Liability (1893–4).
26. Ibid., HO 45/9848/B12393A. Factories: White Lead Poisoning (1892–8).
27. Ibid., HO 45/9854/B12393/H. Factories. Quarries. Committee Report re Rules and Regulations (1893–4).
28. Ibid., HO 45/9849/B12393D. Dangerous Trades. Use of Phosphorous in making Lucifer Matches (1892–1900).
29. *Hansard*, 4th series, 41, cc 556–95. 5 June 1896.
30. See David Brooks, 'Gladstone's fourth administration, 1892–1894', in David. W. Bebbington and Roger Swift (eds), *Gladstonian Centenary Essays* (2000), pp. 226–42.
31. FRO. GG MSS 765. HJG to C. Gladstone, 16 July 1892.
32. Quoted in Leo McKinstry, *Rosebery: Statesman in Turmoil* (2005), p. 131.
33. HJG Papers. BL Add Mss 46054, f 225. T.P. O'Connor to HJG, 1 March 1894.
34. NLS. Rosebery Papers, MS 10152, f 200. HJG to A. Murray, 14 May 1895.
35. Ibid., MS 10130, f 129. Rosebery to HJG, 24 May 1895.
36. Ibid., f 43. Rosebery to HJG, 23 August 1894.
37. BLO. Harcourt Papers, dep. 433, f 36. n.d.
38. FRO. GG MSS 876. HJG to HNG, 11 July, 15 July, 28 July 1895.
39. *The Times*, 5 March 1894.
40. Ibid., 6 December 1897.
41. Ibid., 13 December 1898.

42. BLO. Harcourt Papers, dep. 436, f 49. P. Nickalls to L. Harcourt, 3 November 1898.
43. Gladstone Diary, 9 January 1894.
44. FRO. GG MSS 877. HJG to HNG, 23 September 1894.
45. M. Drew Papers. BL Add Mss 46225, f 157. Copy of HJG to W.E. Gladstone, made by Catherine and sent to Mary, 3 April 1894.
46. E. Hamilton Papers. BL Add Mss 48664. E. Hamilton Diary, 4 July 1894.
47. This is discussed in detail in Ros Aitken, *The Prime Minister's Son. Stephen Gladstone. Rector of Hawarden* (2012), pp. 154–80.
48. Quoted in Pat Jalland, 'Mr Gladstone's daughters', in Bruce Kinzer (ed.), *The Gladstonian Turn of Mind. Essays Presented to J.B. Connacher* (1985), p. 118.
49. FRO. GG MSS 878. HJG to HNG, 16 January 1898.
50. Ibid., 949. M. Drew to HJG, 13 April 1898.
51. *Sunday Times*, 22 May 1898.
52. BLO. Morley Papers, Mss Eng. d. 3595, f 160. HJG to J. Morley, 31 August 1898.
53. Ibid., f 45. A. Bigge to J. Morley, 25 October 1898.
54. FRO. GG MSS 878. HJG to HNG, 29 July 1898.
55. NUL. Trevelyan Papers, GOT 123/75. HJG to G.O. Trevelyan, 1 June 1898.
56. FRO. GG MSS 885. HJG to HNG, 18 March 1927.
57. BLO. Bryce Papers, MSS Bryce 70, f 49. Helen Gladstone to J. Bryce, 6 June 1898.
58. FRO. GG MSS 957. Helen Gladstone to HJG, 12 April 1897.
59. Ibid., 954. C. Gladstone to HJG (dictated to Helen) 28 April 1897.
60. Ibid., 957. Helen Gladstone to HJG, 4 September 1899.
61. Ibid., 878. HJG to HNG, 8 September 1898.
62. Ibid., HJG to HNG, 7 May 1899.
63. Ibid., 970. M. Rendel to HJG, 20 November 1889.
64. Ibid., M. Rendel to HJG, 30 January 1890.
65. Ibid., 877. HJG to HNG, 27 July 1893.
66. SRO. Tennant Papers, GD/510/1/70. HJG to E. Tennant, 14 February 1890.
67. Ibid., HJG to E. Tennant, 16 May 1895.
68. FRO. GG MSS 878. HJG to HNG, 28 July 1898.
69. Richmond, *Letters of Gertrude Bell*, p. 226.
70. HJG Papers. BL Add Mss 46029, f 204. Armitstead to HJG, 3 February 1895; ibid., Add Mss 46030, f 82. Armitstead to HJG, 15 March 1897.
71. FRO. GG MSS 878. HJG to HNG, 2 August 1898.
72. Ibid., HJG to HNG, 28 July 1898.

73. Campbell-Bannerman Papers. BL Add Mss 41215, ff 66–7. HJG to H. Campbell-Bannerman, 12 April 1899.
74. FRO. GG MSS 989. HJG to M. Gladstone, 12 April 1899.
75. HJG Papers. BL Add Mss 46017, ff 153–4. J.F. Leese to HJG, 15 April 1899; ibid., BL Add Mss 46028, f 100. J. Kitson to HJG, 16 April 1899.
76. Ibid., BL Add Mss 46036, f 68. J. Henry to HJG, 14 April 1899.
77. Ibid., BL Add Mss 45997, f 18. L. Harcourt to HJG, 16 April 1899.
78. Mallet, *Gladstone*, p. 173.
79. HJG Papers. BL Add Mss 46036, f 61. J. Henry to HJG, 4 March 1897.
80. FRO. GG MSS 989. HJG to Maud Gladstone, 12 April 1899.
81. HJG Papers. BL Add Mss 46017, f 154. J.F. Leese to HJG, 15 April 1899.

Chapter 4   Resurgence

1. BLO. Bryce Papers, MSS 70, f 72. HJG to J. Bryce, 1 October 1899.
2. HJG Papers. BL Add Mss 45986, f 21. Secret memo on proceedings of 4 October 1899.
3. Campbell-Bannerman Papers. BL Add Mss 41215, f 108. HJG to H. Campbell-Bannerman, 5 October 1899.
4. BLPES. Passfield Papers 1/2/25. B. Webb Diary, 30 October 1899.
5. HJG Papers. BL Add Mss 45986, f 33. HJG to H. Campbell-Bannerman, 3 November 1899.
6. Campbell-Bannerman Papers. BL Add Mss 41215, ff 165–7. H. Campbell-Bannerman to HJG, 9 December 1899.
7. Ripon Papers. BL Add Mss 43543, f 159. HJG to Ripon, 24 May 1900.
8. *Manchester Guardian*, 2 April 1900.
9. FRO. GG MSS 976. E. Wickham to HJG, 19 April 1900. Ibid., 972. S. Gladstone to HJG, 3 April 1900.
10. Ibid., 878. HJG to HNG, 28 September 1900.
11. Ibid., HJG to HNG, 25 July 1900.
12. NLS. Rosebery Papers, MS 10029, f 103. R.B. Haldane to Rosebery, 25 July 1900.
13. FRO. GG MSS 878. HJG to HNG, 27 July 1900.
14. BLO. M. Asquith Papers, MS Eng. d., f 56. HJG to M. Asquith, 27 July 1900.
15. HJG Papers. BL Add Mss 46022, f 110. J. Pease to HJG, 24 January 1900.
16. BLO. Harcourt Papers, MSS dep. 436, f 108. P. Stanhope to L. Harcourt, 30 July 1900.
17. Campbell-Bannerman Papers. BL Add Mss 41215, f 169. HJG to H. Campbell-Bannerman, 12 December 1899.

18. HJG Papers. BL Add Mss 46030, f 163. Armitstead to HJG, 18 September 1900.
19. Schnadhorst, for example, apparently accepted a cheque from Cecil Rhodes who hoped thereby to influence Liberal policy in South Africa. It was not clear what happened to the money. See correspondence between Herbert and R. Hudson. Ibid., BL Add Mss 46020, ff 130–5, 10–14 August 1901.
20. Ibid., BL Add Mss 46483. Notebook, 27 July 1899.
21. Ibid., BL Add Mss 45984, f 98. S. Woods to J.R. MacDonald, 14 March 1900.
22. FRO. GG MSS 976. A. Wickham to HJG, 24 June 1900.
23. Ibid., 981. HJG to A. Wickham, 10 July 1900.
24. HJG Papers. BL Add Mss 46023, f 135. M. Napier to HJG, 3 October 1900.
25. LUL. Birrell Papers, MS 10.2, f 6. News-cutting, 3 January 1900.
26. See his remarks in *Liberal Magazine*, VIII (1900), p. 492.
27. HJG Papers. BL Add Mss 46020, ff 48–9. HJG to R. Hudson, 18 August 1900.
28. Spencer Papers. BL Add Mss 77003, unbound. HJG to Spencer, 7 September 1900.
29. Ibid., HJG to Spencer, 13 September 1900.
30. Ripon Papers. BL Add Mss 43543, f 170. HJG to Ripon, 16 September 1900.
31. Campbell-Bannerman Papers. BL Add Mss 52517, f 14. H. Campbell-Bannerman to HJG, 12 September 1900.
32. NLS. Rosebery Papers, MS 10029, f 111. R.B. Haldane to Rosebery, 4 October 1900.
33. Dilke Papers. BL Add Mss 43902, f 208. H. Labouchere to C. Dilke, 30 October 1900.
34. FRO. GG MSS 960. HNG to HJG, 6 November 1900.
35. Ibid., HNG to HJG, 7 November 1900.
36. Cited in Bentley Gilbert, *David Lloyd George, A Political Life: The Architect of Change, 1863–1912* (1987), p. 201.
37. Quoted in McKinstry, *Rosebery*, p. 433.
38. BUSC. National Liberal Club Papers, DM 668. HJG to C. Geake, 6 December 1901.
39. HJG Papers. BL Add Mss 45986, f 44. HJG to Rosebery, 13 December 1901.
40. FRO. GG MSS 960. HNG to HJG, 18 February 1902.
41. Quoted in John Wilson, *CB: The Life of Sir Henry Campbell-Bannerman* (1973), p. 375.
42. BLO. Bryce Papers, MSS Bryce 70, ff 77–8. HJG to J. Bryce, 18 December 1901.

43. Spender Papers. BL Add Mss 46391, ff 95–6. HJG to J.A. Spender, 17 December 1901.
44. Campbell-Bannerman Papers. BL Add Mss 41216, f 171–2. HJG to H. Campbell-Bannerman, 17 December 1901.
45. HJG Papers. BL Add Mss 45995, ff 34–9. J. Sinclair to HJG, 25 December 1901.
46. BLO. Bryce Papers, MSS Bryce 70, ff 79–80. HJG to J. Bryce, 22 December 1901.
47. Ibid., ff 81–2. J. Bryce to HJG, 23 December 1901.
48. Campbell-Bannerman Papers. BL Add Mss 41216, f 177. HJG to H. Campbell-Bannerman, 27 December 1901.
49. BUSC. National Liberal Club Papers, DM 668. HJG to C. Geake, 28 December 1901.
50. FRO. GG MSS 960. HNG to HJG, 6 January 1902.
51. Ibid., 878. HJG to HNG, 18 February 1902.
52. For example, see NLS. Haldane Papers, MS 5905, f 126. HJG to R.B. Haldane, 17 November 1901.
53. HJG Papers. BL Add Mss 45989, f 72. H. Asquith to HJG, 30 April 1902; Campbell-Bannerman Papers. BL Add Mss 41216, f 208. H. Campbell-Bannerman to HJG, 30 April 1902; ibid., Add Mss 52517, ff 163–5. H. Campbell-Bannerman to J. Sinclair, 24 September 1902. 'Secret'.
54. FRO. GG MSS 947. H. Drew to HJG, 16 December 1902.
55. Campbell-Bannerman Papers. BL Add Mss 52517, f 165. H. Campbell-Bannerman to J. Sinclair, 24 September 1902.
56. Ibid., 41216, f 197. H. Campbell-Bannerman to HJG, 24 February 1902.
57. FRO. GG MSS 878. HJG to HNG, 4 November 1900.
58. Ibid., HJG to HNG, 1 August 1901.
59. Sidney L. Ollard, *A Forty Years' Friendship: Letters from the Late Henry Scott Holland to Mrs Drew* (1919), p. 199.
60. FRO. GG MSS 976. A. Wickham to HJG, 6 January 1902.
61. Campbell-Bannerman Papers. BL Add Mss 41216, f 129. H. Campbell-Bannerman to HJG, 12 September 1901.
62. Raymond A. Jones, *Arthur Ponsonby. The Politics of Life* (1989), p. 33.
63. Spencer Papers. BL Add Mss 77003. Unbound. HJG to Spencer, 12 November 1903.
64. Ripon Papers. BL Add Mss 43543, f 174. HJG to Ripon, 7 October 1900.
65. BLPES. Gardiner Papers, 1/14. HJG to J.L. Gardiner, 21 October 1902.
66. Arthur Porritt, *The Best I Remember* (1922), pp. 51–2.
67. HJG Papers. BL Add Mss 46484. Notebook, 29 September 1903.

68. Randolph Churchill, *Winston S. Churchill II: Young Statesman 1901–1914* (1967), p. 75.
69. RLM. Guardian Archives 124/36. HJG to C.P. Scott, 30 October 1901.
70. *The Times*, 9 October 1901.
71. *Daily News*, 7 July 1903.
72. LUL. Birrell Papers, MS 10.2, f 14. J. Morley to A. Birrell, 22 April 1903.
73. Ibid., MS 10.2, f 7. H. Campbell-Bannerman to A. Birrell, 10 and 13 March 1905.
74. HJG Papers. BL Add Mss 45995, f 166. Memo on J. Sinclair, 1925.
75. This was Herbert's view of his father's political philosophy. See Hamilton Papers. BL Add Mss 48647. E. Hamilton Diary, 30 October 1887.
76. Campbell-Bannerman Papers. BL Add Mss 41217, f 136 and f 141. H. Campbell-Bannerman to HJG, 23 November 1904 and 5 December 1904.
77. Ibid., f 115. HJG to H. Campbell-Bannerman, 23 June 1904.
78. Ibid., f 193. HJG to H. Campbell-Bannerman, 18 February 1905.
79. Ibid., f 203. H. Campbell-Bannerman to HJG, 14 March 1905.
80. Ibid., f 210. HJG to H. Campbell-Bannerman, 17 April 1905.
81. NCO. Gainford Papers, MS 76, f 20. HJG to J.A. Pease, 15 August 1905.
82. Campbell-Bannerman Papers. BL Add Mss 41217, f 248. HJG to H. Campbell-Bannerman, 8 August 1905.
83. Ibid., f 249. H. Campbell-Bannerman to HJG, 9 August 1905.
84. BLO. Bryce Papers, MSS Bryce 70, f 96. HJG to J. Bryce, 24 November 1905.
85. BLO. H.H. Asquith Papers, MSS Asquith 10, f 98. HJG to H.H. Asquith, 29 December 1903. 'Secret'.
86. FRO. GG MSS 960. HNG to HJG, 25 July 1904.
87. BLO. M. Asquith Papers, MS. Eng. d., f 59. HJG to M. Asquith, 3 September 1905.
88. HJG Papers. BL Add Mss 46107, f 82. Notes on the formation of the 1905 cabinet, December 1905.
89. Ibid., 46110, f 151. Memo on meeting with Grey, n.d. 'Secret'.
90. Campbell-Bannerman Papers. BL Add Mss 41238, f 30. HJG to H. Campbell-Bannerman, 30 November 1905.
91. BLO. M. Asquith Papers, MS. Eng d. 3204. Diary, 6 December 1905.
92. Ibid., MS. Eng d., f 63. HJG to M. Asquith, 7 December 1905.
93. Ibid., MS Eng. d. 3204. Diary, 8 December 1905.
94. Acland had previously intimated that his health would not stand the strain of office. Although he eventually received a letter from

Campbell-Bannerman acknowledging his help and one of apology from Herbert for the misunderstanding, he always believed that he had been misled. See HJG Papers. BL Add Mss 45995, ff 142–3. J. Sinclair to HJG, 31 December 1905.

95. Henry W. Lucy, 'The next Liberal ministry', *Nineteenth Century*, LVI (1904), pp. 675–85.
96. HJG Papers. BL Add Mss 46026, f 83. J. Herbert to HJG, 20 December 1904.
97. Ibid., f 86. J. Herbert to HJG, 23 December 1904.
98. BLO. M. Asquith Papers, MS Eng. d. 3204. Diary, 13 November 1905.
99. Ibid., 6 December 1905.
100. CCC. Esher Papers, ESHR 2/10. Journal, 7 December 1905.
101. Graham Jones, 'Entering the cabinet: Lloyd George and the Presidency of the Board of Trade', *Transactions of the Honourable Society of Cymmrodorion*, 6 (1999), p. 114.
102. Cited in Mallet, *Gladstone*, p. 201.
103. FRO. GG MSS 960. HNG to HJG, 3 December 1905.
104. Cited in Mallet, *Gladstone*, p. 201.
105. FRO. GG MSS 950. M. Drew to HJG, nd. Attributed incorrectly by the archivist to 1907.
106. Quoted in John Bowle, *Viscount Samuel: A Biography* (1957), p. 61.
107. BLPES. Passfield Papers,1/2/5. B. Webb Diary, 8 June 1904.
108. HJG Papers. BL Add Mss 46026, f 189. J. Herbert to HJG, 6 February 1906.
109. John A. Spender, *Sir Robert Hudson* (1930), p. 63.
110. *The Times*, 19 May 1905.

Chapter 5   The Home Office

1. The details he reported some years later. NCO. Gainford MS 82, f 50. HJG to J. Pease, 28 January 1910.
2. NA. HO45/10907/R247. Statistics: Number of Civil Servants.
3. HJG Papers. BL Add Mss 45989, ff 141–2. HJG to H.H. Asquith, 24 February 1906.
4. BLPES. Passfield Papers, 1/2/5. B. Webb Diary, 3 May 1907.
5. Quoted in Jones, *Ponsonby*, p. 42.
6. Quoted in ibid., pp. 38–9.
7. NA. H0 45/10326/131787. Aliens: Memorandum on the Administration of the Aliens Act, 1906.
8. John Vincent (ed.), *The Crawford Papers: The Journals of David Lindsay, Twenty-Seventh Earl of Crawford and Tenth Earl of Balcarres, 1871–1940 during the Years 1892 to 1940* (1984), pp. 93–4.

9. Figures from Bernard Gainer, *The Alien Invasion* (1972), p. 201.
10. BLO. Ponsonby Papers, MSS Eng. Hist. c 653. F. Ponsonby Diary, 16 April 1906.
11. HJG Papers. BL Add Mss 46064, f 56. W.S. Robson to HJG, 21 June 1906.
12. NA. HO 144/821/140315. HJG file note, 14 June 1906.
13. HJG Papers. BL Add Mss 45993, f 246. HJG Memo, 23 November 1909.
14. BUL. Masterman Papers 4/2/1. J. Galsworthy to C.F.G. Masterman, 7 July 1909.
15. NA. HO 144/861/155396. J.T. Davies to HJG, 12 August 1907.
16. HJG papers. BL Add Mss 45993, ff 252–8. E. Troup to HJG, 24 March 1910.
17. Ibid., BL Add Mss 45985, f 18. A. Davidson to HJG, 3 April 1907.
18. Quoted in Leslie, *Ruggles-Brise*, p. 150.
19. HJG Papers. BL Add Mss 46064, f 176. HJG to Lord Chief Justice, 29 March 1907.
20. Ibid., BL Add Mss 46018, f 152. Loreburn to HJG, 22 September 1906.
21. Ibid., f 153. HJG to Loreburn, 9 October 1906.
22. Cited in Leslie, *Ruggles-Brise*, p. 80.
23. NA. HO 45/10342/140503. E. Ruggles-Brise to E. Troup, 29 May 1906.
24. NA. HO 45/10356/151410. HJG Memos, 23 January and 23 March 1907.
25. *Hansard*, 4th series, 178, cc 1005–17. 18 July 1907. The affair was again taken up by *John Bull* magazine in 1931, Sir Francis Fremantle in 1935, and in 1956 by Edjali's sister. It also provided the basis of Julian Barnes, *Arthur and George* (2005).
26. *Hansard*, 4th series. 175, cc 177–239. 31 May 1907.
27. BLO. Ponsonby Papers, MSS Eng. hist. c. 652. Diary, 5 August 1906.
28. BLO. M. Asquith Papers, MS Eng. d. 3206. Diary, January 1907.
29. NCO. Mss Emmott, Diary 1/1, 21 April 1907.
30. BLPES. Passfield Papers, 1/2/5. B. Webb Diary, 22 October 1907.
31. BLO. Ponsonby Papers, MSS Eng. hist. c. 653. Diary, 21 January 1907.
32. Burns Papers. BL Add Mss 46324. Diary, 9 May 1906.
33. FRO. GG MSS 976. A. Wickham to HJG, 1 November 1906.
34. Ibid., 950. M. Drew to HJG, 4 December 1906.
35. NA. HO 45/10346/143163. Licensed Victuallers Protection Society of London, 'The Case for the Trade' (July 1906).
36. *Hansard*, 4th series, 162, c 1098. 1 August 1906.
37. Ibid., 172, cc 501–59. 12 April 1907.

38. HJG Papers. BL Add Mss 46018, f 36. Ripon to HJG, 23 March 1906.
39. *Hansard*, 4th series, 162, c 1095. 1 August 1906.
40. Ibid., c 1107. I August 1906.
41. It was a highly emotive issue and Herbert had long gone from the Home Office before any legislation was passed.
42. See Sheila Blackburn, 'Ideology and social policy: the origins of the Trade Boards Act', *Historical Journal*, 34 (1991), pp. 43–64; Duncan Bythell, *The Sweated Trades* (1978).
43. Harold Butler, *Confident Morning* (1950) p. 69.
44. HJG Papers. BL Add Mss 45989, f 173. H.H. Asquith to HJG, 23 December 1907.
45. See, for example, Almeric Fitzroy, *Memoirs* (two vols, n.d.), II, p. 464.
46. FRO. GG MSS 879. HJG to HNG, 7 March 1907.
47. CCC. Esher Papers, ESHR 10/50. Knollys to Esher, 22 March 1908.
48. BLO. M. Asquith Papers, MS Eng. d. 3206. Diary, 7 April 1908.
49. Ibid., 12 April 1908.
50. NCO. Gainford Mss 33. Diary, 5 October 1908. Pease noted that they were joined by Margot, who 'soon let out the differences between her views & Asquith's on some of his colleagues'.
51. Herbert always referred to Asquith by his second name of Henry. BLO. M. Asquith Papers, MS Eng. d., f 68. HJG to M. Asquith, 11 April 1908.
52. HJG Papers. BL Add Mss 45994, f 85. M. Waller to HJG, 13 April 1908.
53. Philip Snowden, *An Autobiography* (two vols, 1934), I, p. 181.
54. Herbert Samuel, *Memoirs* (1945), p. 50.
55. *The Times*, 3 August 1908.
56. *Hansard*, 4th series, 198, cc 537–45. 9 December 1908.
57. Ibid., c 1289. 14 December 1908.
58. HJG Papers. BL Add Mss 45895, f 139. W.S. Churchill to HJG, 30 December 1908.
59. *Hansard*, 4th series, 187, cc 1428–44. 30 April 1908.
60. Ibid., 192, c 1796–7. 21 July 1908.
61. As reported to John Morley. Morley Papers. BLO. Ms Eng d. 3570. f 103. H. Fowler to J. Morley, 10 December 1908.
62. BLO. H.H. Asquith Papers. MSS Asquith 20, f 103. HJG to H.H. Asquith, 5 September 1908.
63. Ripon Papers. BL Add Mss 43543, f 192. HJG to Ripon, 9 September 1908.
64. BLO. H.H. Asquith Papers. MSS Asquith 20, f 107. Ripon to H.H. Asquith, 9 September 1908.
65. Ripon Papers. BL Add Mss 43543, f 196. Ripon to HJG, 10 September 1908.

66. Ibid., BL Add Mss 43543, f 200. HJG to Ripon, 10 September 1908.
67. BLO. H.H. Asquith Papers. Asquith MSS 20, f 122. Ripon to H.H. Asquith, 10 September 1908.
68. Ripon Papers. BL Add Mss 43543, f 203. HJG to Ripon, 13 September 1908.
69. BLO. H.H. Asquith Papers. MSS Asquith 20, f 141. HJG to H.H. Asquith, 12 September 1908; ibid., f 151, 12 September 1908.
70. Ibid., f 154. Crewe to H.H. Asquith, 12 September 1908.
71. Ibid., f 157. L. Harcourt to H.H. Asquith, 13 September 1908.
72. Ibid., f 161. HJG to H.H. Asquith, 14 September 1908.
73. Ibid., f 167. Crewe to H.H. Asquith, 16 September 1908.
74. HJG Papers. BL Add Mss 45989, f 191. H.H. Asquith to HJG, 23 September 1908.
75. CCC. Esher Papers, ESHR 2/11. Journal, 26 September 1908.
76. BLO. H.H. Asquith Papers. MSS Asquith 11, f 194. HJG to H.H. Asquith, 30 September 1908.
77. CCC. Esher Papers, ESHR 10/50. Knollys to Esher, 16 September 1908.
78. *Tablet,* 19 September 1908.
79. NCO. Gainford MS 33. Diary, 4 October 1908.
80. BLO. H.H. Asquith Papers. MSS Asquith 20, f 167. Crewe to H.H. Asquith, 17 September 1908.
81. HJG Papers. BL Add Mss 45985, f 101. HJG to Knollys, 10 August 1909.
82. *Hansard,* 4th series, 159, cc 648–9. 25 June 1906.
83. Ibid., 183, c 284. 13 February 1908.
84. BLPES. Gardiner Papers, 1/14. HJG to A.G. Gardiner, 19 September 1909.
85. *Hansard,* 4th series, 85, c 242. 28 February 1908.
86. Ibid., 5th series, 8, c 1003. 27 July 1909. See also ibid., c 612. 22 July 1909.
87. NA. HO 144/1038/180782. HJG memo, 13 August 1909. The matters referenced in this paragraph were reported in *Hansard,* 5th series, 3, cc 1143–4, 7 April 1909; ibid., 8, cc 507–509, 21 July 1909; ibid., 11, cc 1261–3, 23 September 1909; ibid., 12, cc 1001–3, 27 October 1909.
88. NA. HO 144/882/67074. HJG to his officials, 15 September 1908.
89. Ibid., HO 45/10338/139199. Deputation from Women's Freedom League, 8 July 1909.
90. Ibid., HO 144/1040/182086. HJG to J. Scott, 3 August 1909.
91. Ibid., Report from Holloway Visiting Committee, 4 August 1909.
92. FRO. GG MSS 879. HJG to HNG, 21 September 1909.
93. BLPES. Gardiner Papers, 1/14. HJG to A.G. Gardiner, 23 July 1909.

94. HJG Papers. BL Add Mss 45985, f 104. A. Davidson to HJG, 10 September 1909.
95. Ibid., f 102. F. Ponsonby to HJG, August 1909: ibid., f 104. A. Davidson to HJG, 19 August 1909.
96. NA. HO 144/1038/180782. Treatment of Suffragettes, August 1909.
97. *Hansard*, 5th series, 11, c 1636. 1 October 1909.
98. Ibid., cc 2183–5. 7 October 1909.
99. Ibid., 11, c 1427. 30 September 1909.
100. NA. HO 144/1052/187234. Report from Walton Prison Visiting Committee, 8 January 1910.
101. *The Times*, 23 November 1909.
102. Ibid., 25 November 1909.
103. NA. HO 45/10417. Imprisonment of Nine Suffragettes in Winson Green Prison.
104. HJG Papers. B. L. Add MSS 46068, f 194. HJG to Margaret (indecipherable), 9 January 1910.
105. NA. HO 144/552/185732. Case of Theresa Garnett.
106. NA. HO 144/1038/180172. HJG to E. Troup, 25 July 1909.
107. Ibid.
108. JRM. Guardian Archive 128/133. HJG to C.P. Scott, 7 January 1910.
109. BUL. Masterman Papers, 4/2/4. H.N. Brailsford to C.F.G. Masterman, nd 1909. Theresa Billington thought that Herbert's policies encouraged 'the spirit that always arises under oppression'. Quoted in Roger Fulford, *Votes for Women* (1958), p. 132.
110. NA. HO 45/24665. Index of Suffragette Persons Arrested, 1906–1914.
111. Ibid., HO 144/1042/183256. Tabulation of the Number of Forced Feedings, October 1909.
112. HJG Papers. BL Add Mss 46067, f 292. HJG to E. Hobhouse, 9 November 1909.
113. Ibid., f 182. HJG to E. Richmond, 22 September 1909.
114. Ibid., ff 291–2. HJG to E. Hobhouse, 9 November 1909.
115. NA. HO 144/1043/183461. HJG to E. Troup, 9 September 1909. Handwritten and 'pressing'.
116. HJG Papers. BL Add Mss 45989, f 216. H.H. Asquith to HJG, 11 February 1909.
117. NCO. Gainford MS 33. Diary, 9 September 1909.
118. HJG Papers. BL Add Mss 45986, ff 159–60. HJG to W.S. Churchill, 18 March 1910.
119. The Liberals had retained the Tory appointee, Lord Selborne, as High Commissioner but he had not impressed, Asquith, for example, describing him as deficient in insight and foresight. See CUL. Crewe Papers, C/40. H.H. Asquith to Crewe, 7 May 1908.

120. As reported to an India Office official and quoted in Stephen Koss, *John Morley at the India Office 1905–1910* (1969), p. 118.
121. See, for example, Carol Devlin, 'The Eucharistic procession of 1908: the dilemma of the Liberal Government', *Church History*, 63 (1994), pp. 407–25.
122. Crewe implied that the humanising of the prison system, for example, was due to Herbert's influence. CUL. Crewe Papers, C/16. Crewe to J. Galsworthy, 21 May 1909.
123. Ibid., C/40. H.H. Asquith to Crewe, 28 October 1909.
124. *Hansard*, 4th Series, 184, c 1356. 24 February 1908.
125. Quoted in Lucy Masterman, *C.F.G. Masterman: A Biography* (1939), p. 135.
126. Jill Pellew, *The Home Office, 1848–1914: From Clerks to Bureaucrats* (1982), pp. 76–7.
127. FRO. GG MSS 898. HJG to HNG, 5 October 1909. 'Secret'.
128. Ibid., 879. HJG to HNG, 4 September 1909.
129. Ibid., 898. HJG to HNG, 5 October 1909.
130. HJG Papers. BL Add Mss 45989, f 225. HJG to H.H. Asquith, 30 October 1909.
131. CUL. Crewe Papers, C/47. F. Hopwood to Crewe, 23 December 1909.

Chapter 6   South Africa

1. CCC. Churchill Papers. Chartwell 12/1. HJG to W.S. Churchill, 19 February 1910.
2. FRO. GG MSS 961. HNG to HJG, 13 January 1910.
3. BLO. MSS Selborne, 170, ff 295–303. Notes of conversation with Gladstone on his arrival in South Africa, 17 May 1910.
4. HJG Papers. BL Add Mss 46004, f 61. F. Hopwood to HJG, 28 March 1910.
5. Ibid., BL Add Mss 45997, ff 85–7. HJG to L. Harcourt, 6 December 1910.
6. Ibid., f 239. L. Harcourt to HJG, 19 September 1911.
7. BLO. Harcourt Papers, dep 485, f 159. HJG to L. Harcourt, 21 December 1912.
8. BLO. MS Nathan 379, f 216. C. O'Grady Gubbins to M. Nathan, 6 February 1910.
9. This was claimed, for example, in Frans V. Engelenberg, *General Louis Botha* (1928). Herbert publicly refuted this and when the book appeared in English in 1929 the story had been removed.
10. HJG Papers. BL Add Mss 45996, f 43. HJG to Crewe, 10 May 1910.
11. *Cape Times*, 23 May 1910.

12. FRO. GG MSS 879. HJG to HNG, 3 July 1910.
13. CUL. Crewe Papers C/16. HJG to Crewe, 17 September 1910.
14. Ibid., C/47. F. Hopwood to Crewe, 8 August 1910.
15. Ibid., C/16. HJG to Crewe, 24 September 1910.
16. HJG Papers. BL Add Mss 46023, f 211. A. Ponsonby to HJG, 10 January 1911.
17. CUL. Crewe Papers C/47. F. Hopwood to Crewe, 9 August 1910.
18. Ibid., F. Hopwood to Crewe, 13 November 1910. This was also confirmed to Crewe by a member of the Union Parliament. Ibid., A.P. Crowe to Crewe, 14 October 1910.
19. BLO. Ms Milner, Dep 197, f 6. J. Clunie to A. Milner, 4 June 1910.
20. Ibid., f 208. K.P. Apthorpe to A. Milner, 22 December 1911.
21. FRO. GG MSS 879. HJG to HNG, 30 January 1911. 'Private and Personal'.
22. Ibid., HJG to HNG, 7 December 1910.
23. *Hansard*, 5th series, 21, cc 270–2. 8 February 1911.
24. FRO. GG MSS 879. HJG to HNG, 20 August 1911.
25. HJG Papers. BL Add Mss 46006, f 82. L. Botha to HJG, 25 November 1911.
26. Ibid., BL Add Mss 46006, ff 125–8. Notes on UK Cabinet Practice for Botha, n.d.
27. Ibid., BL Add Mss 46006, f 129. Interview Notes with Botha, 13 June 1912; ibid., BL Add Mss 46006, f 131. HJG to L. Botha, 13 June 1912.
28. Ibid., BL Add Mss 45998, f 194. HJG to L. Harcourt, 29 June 1912.
29. FRO. GG MSS 879. HJG to HNG, 22 January 1911.
30. HJG Papers. BL Add Mss 45997, f 189. L. Harcourt to HJG, 3 August 1911.
31. FRO. GG MSS 951. M. Drew to HJG, Easter 1911, n.d.
32. Ibid., 933. E. Gladstone to HNG, 5 June 1911.
33. Ibid., 879. HJG to HNG, 13 March 1911.
34. This was the rumour that reached Charles Hobhouse in London. See his diary entry for 11 February 1912, cited in Edward David, *Inside Asquith's Cabinet* (1977), p. 111.
35. FRO. GG MSS 951. M. Drew to HJG, 5 February 1912.
36. Ibid., 962. HNG to HJG, 9 February 1912.
37. HJG Papers. BL Add Mss 46033, f 27. Armitstead to HJG, 12 February 1912.
38. Ibid., f 65. Armitstead to HJG, 18 March 1912.
39. Ibid., f 79. Armitstead to HJG, 1 April 1912.
40. FRO. GG MSS 951. M. Drew to HJG, 10 May 1912.
41. NA. CO 417/528. HJG to J. Anderson, 21 December 1912.
42. BLO. Harcourt Papers, dep. 484, f 235. L. Harcourt to HJG, 12 September 1911.

43. Ibid., dep. 485, f 12. HJG to L. Harcourt, 8 October 1912.
44. FRO. GG MSS 879. HJG to HNG, 11 September 1912.
45. *Cape Times*, 6 February 1913.
46. FRO. GG MSS 879. HJG to HNG, 13 March 1911.
47. Ibid., HJG to HNG, 23 July 1910.
48. BLO. Ponsonby Papers, MSS Eng. Hist. c 659, f 6. HJG to A. Ponsonby, 20 February 1911.
49. FRO. GG MSS 880. HJG to HNG, 23 January 1913.
50. H.J. Gladstone Papers. BL Add Mss 45999, ff 138–40. L. Harcourt to HJG, 16 March 1913.
51. FRO. GG MSS 880. HJG to HNG, 4 June 1913. See also ibid., 22 April 1913.
52. NA. CO 417/514. HJG to L. Harcourt, 23 November 1912. 'Private and Personal.' Also HJG Papers. BL Add Mss 45999, f 49. HJG to L. Harcourt, 23 November 1912.
53. BLO. Harcourt Papers, dep. 486, f 161. HJG to L. Harcourt, 28 May 1913.
54. Cited in Ronald Hyam, *The Failure of South African Expansionism, 1908–1948* (1972), p. 87.
55. NA. CO 417/524. HJG to Secretary of State, 28 July 1913.
56. See, for example, FRO. GG MSS 880. HJG to HNG, 10 June 1913.
57. This was a conventional view at the time. See, for example, Cecil Harmsworth, *Pleasure and Problem in South Africa* (1908). See also Andrew Thorpe and Richard Toye (eds), *Parliament and Politics in the Age of Asquith and Lloyd George: The Diaries of Cecil Harmsworth, MP, 1909–1922* (2016).
58. HJG Papers. BL Add Mss 46042, f 73. HJG to H.W. Massingham, 23 August 1914.
59. RLM. Guardian Archive 333/35. HJG to C.P. Scott, 26 August 1913.
60. HJG Papers. BL Add Mss 46002, ff 178–216. HJG to L. Harcourt, 11 July 1914.
61. Information provided later by Gladstone for Harcourt. Ibid., BL Add Mss 46001, f 184. HJG to L. Harcourt, 22 January 1914.
62. FRO. GG MSS 880. HJG to HNG, 20 July 1913.
63. BLO. Harcourt Papers, dep 486, f 213. HJG to L. Harcourt, 7 July 1913.
64. Ibid., f 196. HJG to L. Harcourt, 5 July 1913.
65. HJG Papers. BL Add Mss 46007, f 64. HJG to L. Botha, 5 July 1913.
66. FRO. GG MSS 880. HJG to HNG, 12 July 1913; ibid., HJG to HNG, 13 July 1913.
67. SANA. PM 148/25/1913.
68. *Transvaal Leader*, 30 August 1913.
69. *John Bull*, 23 August 1913.

70. *Hansard*, 5th series, 55, cc 35–40. 7 July 1913.
71. Ibid., c 397. 9 July 1913.
72. Ibid., cc 2023–5. 23 July 1913.
73. Ibid., 56, c 815. 31 July 1913.
74. NA. CO 551/43. Witwatersrand Disturbances Report, 2 October 1913.
75. HJG Papers. BL Add Mss 46007, f 77. HJG to L. Botha, 10 July 1913; ibid., f 87. HJG to L. Botha, 13 July 1913; ibid., f 127. HJG to L. Botha, 9 August 1913; ibid., f 130. HJG to L. Botha, 14 August 1913; ibid., ff 163–4. HJG to L. Botha, 20 September 1913.
76. Ibid., f 127. HJG to L. Botha, 9 August 1913.
77. Ibid., BL Add Mss 46075, ff 186–7. Memo on Draft Factory Act, 31 October 1913; ibid., f 196. HJG to F. Malan, 2 November 1913.
78. NUL. Runciman Papers, WR 82, f 123. H.W. Smyth to W. Runciman, 21 December 1913.
79. NA. CO 551/46. HJG to Secretary of State, 31 December 1913.
80. HJG Papers. BL Add Mss 46000, f 296. L. Harcourt to HJG, 13 November 1913.
81. FRO. GG MSS 880. HJG to HNG, 21 October 1913.
82. HJG Papers. BL Add Mss 46000, f 263. L. Harcourt to HJG, 29 October 1913.
83. FRO. GG MSS 880. HJG to HNG, 20 November 1913.
84. HJG Papers. BL Add Mss 46001, f 184. HJG to L. Harcourt, 22 January 1914.
85. FRO. GG MSS 880. HJG to HNG, 31 January 1914.
86. CO 551/53. HJG to Secretary of State, 14 January 1914; 15 January 1914.
87. BLO. Harcourt Papers, dep. 487, f 212. HJG to L. Harcourt, 10 January 1914.
88. *Hansard*, 5th series, 58, cc 353–429. 12 February 1914.
89. As confided to Almeric Fitzroy. See Fitzroy, *Memoirs*, II, p. 533.
90. FRO. GG MSS 880. HJG to HNG, 14 February 1914.
91. NA. CO 551/54. HJG to Secretary of State, 22 January 1914.
92. BLO. Harcourt Papers, dep. 487, f 242. HJG to L. Harcourt, 31 January 1914.
93. HJG Papers. BL Add Mss 46001, f 91. HJG to L. Harcourt, 7 January 1914.
94. Ibid., BL Add Mss 46002, f 2. HJG to L. Harcourt, 1 February 1914.
95. Ibid., f 78. HJG to L. Harcourt, 9 May 1914.
96. FRO. GG MSS 963. HNG to HJG, 12 February 1914.
97. Ibid., 880. HJG to HNG, 15 January 1914.
98. *Friend*, 3 December 1911.
99. NA. CO 551/14. HJG to Secretary of State, 23 October 1911.
100. Ibid., 551/15. HJG to Secretary of State, 8 January 1912.

101. HJG Papers. BL Add Mss 46006, f 147. HJG to L. Botha, 6 November 1912.
102. NA. CO 551/39. HJG to Secretary of State, 14 May 1913.
103. Ibid., 551/43. L. Botha to HJG, 17 September 1913.
104. *Rand Daily Mail*, 20 November 1913.
105. CUL. Hardinge Papers, 93/96. C. Hardinge to HJG, 19 November 1913.
106. Ibid., 93/117. HJG to C. Hardinge, 20 November 1913.
107. BLO. Harcourt Papers, dep 487, f 124. HJG to L. Harcourt, 24 November 1913.
108. NA. CO 551/46. Emmott's comment was added to a private letter from HJG to L. Harcourt, 11 December 1913.
109. CUL. Hardinge Papers, 93/103. C. Hardinge to HJG, 20 December 1913.
110. Her view was shared with Lord Esher. CCC. Esher Papers, ESHR 2/12. Journal, 7 February 1912.
111. HJG Papers. BL Add Mss 46000, f 340. L. Harcourt to HJG, 27 November 1913.
112. Ibid., BL Add Mss 46008, f 116. J. Smuts to HJG, 20 January 1914.
113. FRO. GG MSS 880. HJG to HNG, 20 March 1914.
114. Ibid., HJG to HNG, 21 April 1914.
115. HJG Papers. BL Add Mss 46007, f 233. L. Botha to HJG, 29 May 1914.
116. Ibid., f 214. HJG to L. Harcourt, 11 July 1914.

Chapter 7   Wars to the Death

1. FRO. GG MSS 880. HJG to HNG, 16 May 1914.
2. Michael & Eleanor Brock (eds), *H.H. Asquith. Letters to Venetia Stanley* (1982), p. 254.
3. Fitzroy, *Memoirs*, II, p. 579.
4. HJG Papers. BL Add Mss 46042, f 10. HJG to J. Spender, 23 October 1914.
5. NA. MH 8/7. HJG memo, July 1916.
6. FRO. GG MSS 981. HJG to A. Wickham, 27 October 1914.
7. Ibid., 881. HJG to HNG, 1 February 1915.
8. C. Harmsworth Diary, 21 October 1914. Cited in Thorpe and Toye (eds), *Parliament and Politics*, p. 174.
9. FRO. GG MSS 881. HJG to HNG, 11 October 1915.
10. Ibid., HJG to HNG, 31 May 1916.
11. HJG Papers. BL Add Mss 46084, f 74. HJG to J. Bradbury, nd 1918.
12. Ibid., f 37. HJG to F.J. Willis 19 July 1918.
13. Ibid., BL Add Mss 46013, f 287. HJG to A. Maudslay, 18 November 1918.

14. FRO. GG MSS 881. HJG to HNG, 11 October 1915.
15. In 1910–12 his annual donations and subscriptions to South African institutions were running at about £900. See HJG Papers. BL Add Mss 46115. Notebook.
16. HJG, *William G. C. Gladstone, A Memoir* (1918). Robert Graves, who trained with Will, hinted at a rather different side to his character in noting that he was known to his comrades as 'Glad Eyes'. See Robert Graves *Goodbye to All That* (Penguin edn, 2000), p. 66.
17. *Outlook*, 21 September 1918.
18. FRO. GG MSS 881. HJG to HNG, 17 March 1917.
19. Ibid., 882. HJG to HNG, 15 February 1918.
20. Ibid., HJG to HNG, 8 January 1918. 'A monstrous list of honours? Worse than ever.'
21. Ibid., 2135. HJG to HNG, 11 September 1918.
22. Ibid., 882. HJG to HNG, 7 December 1918.
23. Ibid., HJG to HNG, 1 January 1919.
24. Ibid., HJG to HNG, 23 September 1919.
25. Ibid., 1965. HJG to HNG, 17 February 1920.
26. Ibid., 882. HJG to HNG, 20 July 1920.
27. Ibid., 965. HNG to HJG, 10 March 1920. See ibid., 963. HNG to HJG, 30 August 1919.
28. Ibid., 882. HJG to HNG, 28 July 1920.
29. BLO. Maclean Papers, dep. c. 465, f 121. R. Hudson to D. Maclean, 12 January 1919; ibid., f 165. R. Hudson to D. Maclean, 4 February 1919; ibid., f 167. R. Hudson to D. Maclean, 5 February 1919.
30. FRO. GG MSS 882. HJG to HNG, 16 December 1920.
31. NUL. Runciman Papers, WR 190, ff 6–8. R. Cecil to W. Runciman, 13 January 1921.
32. BLO. MS Gilbert Murray, 42, f 149. HJG to G. Murray, 22 April 1921.
33. Ibid., f 151. G. Murray to HJG, 24 April 1921.
34. BLO. H.H. Asquith Papers, 34, f 30. Notes of a meeting, 10 August 1921.
35. FRO. GG MSS 883. HJG to HNG, 2 October 1921.
36. HJG Papers. BL Add Mss 46476, ff 27–8. HJG to H.H. Asquith, 29 October 1921.
37. FRO. GG MSS 965 HNG to HJG, 11 December 1921.
38. HJG Papers. BL Add Mss 46840, ff 2–5. HJG, Note on a dinner held on 6 December 1921.
39. FRO. GG MSS 883. HJG to HNG, 18 December 1921.
40. HJG Papers. BL Add Mss 46476, ff 46–9. Cowdray to HJG, 31 December 1921.
41. FRO. GG MSS 883. HJG to HNG, 23 December 1921.
42. NUL. Runciman Papers, WR 192, f 5. HJG to W. Runciman, 27 January 1922.

43. FRO. GG MSS 883. HJG to HNG, 17 January 1922.
44. HJG Papers. BL Add Mss 46476, f 78. HJG to H.H. Asquith, 19 January 1922.
45. Ibid., BL Add Mss 46486. Notebook, 18 January 1922.
46. Ibid., BL Add Mss 46085, f 5. HJG to E. Hatch, 25 January 1922.
47. Ibid., BL Add Mss 46476, ff 118–20. HJG reply to an article on Liberal reunion, 15 March 1922.
48. CUL. Templewood Papers, I, 11. Paper 34. Geoffrey R. Searle, *Corruption in British Politics 1895–1930* (1987), p. 145 rightly observes that Gladstone's moralising in 1922 did not quite square with his 1905 note that 'the ice may have been thin. But transactions should be regarded as a whole. If the letter of the law has not always been observed [...] let everyone ask himself if in tax-rating and other matters, he has always observed the letter of the law.'
49. HJG Papers. BL Add Mss 46486. Notebook, 2 August 1922.
50. Christopher Addison, *Four and a Half Years* (two vols, 1934), II, p. 528.
51. HJG Papers. BL Add Mss 46476, ff 95–6. C.P. Scott to HJG, 3 February 1922.
52. Ibid., BL Add Mss 46110, f 179. Notes on discussion on party policy, 20 July 1922.
53. Ibid., BL Add Mss 46476, f 104. R. McKenna to HJG, 27 February 1922.
54. See for example FRO. GG MSS 883. HJG to HNG, 11 March 1922, 24 April 1922.
55. Cecil Papers. BL Add Mss 51163, f 43. R. Cecil to HJG, 21 November 1921.
56. Ibid., f 47. R. Cecil to HJG, 10 January 1922.
57. HJG Papers. BL Add Mss 46476, f 138. R. Cecil to HJG, 11 April 1922.
58. Cecil Papers. BL Add Mss 51163, f 83. HJG to R. Cecil, 22 April 1922.
59. BLO. MSS Gilbert Murray, 45, f 45. HJG to G. Murray, 20 April 1922.
60. HJG Papers. BL Add Mss 46477, ff 1–14. R. Cecil to HJG, 10 August 1922.
61. Cecil Papers. BL Add Mss 51163, f 114. R. Cecil to D. Gladstone, 15 September 1922.
62. HJG Papers. BL Add Mss 46477, f 30. R. Cecil to HJG, 30 September 1922.
63. See, for example, Michael Bentley, 'Liberal politics and the Grey conspiracy of 1921', *Historical Journal*, XX (1977), pp. 461–78.
64. FRO. GG MSS 883. HJG to HNG, 3 August 1922.
65. Ibid., HJG to HNG, 25 August 1922.
66. HJG et al., *Armenia and the Settlement* (1919), p. 15.
67. Quoted in Trevor Wilson (ed.), *The Political Diaries of C.P. Scott, 1911–1928* (1970), p. 430.

68. *The Times*, 16 October 1922.
69. FRO. GG MSS 965. HNG to HJG, 16 October 1922.
70. HJG Papers. BL Add Mss 46477, f 96. Cowdray to HJG, 2 January 1923.
71. Ibid., BL Add Mss 46474, f 13. HJG to D. Maclean, 14 November 1922.
72. FRO. GG MSS 883. HJG to HNG, 2 December 1922.
73. HJG Papers. BL Add Mss 46474, ff 29–30. HJG to D. Maclean, 23 January 1923.
74. *Daily Chronicle* 15 June 1923.
75. RLM. Guardian Archive 134. C.P. Scott Diary, 1 July 1923.
76. Riddell Papers. BL Add Mss 62967, p. 23. Diary, 17 January 1923.
77. Alfred Henderson-Livesey, *The Intriguers of Abingdon Street* (1926).
78. Desmond MacCarthy (ed.), *Letters of the Earl of Oxford and Asquith to a Friend: Second Series, 1922–27* (1934), p. 83. H.H. Asquith to Mrs Harrison, 21 November 1923.
79. HJG Papers. BL Add Mss 46477, f 112. Cowdray to HJG, 19 November 1923.
80. FRO. GG MSS 884. HJG to HNG, 25 February 1924.
81. HJG Papers. BL Add Mss 46474, f 54. HJG to D. Maclean, 30 December 1923.
82. FRO. GG MSS 884. HJG to HNG, 31 December 1923.
83. Ibid., 989. HJG to M. Gladstone, 5 January 1924.
84. BLO. H.H. Asquith Papers, 34, ff 136–43. D. Lloyd George to H.H. Asquith, 20 August 1924.
85. HJG Papers. BL Add Mss 46474, ff 118–21. D. Maclean memorandum, 12 September 1924.
86. Ibid., f 122. HJG to D. Maclean, 26 September 1924.
87. FRO. GG MSS 884. HJG to HNG, 27 September 1924.
88. Ibid., HJG to HNG, 14 October 1924.
89. HJG Papers. BL Add Mss 46477, f 160. Inchcape to HJG, 15 October 1924.
90. NUL. Runciman Papers, WR 197, f 44. HJG, Narrative of the General Election 1924. Secret. July 1925.
91. FRO. GG MSS 884. HJG to HNG, 1 November 1924.
92. Ibid., HJG to HNG, 25 November 1924.
93. HJG Papers. BL Add Mss 46474, ff 183–4. D. Maclean to HJG, 24 December 1925.
94. Ibid., BL Add Mss 46475, f 180. HJG to R. Hudson, 14 January 1926.
95. Ibid., BL Add Mss 46474, f 192. HJG to D. Maclean, 15 December 1926.
96. Ibid., BL Add Mss, f 197. HJG to D. Maclean, 21 February 1927.
97. Ibid., BL Add Mss 46478, f 176. HJG to R. Muir, 9 January 1930.

98. FRO. GG MSS 951. M. Drew to HJG, n.d. Neither brother contested the accuracy of these claims: their concern was to prevent them becoming public.
99. Peter Wright, *Portraits and Criticisms* (1925), pp. 152–3.
100. FRO. GG MSS 1966. Wright v Bath Club. Notes of First Day Hearing, 13 July 1926.
101. Ibid., 1901. M. Gladstone Memorandum, 1925. This is wrongly attributed in the catalogue to Dolly.
102. BUL. Masterman Papers, 11/1/3/43. HJG to C.F.G. Masterman, 9 April 1926.
103. FRO. GG MSS 966. HNG to HJG, 28 November 1924. This is much higher than the figure of almost 100,000 by 1942 cited in Foot (ed.), *Gladstone Diaries, I, 1825–1832*, p. xxv.
104. FRO. GG MSS 966. HNG to HJG, 28 November 1924, enclosing Masterman's letter dated 27 November 1924.
105. Herbert generally referred disrespectfully to Victoria as the 'O(ld) B(uddha)'. For example ibid., 882. HJG to HNG, 20 July 1920.
106. Gladstone, *After Thirty Years*, p. xvii.
107. FRO. GG MSS 2137. Stamfordham to HJG, 13 November 1928.
108. Macmillan Archive. BL Add Mss 55244, f 96. HJG to Macmillan, 19 December 1928.
109. *The Times*, 31 December 1928.
110. *John O'London*, 12 January 1929: *Manchester Guardian*, 5 January 1929: *Glasgow Herald*, 26 December 1928.
111. *Saturday Review*, 29 December 1928.
112. HJG, *The Story of the Noblemen and Gentlemen's Catch Club* (1930).
113. UCO. P218/C1/4. D. Gladstone to G. Murray, 20 February 1930.
114. Ibid., P218/C1/5. D. Gladstone to G. Murray, 18 March 1930.
115. Ibid., P218/C1/10. D. Gladstone to G. Murray, 28 May 1930.

Epilogue

1. *The Times*, 12 March 1930.
2. FRO. GG MSS 885. HJG to HNG, 15 May 1927.
3. As in Maurice Cowling, *The Impact of Labour* (Cambridge, 1971), p. 231.
4. BLO. Maclean Papers, dep. c. 467, f 27. HJG to D. Maclean, 3 April 1923.
5. HJG Papers. BL Add Mss 46021, f 146. HJG to R. Hudson, 13 October 1913.
6. FRO. GG MSS 886. HJG to HNG, 15 December 1928.
7. Ibid., 885. HJG to HNG, 8 October 1927.
8. Ibid., HJG to HNG, 7 February 1927.

Bibliography

Primary Sources

Private Papers

Lord Althorp
H.II. Asquith
M. Asquith
A. Birrell
J. Bryce
J. Burns
H. Campbell-Bannerman
Lord R. Cecil
J. Chamberlain
W. Churchill
Lord Crewe
C. Dilke
M. Drew
A. Emmott
Lord Esher
E. Evans
Lord Gainford
A.G. Gardiner
H.J. Gladstone
W.E. Gladstone
Glynne-Gladstone
E. Grey
R.B. Haldane
E. Hamilton
L. Harcourt
W. Harcourt
Lord Hardinge
R. Holt

D. Lloyd George
D. Maclean
C.F.G. Masterman
A. Milner
J. Morley
G. Murray
M. Nathan
Lord Passfield
A. Ponsonby
Lord Riddell
Lord Ripon
W. Runciman
H. Samuel
C.P. Scott
J.B. Seely
Lord Selborne
J. Simon
J.A. Spender
W.T. Stead
Lord Templewood
C. Tennant
G.O. Trevelyan

Institutional Papers

Macmillan Publishers
National Liberal Club
University College, Oxford Archives
South African National Archive, Governor General and Prime Minister Series

Government Archives and Official Publications

British Parliamentary Papers
Colonial Office CO 417: 551
Hansard
Home Office HO 45: 144
Metropolitan Police MEPO 2
Ministry of Health MH 8

Newspapers

Cape Times
Daily News
Freeman's Journal
Leeds Mercury
Liberal Magazine
Manchester Guardian
Rand Daily Mail
The Tablet
The Times
Transvaal Leader

Works by Herbert Gladstone

'A first visit to India', *Nineteenth Century*, XXII (1887), 133–48.
After Thirty Years (1928).
Armenia and the Settlement (1919).
'The chief whip in the British Parliament', *American Political Science Review*, 21 (1927), 519–28.
'England's foreign policy', *Nineteenth Century*, CCX (1884), 705–11.
'Ireland blocks the way', *Nineteenth Century*, XXXI (1892), 899–904.
'The Liberal Party and the labour question' (1892). Reprinted from the *Albemarle Review*.
'Obstruction: what is it?', *New Review*, 8 (1893), 390–1.
'Physical training', in F. Wills (ed.), *Lay Sermons for Practical People* (1890), 61–76.
The Story of the Noblemen and Gentlemen's Catch Club (1930).
William G.C. Gladstone: A Memoir (1918).

Secondary Sources

(Place of publication is London unless otherwise stated)

Addison, Christopher, *Four and a Half Years* (two vols, 1934).
Aitken, Ros, *The Prime Minister's Son: Stephen Gladstone, Rector of Hawarden* (Chester, 2012).
Asquith, Margot, *The Autobiography of Margot Asquith* (two vols, 1920).
——, *More Memories* (1933).
Bahlman, Dudley R. (ed.), *Diary of Sir Edward Walter Hamilton* (two vols, Oxford, 1972).
Ball, Stephen (ed.), *Dublin Castle and the First Home Rule Crisis: The Political Journal of Sir George Fottrell, 1884–1887* (2008).
Barber, James, *South Africa in the Twentieth Century* (1999).
Barker, Michael, *Gladstone and Radicalism: The Reconstruction of Liberal Policy in Britain, 1885–94* (Brighton, 1975).
Bassett, A. Tilney, *Gladstone to His Wife* (1936).
Battersea, Constance, *Reminiscences* (1922).
Battiscombe, Georgina, *Mrs Gladstone: The Portrait of a Marriage* (1956).
Bealey, Frank, 'Negotiations between the Liberal Party and the Labour Representation Committee before the general election of 1906', *Bulletin of the Institute of Historical Research*, 29 (1956), 261–74.
——, 'The electoral arrangement between the Labour Representation Committee and the Liberal Party', *Journal of Modern History*, 28 (1956), 353–73.
Bebbington, David, *William Ewart Gladstone: Faith and Politics in Victorian Britain* (Grand Rapids, 1993).
Bentley, Michael, *The Liberal Mind, 1924–1929* (Cambridge, 1976).
——, 'Liberal politics and the Grey conspiracy of 1921', *Historical Journal*, XX (1977), 461–78.
——, *The Climax of Liberal Politics* (1987).

Biagini, Eugenio, *British Democracy and Irish Nationalism 1871–1906* (Cambridge, 2007).

Blackburn, Sheila, 'Ideology and social policy: the origins of the Trade Boards Act', *Historical Journal*, 34 (1991), 43–64.

Bowle, John, *Viscount Samuel: A Biography* (1957).

Boyle, Thomas, 'The formation of the Campbell-Bannerman Government in December 1905', *Bulletin of the Institute of Historical Research*, XLV (1972), 283–302.

Brett Maurice V. (ed.), *Journals and Letters of Reginald Viscount Esher* (four vols, 1934).

Brock, Michael and Eleanor (eds), *H.H. Asquith: Letters to Venetia Stanley* (Oxford, 1982).

Brooks, David, 'Gladstone's fourth administration, 1892–1894', in David. W. Bebbington and Roger Swift (eds), *Gladstonian Centenary Essays* (Liverpool, 2000), 225–42.

Brown, Kenneth D., *John Burns* (1977).

Butler, Harold, *Confident Morning* (1950).

Bythell, Duncan, *The Sweated Trades* (1978).

Cahalan, Peter, *Belgian Refugee Relief in England During the Great War* (1982).

Churchill, Randolph, *Winston S. Churchill II: Young Statesman 1901–1914* (1967).

Cooke, Anthony and Vincent, John, 'Herbert Gladstone, Forster and Ireland, 1881–82', *Irish Historical Studies*, 17 (1970–1), 521–48.

Cowling, Maurice, *The Impact of Labour* (Cambridge, 1971).

Cregier, Donald, *Chiefs without Indians* (1982).

Davenport, Rodney, *South Africa: A Modern History* (1978).

David, Edward, *Inside Asquith's Cabinet* (1977).

Devlin, Carol, 'The Eucharistic procession of 1908: the dilemma of the Liberal Government', *Church History*, 63 (1994), 407–25.

Douglas, Roy, *The History of the Liberal Party* (1971).

———, *Liberals: A History of the Liberal and Liberal Democrat Parties* (2005).

Drew, Mary, *Acton, Gladstone and Others* (1924).

———, *Catherine Gladstone* (1919).

Dutton, David, *Simon: A Political Biography of Sir John Simon* (1992).

Engelenberg, Frans V., *General Louis Botha* (1928).

Farr, Martin, *Reginald McKenna. Financier among Statesmen, 1863–1916* (2007).

Fitzroy, Almeric, *Memoirs* (two vols, n.d.).

Gainer, Bernard, *The Alien Invasion* (1972).

Garrard, John, *The English and Immigration, 1880–1910* (Oxford, 1971).

Garson, Noel, 'Louis Botha or John X. Merriman: the choice of South Africa's first prime minister', *Commonwealth Papers*, 12 (1969), 1–47.

Gilbert, Bentley, *David Lloyd George, A Political Life: The Architect of Change, 1863–1912* (1987).

Gooddie, Sheila, *Mary Gladstone: A Gentle Rebel* (2003).

Grigg, John, 'Herbert Gladstone', in A. Horne (ed.), *Telling Lives: From W.B. Yeats to Bruce Chatwin* (2000), 161–9.

Gutzke, David, 'Rosebery and Campbell-Bannerman: the conflict over leadership reconsidered', *Bulletin of the Institute of Historical Research*, 54 (1981), 241–50.

Hamer, David, *John Morley: Liberal Intellectual in Politics* (Oxford, 1968).

——, *Liberal Politics in the Age of Gladstone and Rosebery* (Oxford, 1972).

——, 'The Irish question and Liberal politics, 1886–1914', in A. O'Day (ed.), *Reactions to Irish Nationalism* (Dublin, 1987), 237–58.

Hancock, Keith, *Smuts. I: The Sanguine Years, 1870–1919* (Cambridge, 1962).

Harmsworth, Cecil, *Pleasure and Problem in South Africa* (1908).

Harris, Wilson, *J.A. Spender* (1946).

Havighurst, Alfred, *Radical Journalist: H.W. Massingham, 1860–1924* (Cambridge, 1974).

Hazlehurst, Cameron, 'Asquith as prime minister, 1908–1916', *English Historical Review*, 85 (1970), 502–31.

Hazlehurst, Cameron and Woodland, Christine (eds), *A Liberal Chronicle: Journals and Papers of J.A. Pease, 1st Lord Gainford, 1908–1910* (1994).

Henderson-Livesey, Alfred, *The Intriguers of Abingdon Street* (1926).

Hopkins, Eric, *Charles Masterman 1873–1927: Politician and Journalist. Splendid Failure* (1999).

Hyam, Ronald, *The Failure of South African Expansionism, 1908–1948* (1972).

Jackson, Alvin, *Home Rule: An Irish History, 1800–2000* (2003).

Jalland, Patricia *The Liberals and Ireland* (1980).

——, 'Mr Gladstone's daughters', in Bruce Kinzer (ed.), *The Gladstonian Turn of Mind: Essays Presented to J.B. Connacher* (Toronto, 1985).

James, Robert, *Rosebery. A Biography of Archibold Philip, 5th Earl of Rosebery* (1963).

Jenkins, Terence, *Gladstone, Whiggery and the Liberal Party, 1874–1886* (1988).

Jones, Graham, 'Entering the cabinet: Lloyd George and the Presidency of the Board of Trade', *Transactions of the Honourable Society of Cymmrodorion*, 6 (1999) 104–18.

Jones, Raymond A., *Arthur Ponsonby: The Politics of Life* (1989).

Keiser, Richard, 'The South African Governor-General, 1910–1921' (Oxford D. Phil thesis, 1975).

Kinnear, Michael, *The Fall of Lloyd George* (1973).

Koss, Stephen, *John Morley at the India Office, 1905–1910* (New Haven, 1969).

——, *Asquith* (1976).

——, 'Asquith versus Lloyd George', in A. Sked & C. Cook (eds), *Crisis and Controversy: Essays in Honour of A.J.P. Taylor* (1976), 66–89.

Leslie, Shane, *Sir Evelyn Ruggles Brise* (1938).

Letters of Lord Acton to Mary, Daughter of the Right Hon. W.E. Gladstone (1913).

Lloyd, Trevor, 'The whip as paymaster: Herbert Gladstone and party organisation', *English Historical Review*, 89 (1974), 785–813.

Lucy, Henry W., 'The next Liberal ministry', *Nineteenth Century*, LVI (1904), 675–85.

MacCarthy, Desmond, *Letters of the Earl of Oxford and Asquith to a Friend: Second Series, 1922–27* (1934).
Mallet, Charles, *Herbert Gladstone: A Memoir* (1932).
Masterman, Lucy, *Mary Gladstone: Her Diaries and Letters* (1930).
———, *C.F.G. Masterman: A Biography* (1939).
Matthew, Colin, *Gladstone, 1809–1898* (Oxford, 1997).
McCready, Herbert, 'Chief whip and party funds: the work of Herbert Gladstone in the Edwardian Liberal Party, 1899 to 1906', *Canadian Journal of History*, VI (1971), 285–303.
McKenna, Stephen, *Reginald McKenna, 1863–1943: A Memoir* (1948).
McKinstry, Leo, *Rosebery: Statesman in Turmoil* (2005).
Morris, Anthony J.A., *C.P. Trevelyan: Portrait of a Radical* (1977).
Ollard, Sidney L., *A Forty Years' Friendship: Letters from the Late Henry Scott Holland to Mrs Drew* (1919).
Pellew, Jill, *The Home Office, 1848–1914: From Clerks to Bureaucrats* (1982).
Ponsonby, Frederick, *Recollections of Three Reigns* (1951).
Pope-Hennessy, James, *Lord Crewe, 1858–1945: The Likeness of a Liberal* (1955).
Porritt, Arthur, *The Best I Remember* (1922).
Porter, Bernard, *Critics of Empire* (1968).
Pugh, Martin, *Lloyd George* (1988).
Pyrah, Geoffrey, *Imperial Policy and South Africa, 1902–1910* (1955).
Reid, Stuart J. (ed.), *Memoirs of Sir Wemyss Reid, 1842–1885* (1905).
Richmond, Elsa, *The Earlier Letters of Gertrude Bell* (1937).
Robbins, Keith, *Sir Edward Grey: A Biography of Lord Grey of Falloden* (1971).
Rowland, Peter, *The Last Liberal Governments: the Promised Land, 1906–1910* (1968).
———, *Lloyd George* (1975).
Russell, Alan, *Liberal Landslide: The General Election of 1906* (Newton Abbot, 1973).
Samuel, Herbert, *Memoirs* (1945).
Searle, Geoffrey, *The Liberal Party: Triumph and Disintegration, 1886–1929* (2001).
Snowden, Philip, *An Autobiography* (two vols, 1934).
Sommer, Dudley, *Haldane of Cloan: The Life and Times, 1856–1928* (1960).
Spender, John A., *Life, Journalism and Politics* (two vols, 1927).
———, *Sir Robert Hudson* (1930).
———, *Life of Herbert Henry Asquith, Lord Oxford and Asquith* (two vols, 1932).
Stray, Christopher, *Contribution towards a Glossary of the Glynne Language* (2005).
Thomas, Ivor, *Gladstone of Hawarden: A Memoir of Henry Neville, Lord Gladstone of Hawarden* (1936).
Thorold, Algar L., *The Life of Henry Labouchere* (1913).
Thorpe, Andrew and Toye, Richard (eds), *Parliament and Politics in the Age of Asquith and Lloyd George: The Diaries of Cecil Harmsworth, MP, 1909–1922* (2016).

Troup, Edgar, *The Home Office* (1925).

Vincent, John, *The Crawford Papers: The Journals of David Lindsay, Twenty-Seventh Earl of Crawford and Tenth Earl of Balcarres, 1871–1940 during the Years 1892 to 1940* (1984).

Waley, Daniel, *A Liberal Life: Sidney Earl Buxton, 1853–1934* (1999).

Walker, Eric, *Lord de Villiers and His Times: South Africa, 1842–1914* (1925).

——, *A History of South Africa* (3rd edn, 1968).

Wasserstein, Bernard, *Herbert Samuel: A Political Life* (1992).

Wilson, John, *CB. The Life of Sir Henry Campbell-Bannerman* (1973).

Wilson, Trevor, *The Downfall of the Liberal Party, 1914–1935* (1968).

——, *The Political Diaries of C.P. Scott, 1911–1928* (1970).

Wright, Peter, *Portraits and Criticisms* (1925).

Index

Plate 1 Hawarden Castle, Herbert's much-loved family home. Credit: Alamy.

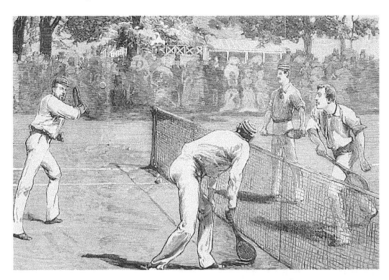

Plate 2 Parliamentary tennis match. A keen sportsman, Herbert (top right) playing tennis for the Liberals against the Conservatives in 1883. Credit: Getty Images.

Plate 3 Herbert Gladstone MP, the new member for Leeds, 1880. Credit: Alamy.

Plate 4 A Gladstone family group. Relaxing on the steps at Hawarden during the 1880s, Herbert is surrounded by three generations of Gladstones. Harry is sprawled rather awkwardly at the front left of the picture. Credit: National Portrait Gallery.

Plate 5 Margot Tennant, *c*.1890, object of the youthful Herbert's affections. Credit: Victoria and Albert Museum.

Plate 6 Herbert Gladstone as home secretary at his desk in Whitehall, *c.*1906. Credit: Getty Images.

THE NEW LIBERAL GOVERNMENT: MEMBERS OF THE CABINET.

Mr. H. Gladstone. Mr. Haldane. Mr. Sydney Buxton. Earl Carrington. Lord Tweedmouth.
Earl of Crewe. Mr. Bryce. Mr. Lloyd-George. Sir H. Fowler. Mr. Augustine Birrell. Mr. J. Sinclair.

Sir H. Campbell-Bannerman.
Sir R. Reid. Sir E. Grey. Earl of Elgin. Mr. Morley. Marquis of Ripon. Mr. Asquith. Mr. John Burns.

Plate 7 The Campbell-Bannerman Cabinet in 1906. Despite the seniority of his own ministry, Herbert's position at the left hand end of the back row was somehow symbolic of his self-effacing nature. Credit: Alamy.

Plate 8 The London Eucharistic Procession of 1908 which drove Herbert to offer his ministerial resignation. Public Domain.

Plate 9 Suffragette leaflet. An example of the suffragette propaganda which Herbert sought, with little success, to counter. Public Domain.

Plate 10 Herbert Gladstone in court. Subpoenaed in 1908 to appear as a witness to a suffragette demonstration, Herbert was given a rough time in the witness box by Christabel Pankhurst. Credit: Alamy.

Plate 11 Dorothy Gladstone, Herbert's wife in 1910 shortly after her husband was made a viscount. Credit: Alamy.

Plate 12 The Rand Strike. Police dispersing strikers in Johannesburg. As governor-general, Herbert's handling of the 1913 strike generated criticism from organised labour in both Britain and South Africa. Public Domain.

Plate 13   Belgian refugees in London; outside the Aldwych offices of the War Refugees Committee, 1914. Public Domain.

Plate 14   Little Munden church and graveyard where Herbert was buried in 1930. Public Domain.